T0291352

Holy Hype

Holy Hype

A Guide to Religious Fervor in the Advertising of Goods and the Good News

Susan H. Sarapin
Pamela L. Morris

LEXINGTON BOOKS
Lanham • Boulder • New York • London

Published by Lexington Books
An imprint of The Rowman & Littlefield Publishing Group, Inc.
4501 Forbes Boulevard, Suite 200, Lanham, Maryland 20706
www.rowman.com

86-90 Paul Street, London EC2A 4NE, United Kingdom

British Library Cataloguing in Publication Information Available

Library of Congress Cataloging-in-Publication Data

Names: Sarapin, Susan H., 1951– author. | Morris, Pamela L., 1971– author.
Title: Holy hype : a guide to religious fervor in the advertising of goods and the good news / Susan H. Sarapin, Pamela L. Morris.
Description: Lanham : Lexington Books, [2022] | Includes bibliographical references and index. | Summary: "This book discusses the advertising technique of using religious symbols, themes, and rhetoric in the promotion of secular consumer goods and services and, inversely, the use of nonreligious themes in the promotion of religious goods, institutions, and services"—Provided by publisher.
Identifiers: LCCN 2021040925 (print) | LCCN 2021040926 (ebook) | ISBN 9781793629340 (cloth) | ISBN 9781793629357 (epub) Subjects:
LCSH: Religion in advertising. | Advertising—Relgious aspects.
Classification: LCC HF5821 .S327 2022 (print) | LCC HF5821 (ebook) | DDC 659.1—dc23
LC record available at https://lccn.loc.gov/2021040925
LC ebook record available at https://lccn.loc.gov/2021040926

Contents

1 Preface: Let There Be Light 1

2 Holy Hype: What, in Heaven's Name, Is It? 9

3 Religion and Advertising: Scrambling the Sacred and the Profane 29

4 In the Beginning: At the Intersection of Damascus Road and Madison Avenue 47

5 Selling the Goods Amidst the Good News 65

6 Apparel: The Fabric of American Faith 159

7 Marketing Religion on the Streets 179

8 The Bible Tells Me So: Scriptural Stories of Survival Create Metaphors for the Advertising of Nonprofits 205

9 Revelations of the Future of Holy Hype 227

Index 237

About the Authors 251

Chapter 1

Preface

Let There Be Light

In 1975, American sociologist Robert Neely Bellah wrote an oft-quoted sentence that is the perfect opening for this book on the intersection of religion and advertising: "[H]appiness attained through limitless material acquisition is denied by every religion and philosophy known to mankind, but is preached incessantly by every American television set" (p. 134). Advertisements are word-and-picture exercises used in the persuasion of consumers to purchase products or services in addition to the promotion of a particular brand of product or service. The object is to get targeted, or specifically chosen, consumers to buy in enough quantity to bring in revenue significantly over and above the cost of publishing the ads. Whether by picture tube, pixels online, or paper, they are the mechanism by which producers of things sell their products to the public to make a profit. But that is not the only reason or most important reason to study ads. Judith Williamson writes in the introduction to her book *Decoding Advertisements* (1978):

> Advertisements are one of the more important culture factors moulding (*sic*) and reflecting our life today . . . Obviously it has a function, which is to sell things to us. But it has another function, which I believe in many ways replaces that traditionally provided by art or religion. It creates structures of meaning. (pp. 11–12)

Successful ads home in on those characteristics of social life that are particularly salient to large swaths of the consumer culture. Some people respond best to sexual stimuli; some others respond to fear appeals. For another group of consumers, humor is the way to engage them and build a positive connection between them and the product. Which subjects are found to be the major attention getters or most pertinent and arresting to the greatest number of viewers? The answer to this question comes from the assessment of the targeted audience. Despite the contradictory and enigmatic relationship between conspicuous consumption and the nineteenth-century Protestant value of frugality, religious themes are some of the most charismatic in advertising for unsacred, worldly goods, an approach we call "holy hype." Budde, a scholar in Catholic studies and political science, calls the paradox "postmodern hedonism simultaneous with a 'return to traditional values'" (1997, p. 37) and explains how it happened once the Industrial Revolution had truly kicked in:

> [I]n the postmodern era problems of productive capacity have been largely overcome in the advanced capitalist countries, only to be replaced by those of consumptive capacity. Capitalism now needs high, even profligate, levels of consumer spending to function smoothly; were people to cease consuming once their basic needs were met, the system would collapse. (p. 37)

Holy hype is primarily the use of religious images, themes, words, and sometimes music in advertisements to sell secular products. I, Dr. Susan Sarapin, believe that the first example of holy hype that I actually perceived as such was the Xerox® "It's a miracle" campaign in the mid-1970s (see figure 2.1d). My undergraduate education in art inculcated in me the artistic sophistication to be aware of this holistic (or, rather, holy-istic) advertising approach and to appreciate what ability it was that I would eventually praise in gifted copywriters, art directors, and photographers. My graduate studies leading to a doctoral degree in communication filled in the psychological and sociological aspects of audience response. As a lifelong, incurably curious observer of human conduct in general and human religious behavior in particular, stimulated by our family habit of discussing news events over dinner and creating puns about them, I had also begun to notice billboards, church marquees, and signs of all sorts.

I began collecting vintage and current tear sheets from magazines and newspapers that featured holy hype and took notes on TV commercials using this approach. This hobby was significantly facilitated by the introduction of the internet and sites such as eBay.com. In graduate school, I explored this subject matter through academic research just to satisfy my own inquiring mind. It was not my chosen specialty. Academic reception of the articles that emerged from the research was highly approbative. The work on holy hype was a labor of love for me, but I discovered that many of my colleagues also found it fascinating, elucidating, and instructive in other types of advertising. Fortunately for me, among those communication scholars was my coauthor, Pamela L. Morris, PhD. She was captivated by what I discovered in the phenomenon of holy hype—an approach to advertising that had a complicated, centuries-long history, sociological aspects, humor, irony, and communicative insights. Dr. Morris comes from the same communication philosophy as I do, but with a chosen emphasis on media literacy, answering questions regarding what is really being sold or told. Her studies balanced my emphasis on the communicative channels of television, radio, and print and their effects, and these contributed the illuminating complement to our investigation.

About four years ago, I became convinced that the best way to share a portion of my 2,500-plus ads was to write a book about holy hype. As instructors and mentors, Dr. Morris and I understand that part of our obligation to the academy and to students everywhere is the enrichment of the body of literature by contributing our knowledge, research analyses, and insights. Students and teachers of advertising, persuasion, religion, visual communication, public relations, sociology, history, and marketing along with practicing clergy and others could benefit from a resource like this book. There are some excellent journal articles and books that touch on this topic textually from a chiefly sociological perspective and as a minor facet of the practice of advertising; however, there is none aside from this book with such a clear and expansive focus on the actual ads. We show almost 300. Some may suggest that our perspective on holy hype, that is, concentrating on hundreds of single ads, is "unjustifiably reductionist" (Budde, 1997, p. 38). On the contrary, Budde observes:

> Whatever effects derive from commercial culture, such can only be effects of the total flow—and the significance of any single item in that flow can be ascertained only in relation to other items in that flow. In place of a linear, behaviorist epistemology ("Does commercial A produce the expected behavior/attitude change?"), one must necessarily substitute a more interpretive, subjective methodology. (p. 38)

And that is exactly what we have chosen to do here. We leave it to other academic scholars to find other contextual criteria by which to compare ads—whether by an economic, social, religious, or any other standard—or by decade, by industry, or some other category. The foundations are here for much more research.

Meanwhile, the popular audience in many countries, but especially in the United States, would welcome this type of information to satisfy their curiosity about this ancient advertising phenomenon. Investigating the promotional industry messages that use this approach most frequently assists us in learning new ways to attract consumers, proselytize, use humor, use religious themes that resonate with but do not offend viewers, and formulate persuasive appeals—skills that are beneficial in advertising for all sorts of clients. As media scholars, we do not wholly subscribe to the critical school of thought. We believe that audiences have agency; they have the power to critique the messages they receive, and the power to make decisions from whether to buy to whether to speak up in favor or in protest of those messages. We also believe that media creators can be guided by both audience demands and ethical considerations, although we acknowledge the importance of scholarship and public involvement toward those ends.

Although sacred- or religion-related themes are highly conspicuous in the marketplace through advertising, they are not pervasive. Yes, this approach clearly stands out in the cacophony of the mass media. Maguire and Weatherby (1998), who searched for "visuals only" in their study, find that only 1.25% of advertising contains referents to religion. We estimate that when we search ads (a) using an inclusive array of keywords, (b) looking for words as well as images, (c) and checking a wider variety of mass-mediated channels, including magazines, that about 2.5%–3%, perhaps even more, of all advertisements would be found to contain religious symbolism in the picture and/or rhetoric, even if only tangentially.

By way of clarification, this book is not a treatise on religion, nor is it a discourse on advertising in general. There are many books for the student covering each of these areas of interest. However, the student of either of these disciplines will find enough new material in the other to see these domains and their intersections in a whole new light. Our approach focuses on parts of advertising that are not often treated academically. To further explain our purpose, we want readers to understand that we use the word "student" loosely. The term could have an academic meaning, or it could refer to people among a popular audience who are simply fascinated by the holy hype phenomenon and are devotees of these topics. This book may also appeal to people who consider themselves basic observers of human behavior, people who want to know why there is such a concept as holy hype, how it came to be, and how it might be affecting us and our consumer decisions, often without our awareness.

We must emphasize that in the examination of the book's ads, we do not indulge in deep sociological analysis. Although sociology is the study of the petri dish in which advertising and any other human activities or interests flourish or dwindle, our route through the study of holy hype is much more aligned with communication principles than with sociological ones. As such, it leads us to explore questions such as these: *What are the actual messages being disseminated? How do the messages work on the receivers of those messages, and do they work effectively or not?* We have opted to use print media primarily, although we do include a handful of still images from some television commercials. Video analysis is more complex, and would require the reader to exit this book to fully appreciate the item being analyzed. Print ads, on the other hand, are shown as they were or are seen by the public and can be analyzed more expeditiously and in fewer words. Additionally, we show a few stock photos to demonstrate that not all holy hype ads require original photography or illustration. This saves money for the advertiser and makes complicated concepts doable because the problems of image production have already been solved.

Although this book focuses on holy hype in the United States, it contains numerous advertising examples from other countries—countries that did not engage in this type of advertising just one or two decades ago. Some of the governments of these other nations use censorship in cases of public expression that officials deem to be blasphemous or socially out of bounds in other ways—for example, those that are sexually explicit or show behavior considered irreligious, such as smoking or drinking alcohol. In America, the First Amendment protects potentially offensive ads as free speech, the suppression of which is determined by "righteous" public outrage and pushback through negative commentary, protests against, and boycotts of corporations, putting economic pressure on the "offenders." We include comments by businesspeople defending their use of extreme holy hype. Most have not felt the need to tamp down any perceived impiety or sacrilege because the repudiation of their ads has not resulted in harm to their financial or reputational bottom lines.

There may be issues in the ads we show that we do not fully address in our commentary. For example, we may notice and even point to a potential issue with race or sexuality, such as what we have seen in the "Ebony and Ivory" advertisement by Benetton® (not shown in this book due to the inability to contact the people responsible for giving usage permission), in some of the Nike® ads (see figure 5.14), or in ads such as in figures 5.2b, 5.5b, and 5.7b. Are some of these ads designed to shock us into conversations or into changing our minds about things? Undoubtedly. Are some designed to take advantage of cultural differences between races? In other words, are certain audiences purposely being manipulated? It seems likely, but we leave that discussion to other scholars whose main focus is something other than religion. Cultural context will always need to be taken into consideration in advertising decisions.

After reading this book, you may wonder why, of all ads that would perfectly represent our main topic, Christmas ads are almost nonexistent in this volume. The answer is this: We could probably write three books on Christmas ads alone. Also, Christmas ads by their very nature are holy hype: the promotion of consumer goods at a religious holiday. If these ads did not contain any references to religion or the holiday, the products might fail in the marketplace at the biggest selling time of the year. It is far more instructional to see the holy hype approach used more ingeniously in situations that do not compel religiosity, especially for products that normally have absolutely nothing to do with religion or spirituality.

This book is organized into nine chapters, including this introduction as Chapter 1 and the conclusion as Chapter 9. Chapter 2 explains the holy hype phenomenon in all of its manifestations, helping the reader identify this advertising approach. Chapter 3 explores the seemingly illogical link between religion and advertising, between the piety of faith and the irreverence of selling. Chapter 4 delves into some of the early forms of holy hype all the way back to the Middle Ages, and provides a historical, theoretical, and sociological framework for the ancient and modern modes of holy hype. Chapter 5 focuses on the visual evidence of the use of religious themes and images in the advertising of consumer goods and services as well as the use of secular themes and images in the advertising of religious goods and services, representing most major religions. It illustrates and explains this approach in the nineteenth, twentieth, and twenty-first centuries. Chapter 6 explains and illustrates the use of apparel, mostly T-shirts and sweatshirts, plus jewelry and other tchotchkes, Yiddish for inexpensive trinkets, to identify oneself by faith and religion and to express personal beliefs and associations. Chapter 7 explicates much of the God-related promotion we see on highway billboards and church marquees. With an outdoor audience in the hundreds of thousands every day, these signs of God are powerful, inspirational, and persuasive and, sometimes, quite amusing. Chapter 8 is an explanation of the use of Bible stories as metaphor, such as the Noah's Ark theme in survival-communication advertising for nonprofit organizations specializing in the promotion of environmental stewardship and the protection of the earth's natural resources.

We would like to thank some people who contributed to the production of this book. Our gratitude goes to: Dr. Christine Spinetta-Ganguly for her help with Chapter 4, both in conducting research and in writing; David Hamburg (Dr. Sarapin's brother), Hanna Hodnett, and Zachary Huelsing (Dr. Sarapin's younger son) for their work in copyediting, proofreading, and formatting; and our husbands Marvin and Mike for their supreme patience while we focused almost completely on our writing. Dr. Sarapin thanks the late Mira and Alvin Hamburg, her parents, above all. They sacrificed so much for her and were always her biggest cheerleaders. Dr. Sarapin would also like to give her appreciation and thanks to: Linda Hamburg Missler (her sister); Nathaniel Huelsing (her older son); mentors Dr. Glenn Sparks, Dr. Sorin Matei, Dr. Melanie Morgan, Dr. Robert Ogles, Dr. John Greene, Dr. Pamela Morris, Dr. Maryjo Cochran, and Dr. Jefferson Spurlock; dear friends and boosters Gerri Kuna and Cheryl Ford. Dr. Morris wishes to thank those who have believed in her throughout the years, especially Dr. Earl and Sharon Morris (her parents), Jennifer Lindsay (who told her that "It is never too late to change your dreams"), Dr. Cheri Niedzwiecki, Dr. Stacey Connaughton, Dr. Sorin Matei, and the late Dr. Robert Yale.

Perhaps a reading of this book may stimulate some of you to become "fans" of holy hype. Using a bit of wordplay in an effort to whet your appetite, we show you an old form of holy hype in figure 1.1. Before the days of air conditioning in the 1950s, and even continuing into the 1960s and 1970s in churches that could not afford to install central air conditioning, sitting in a crowded sanctuary for hours could get uncomfortably warm. Commercial printers began creating church fans, handheld devices made of an inexpensive wooden handle with a "fan blade" constructed of thick paper stock and attached to the handle by a staple. One side of the blade would be printed with a photo or drawing of the church or biblical image usually of Jesus, and the reverse side would be imprinted with an advertising message by the community business footing the bill for the fans or paying the church for use of the advertising space. These fans became a standard at worship services and are still used today in some churches, even when air conditioning is available.

We sincerely hope that this book and its hundreds of ads serve to inspire, educate, and amuse people of all ages and from all walks of life. We also hope that it sheds much light on an under-researched subject of broad interest. As we get into Chapter 2, we begin to examine the finer points of holy hype within the context of advertising in general—how holy hype both conforms to and occasionally breaks the rules of advertising.

Figure 1.1 An Array of the Front and Back Sides of Four Vintage Church Fans from the 1940s and 1950s, Both Folding and Non-Folding. *Source: Image created by author.*

REFERENCES

Bellah, R.N. (1975). *The broken covenant: American civil religion in time of trial.* Seabury Press.

Budde, M. (1997). *The (magic) kingdom of god: Christianity and global culture industries.* Westview Press.

Maguire, B., & Weatherby, G. A. (1998). The secularization of religion and television commercials. *Sociology of Religion, 59*(2), 171–178. doi: 10.2307/3712079

Williamson, J. (1978). *Decoding advertisements: Ideology and meaning in advertising.* Marion Boyars.

Chapter 2

Holy Hype

What, in Heaven's Name, Is It?

OVERVIEW

Thomas Merton, an American Trappist monk, wrote that "Advertising treats all products with the reverence and the seriousness due to sacraments" (1966, p. 211). Our purpose in illuminating the holy hype approach in advertising is to raise awareness of the substantial persuasive effects of this communication viewpoint and to demonstrate how holy hype complies with the principles of advertising. In fact, holy hype expands upon the tenets of advertising in a noticeable yet rarely studied way. O'Shaughnessy and O'Shaughnessy (2004), directing their attention to symbolic systems and these systems' efforts to appeal to a target audience put it simply: Symbolic systems like religion "can evoke relevant meanings by resonating with the concerns of the target audience" (p. 40).

If you have ever seen a metallic fish decal affixed to the rear of a vehicle, a billboard exhorting attendance at church, a T-shirt sporting a special take on a verse or concept from the Bible, a sign in front of a church proclaiming a humorous or inspirational message, or a print ad audaciously announcing the resurrection of a twenty-five-year-old athletic shoe as the "Second Coming," then you have witnessed holy hype in action. And in the process, perhaps, someone has "witnessed" to you. While these may attract the attention of and even persuade a great many Christians, ads resembling these approaches may also repel or annoy others through their perceived irrelevance or inappropriateness.

These and many other acts of faith- or religion-themed advertising, or holy hype, are seen everywhere in our highly spiritual, consumer culture—at the intersection of Madison Avenue and Damascus Road. Ubiquitous, yes. Novel? No way. Ecclesiastes 1:9 (NIV) states, "What has been will be again, what has been done will be done again; *there is nothing new under the sun*" [author emphasis]. The concept behind holy hype originated at least five millennia ago, thousands of years before the advent of print, and long before the establishment of advertising as a professional discipline shortly after the Industrial Revolution. Presbrey looks to the ancient Babylonians as the first promoters, by virtue of their stamping the soft, clay bricks used to build temples with the pictographic mark, or "logotype," of the king who built them. Remarking further on this advanced civilization that prospered 3,000 years before Jesus, Presbrey states, "The kings who did this advertised themselves to such of their subjects as could read hieroglyphics. The modern advertising man would say they ran an institutional campaign for themselves and their dynasties" (1929, p. 1). It is possible that this type of advertising was the first blending of the sacred and the profane.

Modern and postmodern holy hype have increased in frequency and breadth of exposure with the development of more conspicuous and portable forms of media technologies; greater acceptance and adoption of advertising in general by the leaders of certain religious denominations; the inculcation of religious belief or spirituality into the consciousness of the American consumer culture; and the blurring of the line between our sacred and secular lives.

The medium of print antedated all other forms of mass media, thanks to the invention of the Gutenberg printing press centuries before the founding of America. The Bible, itself, was the first book to be produced for a large, international market, and this period is known as the actual beginning of mass communication. The printing press enabled the increasingly literate public to read the writings of thinkers such as Erasmus and Luther, whose ideas were now able to spread across Europe in the form of books and to influence minds to this very day. Some of the earliest instances of mass-produced holy hype were colonial-era flyers distributed or read aloud by town criers and newspaper ads announcing either the appearance of an itinerant evangelical preacher or a special worship service at a particular church. In modern times, print advertising using religious imagery for the promotion of consumer products has been employed by some of the largest and most widely known brands, such as Xerox®, Nike®, Benetton®, and Reebok®. Print advertising in an evangelical vein, using either sacred or secular themes, has become more prevalent, and even daring in some cases, for religious denominations and organizations such as the United Church of Christ, Damascus Road Church, CAIR (Council on American-Islamic Relations), and Catholic Charities.

SOURCE OF THE TERM "HOLY HYPE"

This phenomenon was originally dubbed "godvertising" by Dr. Read Schuchardt, a professor of communication at Wheaton College in Wheaton, Illinois. He used it in an article in the 1990s, which was published in a scholarly journal. There is an internet dotcom URL by that name, godvertising.com, which was registered on July 31, 2002. It has been online at least since July 2004. The owner of the site encapsulates the gist of his digital gallery in the succinct tagline, "Church Signs—Sermons in 25 words or less." And that pretty much sums up the content of the website—hundreds of photos of church reader boards spotted all over the United States, and submitted by the site's numerous visitors.

Although the word "godvertising" has been in use for about 25 years, there has been little consensus on what it means or signifies and little to no published academic research about it. The term "godvertising" refers to advertisements that promote God, and the website dedicated to it exemplifies godvertising by displaying hundreds of interesting, ironic, and humorous reader boards on signs installed on the front lawns of churches. Holy hype can promote God, but it can promote many other things as well, such as religion in general, particular religions and houses of worship, atheism, liquor, cars, and just about anything else under the sun. Consequently, godvertising is much too narrow a definition and name to fully explain the holy hype phenomenon in American culture. Holy hype was coined by Dr. Susan Sarapin in 2019.

DEFINITIONS OF "HOLY HYPE"

Simply put, holy hype as a unique phenomenon in advertising is characterized by four main dimensions: (1) the use of religious themes to advertise nonreligious or secular consumer products; (2) the use of religious themes to advertise God or religion or to identify oneself as an adherent (which could be anything from the knowledge of a divine being to the welcoming fellowship of a particular church to the support of a faith-based cause or organization); (3) the use of secular themes to advertise God or religion; and (4) the use of religious themes to advertise religious products. Each of these dimensions represents a distinct meaning within the definition. Lest anyone assume that the word "hype" in this terminology implies negativity, we must clarify. Although hype can refer to deceptively unwarranted claims, our meaning of the word is that of the promotion, or advertising, of things and concepts, indeed sometimes shockingly intensified, through ingenious or dramatic methods.

Here, corresponding with the dimensions above, are the definitions of holy hype we believe are most accurate for this review.

Type 1—Secular Holy Hype

One of the earliest and most venerable campaigns of secular holy hype ran from 1961 into the 1970s. It was created by the Doyle Dane Bernbach advertising agency, whose copywriter, Judy Protas, conceived of the famous slogan, "You don't have to be Jewish to love Levy's Rye Bread." This series of ads appears in AdAge's listing of the top 100 ads of the twentieth century (AdAge, 1999; Fox, 2014) (see figure 2.1c). There is no clearer indication of times changing than the fact that these ads today, almost 60 years later, would be almost meaningless for some and highly racist and anti-Semitic for others. Jews in the 1960s and 1970s were predominantly White and were characterized by a one-size-fits-all typology. Back then, a Black man, a Native American, an Irish policeman, and others were thought of as "conspicuously non-Jewish New Yorkers" (Fox, 2014). In 2019, the US Census Bureau reported the racial makeup of Jews in America to be 2% Black, 5% Hispanic, and 4% of another ethnicity (Sales, 2019). Following decades of intermarriage and conversion to Judaism resulting in 11% of Jews being something other than "White," the photographs in these advertisements for Levy's would not be of individuals so "obviously" *not* Jewish. Good timing and a keen awareness of social norms are critical in the development of effective advertising. Some excellent publications are littered with really good ideas that did not hold up to changing social sensitivities and mores, and the agency responsible for Levy's campaign knew when it had outlived its usefulness. During its run, it took the company's rye bread from New York notoriety to the rest of the nation.

Another of the most beloved and memorable of the modern commercial television and print advertising campaigns that employed an explicitly religious or spiritual theme was the "It's a Miracle" series for Xerox® duplicators. Created by Needham, Harper & Steers agency in 1975, this ad is another notable entry in the list of top ads of the twentieth century (AdAge, 1999). The scene is set inside a medieval monastery, and the actor-models are Catholic monks (figure 2.1d). The brothers greet the customers with a humble acceptance of their duplicating jobs, and then turn their eyes skyward, beseeching God for a miraculous solution to the laborious task ahead of them. God delivers for the church scribes with the Xerox 914 workhorse, often hidden by the monks in an adjacent room. The customer must believe that the monks themselves are copying the documents by hand, as they do with their beautiful illustrated manuscripts. The effectiveness of the Xerox ads could live on for years, as long as the company were to continue to produce copiers,

Figure 2.1 a) A Billboard Advertising the Historic Anglican Church Behind It, St. Matthew-in-the-City, in Auckland, New Zealand. The church is known for its progressive theology and this often-humorous sign. b) This is the same billboard with a different image, one of Mary discovering from a home pregnancy test that she is with child. c) Ad from the 1961–1970s campaign for New York's Levy's bread. The slogan became "You don't have to be Jewish to love Levy's Jewish rye bread," and the ad series found its way into AdAge's list of 100 all-time best ads of the twentieth century. d) A Xerox ad from the "It's a miracle" campaign from the mid-1970s, which likewise was noted as one of the best of the 20th century. Headline: "The duplicators for those who appreciate the virtues of simplicity." e) An ad about the "Seven Capital Sins" for EF Hutton, a financial services company that went out of business. f) A bottle label for Unholy Ale from Coppertail Brewing. The art by Evan Harris is reminiscent of medieval manuscript illustrations. *a) Courtesy of St. Matthew-in-the-City. b) Courtesy of St. Matthew-in-the-City. c) Levy's; no longer in business. d) Courtesy of Xerox, ©Xerox Holdings Corporation. e) EF Hutton; no longer in business. f) Courtesy of Coppertail Brewing, ©Coppertail Brewing Co.*

and its salience was demonstrated in 2017, when Young & Rubicam brought back the Xerox 1977 Super Bowl ad and Brother Dominic for a new audience of digital natives (Coffee, 2017). We may have seen our favorite monks for the last time because Hiltzik (2018) predicts an imminent end to the once-indestructible Xerox. The monastic scribes' durability and longevity in the advertising world, speaking for Xerox, will depend on articles and books like these in which the ad agency's creativity is remembered and lauded. As long as journalism, communication, and religion professors teach students about the important period dating to the sixth century CE up to the invention of the printing press, the connection between monks and the production of textual copies will live on (Corwin, 2016).

These ads and the Levy's rye bread ads would be examples of definition one of "holy hype," below:

> (1) The act of promoting or calling public attention to non-religious consumer products or services by communicating, through the explicit use of religious imagery, rhetoric, or music, a commercial message designed to influence the behavior or thought patterns of an audience of current and potential consumers of those secular consumer products or services.

This form of holy hype, which we call secular holy hype, is characterized by two distinct attributes: (a) It draws attention to a nonreligious product or service; and (b) The purpose of the advertising is strictly commercial. The mission of these messages is not evangelical or the spreading of the gospel. These are not reverent paeans to the Almighty—rather, they are fervent, and frequently irreverent, exaltations to the almighty dollar (see Chapter 5 for more). Two other examples of secular holy hype can be seen in the bottom two ads in figure 2.1. The EF Hutton ad in figure 2.1e speaks about sin in relation to financial services, and the Unholy ad by Coppertail Brewing in figure 2.1f promotes an ale as "not so sacred."

Type 2—Proselytistic and Self-Identifying Holy Hype (Witnessing)

> (2) The act of promoting or calling public attention to God, the gospel, a sacred text, a church, a denomination, or a religious cause by communicating, through the explicit use of religious imagery, rhetoric, or music, a noncommercial message designed to influence the behavior or thought patterns of an audience of current and potential consumers of religion or to identify oneself as an adherent.

This style of holy hype is frequently seen in American culture and is characterized by two distinct properties: (a) It draws attention to God, a religion, or a religious tenet; and (b) The purpose of the advertising or the use of the product is *not* commercial. From mostly the Christian angle, the mission of these messages is primarily that of evangelical proselytizing, spreading the word, and making converts. This definition would include, but is not limited to, religious-tradition-specific signs promoting faith in general or a specific religion or denomination in particular; signs promoting a specific church; and wearable art such as T-shirts and jewelry, bumper stickers, car decals, and more. This category would even extend to such unusual products as the Grilled Cheesus, which debosses a slice of bread around an image of Jesus, producing a darkened, raised image after toasting, Jesus belt buckles, and inflatable nativity scenes for the front yard at Christmas (see figure 2.2).

Although other religions participate in some religious holy hype, Jews, for example, are generally not involved in proselytizing. Some Jews do wear religious jewelry, such as a Star of David or a mezuzah on a necklace, but this is not nearly as overt a statement as the displays created by some members of certain Christian denominations. This would not include religious images or signs that would be more accurately described as belonging to the domain of

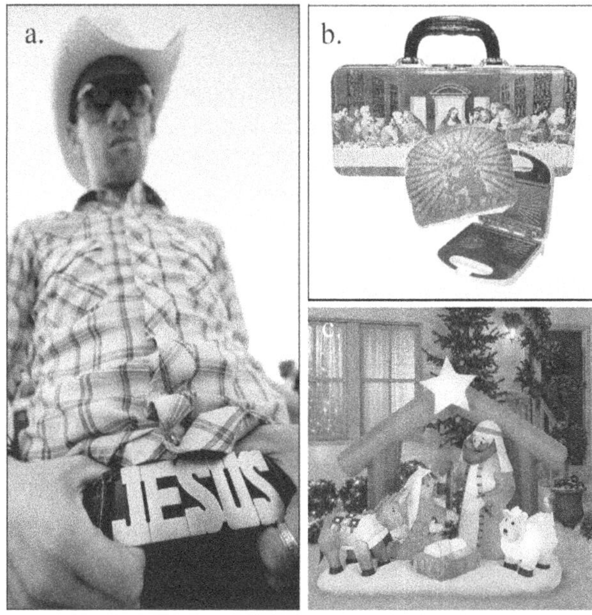

Figure 2.2 a) A wannabe cowboy unambiguously promotes his religious affiliation through his belt buckle. b) A "Last Supper" lunchbox and a grilled CHEESUS sandwich maker from OMRgoods. c) Inflatable nativity scene for the front yard at Christmas. *a) Photo from iStockphoto, photographer Mlenny. b) Photo courtesy of Susan Sarapin. c) Photo courtesy of Gemmy Industries, ©Gemmy Industries Corp.*

civil religion, such as "In God We Trust" appearing on our nation's currency (read about civil religion and its differences from holy hype in Chapter 3).

Type 3—Institutional Holy Hype

The third form of holy hype, as defined below, is exemplified by campaigns produced by sectarian organizations such as churches and associations to promote their form of religion.

> (3) The act of promoting or calling public attention to God, the gospel, a sacred text, a church, a denomination, or a religious cause by communicating, through the explicit use of secular imagery, rhetoric, or music, a noncommercial message designed to influence the behavior or thought patterns of an audience of current and potential consumers of religion.

This type of holy hype, which we refer to as institutional, is identified by two distinct characteristics: (a) It promotes or draws attention to a religious and/or charitable organization or cause, usually a specific church; and (b) The purpose of the advertising is not commercial. The objective of these messages is primarily recruitment into the institution or getting the public to attend or participate in a function. The ads numbered figures 2.1a and 2.1b fall under this category. There is a billboard, which advertises the historic Anglican Church behind it, St. Matthew-in-the-City, in Auckland, New Zealand. The first of these shows Joseph and Mary in bed with the accompanying title: "Poor Joseph. God was a hard act to follow." Figure 2.1b is the same billboard with a different theme. Mary has just run a pregnancy test on herself and discovered, in shock, that she is heavy with child. The ads that represent this category are commonly friendly, ironic, humorous, or thought-provoking invitations to join the group in fellowship (see figure 2.3).

Early in the twentieth century, experts in church publicity began publishing stand-alone books and reports for members of the clergy, whereas previous treatises on this topic had been relegated to religious journals that were available to ministers of specific denominations. Among these authors, Ernest Eugene Elliott was prolific. Some of his book titles are *Making Good in the Local Church* from 1913, *How to Fill the Pews* from 1917, and *How to Advertise the Church* from 1920. He hit the nail on the head when he wrote,

> It is with considerable hesitancy that one undertakes to point out the method of a practical application of modern principles to the work of the Church. Religious workers as a rule have a natural prejudice against attempts to apply worldly methods, though modern, to the work of the Church, and this feeling is so strong on the part of many that one almost seems to proclaim himself a reformer indeed when he attempts to draw practical inferences as in these studies and to make these inferences generally and quickly applicable. (Elliott, 1917, n.p.)

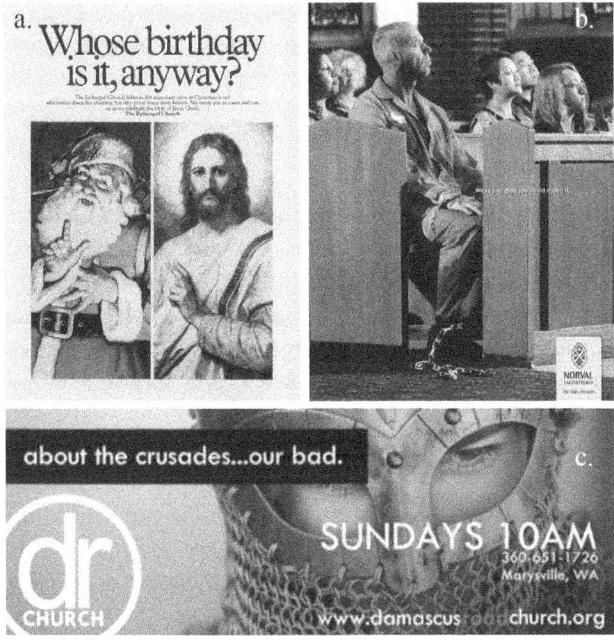

Figure 2.3 a) One of Tom McElligott and Nancy Rice's exceptional ads for The Episcopal Church. b) One of a campaign of ads for Norval United Church. Prisoner in orange jumpsuit sitting in a pew without causing a stir. "We're just glad you could make it." c) An early ad for a new type of church in Marysville, WA. *a) ©The Episcopal Church, courtesy of Father Martin. b) Courtesy of Norval United Church, The United Church of Canada. c) ©Damascus Road Church.*

One of those modern worldly methods was advertising. Churches and religious organizations, for the most part, have discovered that they compete with hundreds of other activities available to the consumer on Wednesday nights, Friday nights, Saturday mornings, and Sundays. The church, synagogue, or temple must find a way to break through the advertising for those rival venues, including other houses of worship. Tom McElligott is the copywriter for numerous ads for The Episcopal Church in the 1980s, one of which is figure 2.3a. A few of his dozens of ads in this campaign are sprinkled throughout this book. McElligott and his agency, Fallon McElligott, created them pro bono. Figure 2.3b is one of a campaign similar to McElligott's in its use of "outside-the-box," unorthodox situations. In this ad for the Norval United Church, a prisoner in shackles and orange jumpsuit sits attentively in the pew. Nobody looks upon him as being strange or out of place. He is welcomed just like everyone else around him is. The headline is: "We're just glad you could make it." In one more ad in the figure, the one for Damascus Road Church at figure 2.3c, we see a remnant of the Crusades, dressed in chain mail, head down in an apologetic stance. The memorable headline in our modern language is: "About the crusades . . . our bad."

Type 4—Religious Holy Hype

The fourth category of holy hype, as defined below, is seen in most traditional media as well as some unique new forms of media. One example of this form of religious advertising would be some of the items sold in association with the movie *The Passion of the Christ*. It may include advertisements of consumer items such as kosher foods, items used for worship, tangible symbols to hang in homes or churches, head scarves, and services such as religious dating services.

> (4) The act of promoting or calling public attention to religious consumer products or services by communicating, through the explicit use of religious imagery, rhetoric, or music, a commercial message designed to influence the behavior or thought patterns of an audience of current and potential consumers of those products or services.

This could be the most humdrum of the categories of holy hype if it were not for the imaginative efforts of talented advertising agencies. The overwhelming challenge for them is to outperform the effectiveness of innovations in institutional holy hype. Searching through hundreds of examples of this type of ad on the internet reveals just how difficult this task really is. We, as communication scholars, find that this type of advertising is not necessarily produced by advertising specialists. These ads are commonly designed by account executives at newspapers who sold the ad space, or they are put together by clerics or office employees at the church or synagogue, whose belief is that the more words in the ad, the more effective the "tell-them-everything-you-can-in-the-space-you-can-afford" approach. Those who think of the ad campaign as an investment will make the financial commitment necessary to hire experienced advertising copywriters and designers. We looked at ads for Christian book stores, religious jewelry, clerical apparel, churches, and many more, the type of religious goods retailers and religious institutions would be apt to advertise as their services and products. Finally, after an extensive exploration, we located a couple of high-quality ads that we could use to illustrate this category. The paucity of professional-looking and innovative advertisements in this category points to an area of holy hype that remains inadequately explored in terms of creativity and individualization. The two ads shown in figures

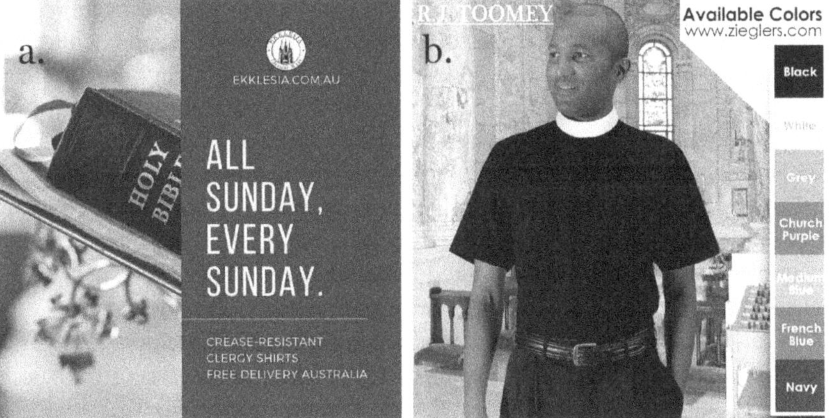

Figure 2.4 a) An Australian company that sells clerical apparel advertises the durability of its crease-resistant clerical shirts. b) R. J. Toomey on Zieglers.com. *a) Screenshot taken from ekklesia.com, ©Ekklesia. b) Screenshot taken from zieglers.com.*

2.4a and 2.4b are two examples. They make use of stock photography (figure 2.4a) and professional photography (figure 2.4b), and yet there is no overall compelling headline to draw in viewers. There are companies, which identify as religious marketers, that do offer off-the-rack designs for postcards. Just insert the name of the church, and print off a few thousand for bulk-mail processing.

EXPLORING THE DEFINITION

Some more fundamentalist-leaning religious men and women would point to this cultural curiosity, holy hype, and suggest that it is an actual *act of God*—that is, God is the divine author of these messages. And in much the same way He inspired men to proclaim His Word through written medium thousands of years ago, God is now inspiring people to put His messages on highway billboards, in skywriting, in newspapers and magazines, on television and radio, and on clothing. According to the Jewish scriptures, known as the Torah, or what Christians call the Old Testament, God actually "engraved" His words into stone tablets, in His own inimitable style, for the purpose of disseminating His message to a large, public audience to influence the behavior and thinking of the Hebrew people.

However plausible this act-of-God theory may be, this book will be limited mostly to scholarship within the discipline of communication, specifically media effects, although elements of religious doctrine and sociology will be necessary considerations to explain such things as the justification for holy hype. Although many would like to claim that God is the true client in this marketing activity, we are going to take a less otherworldly approach to this investigation. Consequently, despite the fact that the Almighty may, in fact, be the ultimate beneficiary of a successfully implemented holy hype campaign, we will examine this topic under the assumption that mere mortals are the producers, distributors, and consumers of these messages.

Let's look at another couple of key considerations regarding holy hype. First, it does not matter whether the use of the medium is paid for or not. For example, a billboard company could come up with a holy hype message or receive one from an anonymous partner and decide to donate sign space for it. Wearables, likewise, are not a paid advertisement for religion. The "God Speaks" campaign, which hit Florida in 1999, began as a series of billboards commissioned by a citizen who wished to remain anonymous. Charlie Robb of the Smith Agency in Fort Lauderdale designed the holy hype, intended to provide a spiritual yet nondenominational message to passersby to remind them of God's presence (Kuntz, 1999). So clever and original was the campaign that it came to the attention of the Outdoor Advertising Association of America. The organization, which includes billboard companies among its membership, succeeded in persuading its members to design and display the ads as a public service. A few of the holy hype sayings were (a) "What part of 'Thou Shalt Not . . .' didn't you understand?—God"; (b) "That 'Love Thy Neighbor' thing—I meant it. —God"; (c) "I can think of 10 things that are carved in stone. —God" (see figure 7.2e). For the most part, the campaign was well-received by the public and by advertising associations that presented it with awards. There were some—a portion of the most fundamentalist of Christian sectarians—who felt the boards treated the serious topic of God too irreverently and too glibly (Sarapin & Spinetta, 2010). An accommodation was made for non-Christians or any others who worship on other days of the week. This planned billboard message, "Let's meet at my house Sunday before the game. —God," was scuttled (Kuntz, 1999).

Another consideration we must make about holy hype is this: John Jantsch of Duct Tape Marketing riffs off of one of legendary advertising guru David Ogilvy's memorable pearls of wisdom, "Ninety-nine percent of advertising does not sell much of anything," (Jantsch, n.d.) or the quote most often inaccurately attributed to John Wanamaker, "Half the money I spend on advertising is wasted; the trouble is, I don't know which half" (Searls, 2016). On the contrary, holy hype informs and/or influences a decision or intent to act. It plants an image or impression of the product or service in the potential consumer's mind, good or bad, positive or negative. It creates, enhances, reinforces, or inadvertently destroys a brand for a segment of the viewers. Similarly, holy hype does not *sell* God. It brings God or religion into the conversation, into the audience's consciousness, even if merely tangentially.

It makes the audience *aware* of God through a humorous, ironic, wry, or serious reference.

SEMANTICS AND AUDIENCES

Precisely because this book deals with an image-heavy style of advertising, we look to a distinguished professor of film and visual communication, Paul Messaris (1996), for the essentials of the roles of images in persuasion. He explains that images (a) "elicit emotions," (b) "serve as photographic proof that something did happen," and (c) "establish an implicit link between the thing that is being sold and some other images" (p. vii). Visual communication is often analyzed using semantics, in particular the system created by semiotician Charles Sanders Peirce, which "classifies relationships between signs and their meanings (or more precisely, between 'signifiers' and 'signifieds')" (Messaris, 1996, p. viii). The three main categories of Peirce's categorization are the icon, the index, and the symbol.

Most relevant to the use of images is iconicity, which evaluates the similarity between the sign and the object (signifier and signified). One characteristic of an icon is its authenticity, an important attribute of images that lends credibility to the advertising message and is expected to favorably influence buying decisions. However, one characteristic of postmodern culture that affects the semiotics of advertising, and holy hype in particular, is fragmentation, "that all things are disconnected and disjointed in their representations from each other, their origins and history, and contexts" (Furat, 1991, p. 71). Budde (1997) writes that this fragmentation is a result of

> the sheer volume, diversity, and transitoriness of cultural production (that) have largely sundered ties between symbols and their referents . . . Symbols can no longer be assumed to have a constant, universally understood relationship to some independent, "real" referent; rather, symbols in the commercial culture are constantly recombined, reshuffled, and replaced with an eye toward conveying novel "meanings" to various products and consumption opportunities. (p. 36)

Meaning in the postmodern word, writes Budde, "is constructed from a goulash of symbols, narratives, and prior 'meanings' in play in the cultural environment" (p. 36). Symbols detached from their original meaning now have polyvalent meaning, multiple interpretations, depending the way they are "appropriated by different sub-groups within an audience" (p. 36). Many possibilities open up for the use of religious symbols and rhetoric as they are shuffled into a deck of advertising techniques, and are drawn out of the deck in combination with other techniques.

The use of icons in advertising messages must also take into consideration the culture within which the targeted audience lives. O'Shaughnessy and O'Shaughnessy (2004) explain that the larger culture can be broken down into subcultures on the basis of just about any characteristic of a group of people who associate with each other because of that trait: age, religion, gender, ethnicity, and more. They contend that subcultures

> May be so distinct as to require different persuasive appeals. Even where there is no need to modify a product, the advertising may have to be changed to suit the "foreign" culture. This is because the persuasive job to be done may have to be tailored to the beliefs and/or values of the culture while various persuasive appeals vary in cultural appropriateness. (p. 10)

Subcultures can be so narrow in their interests that an ad created to sell a product or service to Orthodox Jews may have little or no significance for audiences of Reform Jews. It is our common experiences that predispose us, the members of each subculture, to notice certain concrete and abstract items and situations and respond in certain "learned" or remembered ways.

Religious versus Spiritual

We are sure the reader has already noticed that the word "church" has been used, to the exclusion of the name of any other house of worship, such as synagogue, temple, or mosque. There is a good reason for this. Indeed, there will be a noticeable emphasis on Christianity in general, and on Protestant Christianity in particular, because this group is the one most responsible for the religiously themed advertising and branding we see on the American landscape. The reasons for this will become evident as we delve more deeply into the social, economic, and political movements and trends since the birth of our nation in the late eighteenth century.

One effect of holy hype, regardless of its persuasiveness in "selling," is its degree of offensiveness to viewers, which depends on the amount and type of humor or sarcasm, the object of the humor, and the viewer's self-identification as spiritual or religious. This aspect is what makes holy hype a risky approach for advertisers. Those who regard themselves as highly "religious" may find the use of sacred images or themes to sell secular products as sacrilegious regardless of the actual rhetoric, images, or meanings. These symbols of their faith belong completely in that divine realm, they may think, and "mocking" them in order to makes sales or a joke is unthinkable, unfunny, and repulsive. Gubanov, Gubanov, and Rokotyanskaya (2019) explain that the joke or humorous criticism may be met by "unlaughter" if the mockery hurts, and that response "is perceived as a flawed inability to laugh at oneself and as a lack of a sense of humor, which, in its turn, further exacerbates the opposition of the Other (believers—atheists, West—East, etc.)" (p. 2143). Humor in this vein, as perceived by fundamentalist religionists, "negatively affects the overall image of religion and its followers" (p. 2143). A spiritual viewer of the ad may not find the satirical manipulation of "sacred" symbols offensive because the spiritual person may not connect with these symbols theologically.

N. D. Bell et al. (2011) explain why there is this stark difference of opinion on whether church marquees that are meant to be humorous are actually funny. They attribute the varying responses to the divergent natures of religious values and the values of those who use humor. They explain: "Humor flourishes where there is tolerance of ambiguity, chaos, passion, openness and nonconformity. Religion, and especially fundamentalism, on the other hand, lacks tolerance of ambiguity and encourages order, control, conservativism, and conformity" (p. 188).

An example of this predicament is a recent one from the arts, advertisements for the Tony Award-winning musical, "The Book of Mormon." The production itself was a caricature of a young, naive Mormon man's two-year mission experience to Uganda. To say that the LDS Church's members were not pleased with the irreverent musical would be an understatement. In a discussion on NPR in 2015, participant Timothy Emery commented during intermission:

> "I'm deeply Mormon, was raised in the church, really terribly offended by this play." He continued, "I might leave, yeah—except that I keep laughing. And that bothers me because it's so funny. So, my outsides are telling me, don't go forward. Don't see it. But my insides are telling me, this is really funny. So, I'm very conflicted at this point" (Smardon, 2015, n.p.) He did go back in for the second half.

The LDS Church, though, chose to take the high road in its response to the musical and its content rather than fight it (see figure 2.5). Public relations professional Chris Thomas states,

> The Playbill ad is another example of the LDS Church's savvy response to "The Book of Mormon" musical. Instead of protesting the musical, which is something that many would do, especially religious organizations, they made a bold and deliberate decision to embrace the situation. They have taken something that could have been detrimental to the church's missionary efforts and made it positive. (Jones, 2016, n.p.)

Notwithstanding the variety of Playbill ads the church ran, the official comment from the church was this: "The production may attempt to entertain

Figure 2.5 a) This is the Playbill publication from the performance of "The Book of Mormon." b) This ad appeared in some copies of the Playbill. c) This ad also appeared in some versions of the Playbill. Rising to the occasion, the Church of Jesus Christ of Latter-day Saints chose to counter the criticisms and derogation of the musical by promoting the actual sacred text. *All images courtesy of the Church of Jesus Christ of Latter-day Saints, © by Intellectual Reserve, Inc.*

audiences for an evening, but the Book of Mormon as a volume of scripture will change people's lives forever by bringing them closer to Christ" (Kirkland, 2011, n.p.).

Advertising versus Marketing and Branding

It should be noted that "marketing" is a term for the totality of activities involved in the transfer of goods and/or services from the producer or seller (i.e., the advertiser) to the end-user or consumer. According to the American Marketing Association, "Marketing is the activity, set of institutions, and processes for creating, communicating, delivering, and exchanging offerings that have value for customers, clients, partners, and society at large" (2017, n.p.). The goal is satisfying the identified "customer" to a greater degree than can competitors within the same marketplace or niche. Marketing includes analyzing the ultimate consumer's needs and wants and the understanding of how these consumer expectations complement or conflict with the goals of the organization. The consumer research results, or demographics, enable the organization to make strategic judgments that run the gamut from product design to package design to pricing to the eventual distribution of the product or service. Advertising is merely one of those numerous activities involved in marketing.

Branding is yet another concept in the marketplace. It is defined as "The marketing practice of creating a name, symbol or design that differentiates a product from other products" (Entrepreneur, 2020, n.p.). It is one activity of marketing. Advertising can be a large part of branding or reinforcing the brand of a product or service, but advertising and promotional campaigns change over time depending on changes in consumer trends, politics and political language, the economy, and many other variables. A brand, once established, is designed to become a fixture in the commercial, and sometimes cultural, realm. In other words, it is supposed to be relatively permanent. As we will see later, sometimes unexpected, external forces necessitate the tweaking of a time-honored brand—even a religious identity. Landor, an international giant in the branding business, defines a brand as "the sum of all the characteristics, tangible and intangible, that make the offer unique." Notice that they do not try to make the product unique, but rather the offer—what the product or service does for the consumer at this particular time under these particular conditions. They expound upon this concept by defining brand "identity" as those elements, such as the name, logo or symbol, and colors, by which an offer can be recognized (Gilmore, 2015, n.p.).

One might ask, "What do you mean by an 'intangible' characteristic of a company, product, or service?" Basically, it is an emotional association, preferably a positive one that the potential consumer makes with the product. A successful product's (or organization's) name or brand makes a consistently good impression, or in this case, a *God* impression, and evokes from the audience a perceived beneficial connection. Lance Strate, a professor of communication and media studies, concurs, stating that today's advertisements "generally do not present logical arguments and claims for their products. Instead, they seek to associate their product with evocative images and themes" (1991, p. 113). In other words, we have moved further away from the twentieth-century features and benefits into ads that make you *feel* a certain way about the product. This emotional association recalls the old expression introduced by Supreme Court Justice Potter Stewart in his attempt to define the indefinable, obscenity, in *Jacobellis v. Ohio* (1964),

> I shall not today attempt further to define the kinds of material I understand to be embraced within that shorthand description, and perhaps I could never succeed in intelligibly doing so. But *I know it when I see it* [author emphasis], and the motion picture involved in this case is not that. (Stewart, 1964)

The people at one of the country's leading brand consulting firms describe this mysterious yet very real feature of branding in a way we can all understand:

> While Brand X cola or even Pepsi-Cola may win blind taste tests over Coca Cola, the fact is that more people buy Coke than any other cola and, most importantly, they enjoy the experience of buying and drinking Coca Cola. The fond memories of childhood and refreshment that people have when they drink Coke is often more important than a little bit better cola taste. It is this emotional relationship with brands that make them so powerful. (The Brand Company, 2004, cited in Henriques, 2007, p. 45)

The holy hype approach can either brand a product or service or it can be used sporadically. Nike's advertisements use religious themes or phrases on occasion and for certain targeted audiences, but Hell Pizza's ads and Brimstone Brewery's ads do incorporate holy hype on a regular basis, making it part of their brands (read more about these brands in Chapter 5).

CONCLUSION

We have defined holy hype in its major dimensions to assist the viewer in discerning who it is meant to affect, what it is trying to persuade consumers to do, and whether it is successful. The various sub-definitions also help us glean information about the principles of advertising in general. It is our hope that as the reader sees the ads throughout the entirety of this volume, these definitions will be kept in mind and help the reader not just to see them but also to perceive them.

With all due respect to Canadian thinker and celebrity Marshall McLuhan, the designation of holy hype has more to do with the message than with the medium, venue, producer, or targeted message receiver. Without a convincing message that either sells a product or service, or facilitates engagement with and feeling for a brand, all of the well-conceived irony, humor, or mystery in advertising will be wasted effort and investment on the part of the creator, advertiser, and consumer. Unless it is strictly informational, the religious communication within a sacred or secular context, or the religiously cloaked consumer message, must be constructed as persuasive in essence, as all advertising messages should be. If one's purpose is persuasion, something in the rhetoric should impart a sense of urgency, fill a consumer's material or psychological need, or stand as a convincing argument for the product or service being advertised. The contextual whole of visual element plus language should create within the receiver a favorable inclination toward the product or service, and the whole should be greater than the sum of its parts. In other words, the message should communicate more than the literal content. Holy hype, like other types of advertising, should let you know *what's in it for you.* As in general marketplace advertising, the message should explicitly or implicitly communicate the benefits of the product or service.

REFERENCES

American Marketing Association. (2017). Definitions of marketing. https://www.ama.org/the-definition-of-marketing-what-is-marketing/

Branding. (2020). Entrepreneur.com. https://www.entrepreneur.com/encyclopedia/branding

Budde, M. (1997). *The (magic) kingdom of God: Christianity and global culture industries*. Westview Press.

Coffee, P. (2017). Xerox updates its iconic 1977 "Brother Dominic" Super Bowl spot for our digital age. https://www.adweek.com/brand-marketing/xerox-updates-its-iconic-1977-brother-dominic-super-bowl-spot-our-digital-age-175352/

Corwin, V. (2016). Medieval book production and monastic life. *Dartmouth Ancient Books Lab*. https://sites.dartmouth.edu/ancientbooks/2016/05/24/medieval-book-production-and-monastic-life/

Duhamel, P. A. (1949). The function of rhetoric as effective expression. *Journal of the History of Ideas, 10*(3), 344–356. doi: 10.2307/2707041

Elliott, E. E. (1917). *How to fill the pews*. The Standard Publishing Company.

Firat, A. Fuat. (1991). The consumer in postmodernity. *Advances in Consumer Research 18*, 70–76.

Fox, M. (2014). Judy Protas, writer of slogan for Levy's Real Jewish Rye, dies at 91. *The New York Times*. https://www.nytimes.com/2014/01/12/business/judy-protas-writer-of-slogan-for-levys-real-jewish-rye-dies-at-91.html

Gilmore, T. (2015). What is branding? https://www.linkedin.com/pulse/what-branding-thomas-gilmore/?trk=related_artice_What%20is%20Branding%3F_article-card_title

Gubanov, N. N., Gubanov, N. I., & Rokotyanskaya, L. (2019, July). Conflicts based on humor and religion. In *4th International Conference on Contemporary Education, Social Sciences and Humanities (ICCESSH 2019)*. Atlantis Press.

Henriques, A. (2007). *Corporate truth: The limits to transparency*. Taylor & Francis.

Hiltzik, M. (2018). Xerox, once a business icon, is about to disappear—Take heed, Amazon and Google. *Los Angeles Times*. https://www.latimes.com/business/hiltzik/la-fi-hiltzik-xerox-20180213-story.html

Jantsch, J. (n.d.). 99% of advertising doesn't sell a thing. *Ducttapemarketing.com*. https://ducttapemarketing.com/99-of-advertising-doesnt-sell-a-thing/

Jones, M. (2016). How the LDS Church's response to "The Book of Mormon" musical is actually working. https://www.deseret.com/2016/11/16/20600593/how-the-lds-church-s-response-to-the-book-of-mormon-musical-is-actually-working#the-eugene-oneill-theatre-and-the-marquee-for-the-book-of-mormon-are-seen-in-new-york-thursday-jan-19-2012-ap-photo-charles-sykes

Kirkland, L. (2011). "Book of Mormon" musical: Church's official statement. *Newsroom Blog*. https://newsroom.churchofjesuschrist.org/article/church-statement-regarding-the-book-of-mormon-broadway-musical

Kuntz, T. (1999, July 18). Word for word/billboards for God; Did somebody say, "Give me a sign, Lord?" *The New York Times Week in Review*. https://www.nytimes.com/1999/07/18/weekinreview/word-for-word-billboards-from-god-did-somebody-say-give-me-a-sign-lord.html

Merton, T. (1966). *Conjectures of a guilty bystander*. Doubleday.

Messaris, P. P. (1996). *Visual persuasion: The role of images in advertising*. SAGE Publications, Inc.

O'Shaughnessy, J., & O'Shaughnessy, N. J. (2004). *Persuasion in advertising*. Routledge.

Presbrey, F. (1929). *History and development of advertising*. Doubleday, Doran & Company.

Sales, B. (2019). America's 7.5 million Jews are older, whiter, and more liberal than the country as a whole. *Jewish Telegraphic Agency*. https://www.jta.org/2019/10/07/united-states/americas-7-5-million-jews-are-older-whiter-and-more-liberal-than-the-country-as-a-whole

Sarapin, S. H., & Spinetta, C. M. (2010, November). Selling their souls: When sacred images and consumer advertising met in the Middle Ages. [Unpublished.]

Searls, D. (2016). Rethinking John Wanamaker. *Medium.com*. https://medium.com/@dsearls/rethinking-john-wanamaker-3f9cfac3ea03

Shepard, R. N. (1990). *Mind sights: Original visual illusions, ambiguities, and other anomalies*. Freeman.

Smardon, A. (2015). In Utah, "Book of Mormon" strikes a chord. *NPR.com*. https://www.npr.org/2015/08/02/428643358/in-utah-book-of-mormon-strikes-a-chord

Stewart, P. (1964). Concurrence to *Jacobellis v. Ohio*. https://www.law.cornell.edu/supremecourt/text/378/184#writing-USSC_CR_0378_0184_ZC1

Strate, L. (1991) The cultural meaning of beer commercials. *Advances in Consumer Research* (18), 115–119.

"Top 100 ads of the 20th Century." 1999. *AdAge*. https://adage.com/article/special-report-the-advertising-century/ad-age-advertising-century-top-100-advertising-campaigns/140150

Chapter 3

Religion and Advertising

Scrambling the Sacred and the Profane

In Chapter 2, we defined and described the advertising strategy we call holy hype. Before we further explore holy hype advertisements themselves, we will explore the unique relationship between advertising and religion. In an article titled "Close encounters of a religious kind," Laurel Burton wrote about the religious aspects of advertising:

> The religion of Madison Avenue is a slickly packaged (and well researched) blend of doctrine and sacrament. The primary tenet of the new faith is salvation through social acceptance . . . with the "means of grace" ranging from deodorant to toothpaste to feminine hygiene aids to automobiles. (1983, p. 141)

This relationship and the differing perspectives on it are part of what makes holy hype such a fascinating area of study. This chapter explores how connections between religion and advertising go beyond the use of symbols and rhetoric in individual advertisements, also meeting at the level of larger societal structures and influences.

The intersection of religion and advertising has been explored by both scholars and professional practitioners. Sut Jhally and John Kavanaugh, among others, have argued that advertising *is* a religion, that is, that the elements of religion such as rituals and rites, belief and meaning, and the sacred and divine, can be experienced through advertising. Others, notably Tricia Sheffield and Mara Einstein, have countered that it is not a religion, but has *dimensions* of religion. Many scholars do agree that, as Sheffield writes: advertising "certainly contains, and has used, the religious to be culturally powerful by drawing from traditional institutions as a source for providing meaning" (2006, p. 23). We will see many examples of that throughout this book. However, the mixing of sacred and profane goes beyond the use of religious symbols, stories, and concepts in persuading us to buy goods and services. In her book *Brands of Faith* (2008), Einstein lists some of the similarities:

> There is a symbiotic relationship between religion and marketing. Religion and marketing are both forms of meaning making. Religion and marketing are both part of identity creations. Religion and marketing share a similar process of acceptance by their users. In all, these institutions are much more alike than they are different. (p. 14)

Religion and advertisements both communicate values that provide structures to live by, influence identity and self-perception, fulfill a human desire for the transcendent, and use persuasion and stories as techniques (Sullivan, 2010). Scholars have invoked such well-known names as Karl Marx and Émile Durkheim in their discourse on the overlap of these two institutions. Religion also makes appearances in American civil society in ways that are unique, but which we do not consider part of our definition of holy hype, so it is important to explore this area. Yet another intersection of religion and advertising is the people. When advertising first took off in the United States, it was, in many cases, those closely related to the church who were the stars of advertising. We begin by reviewing the perspectives on the relationship between religion and advertising.

A NEW RELIGION

Consumer culture has been described in religious terms many times. Phrases such as the worship of goods, the idolizing of things, and the shopping mall as the new church have enlivened essays and scholarly writings. In 1962, literary critic Leo Spitzer analyzed an orange juice ad for its religious themes, and commented that "to a great extent, present-day advertising has taken over the role of the teacher of morals," but also has taken on the role of making the audience want the goods: "the advertiser, like the preacher, must 'create the demand' for the better" (p. 273). He continued by saying that "it would not, perhaps, be wrong to see a sermon in all advertising" (1962, p. 274).

Sut Jhally wrote an essay based on a small portion of his work *The Codes of Advertising* (1987). By far, not the only scholarly writing on the subject, his essay, written in 2000 and titled "Advertising and Religion: The Dialectic of Technology and Magic," is well known, short, easy to comprehend, and has inspired scholars to take up the topic in response. In it, Jhally, a professor of communication at the University of Massachusetts-Amherst, who focuses on cultural studies, advertising, media, and consumption, argues that advertising is a religion using a Marxian analysis. In *Das Kapital* (Volume 1, 1867), Marx used "mist-enveloped regions of the religious world" (p. 48) as an analogy to describe the relationship between humans and things. Marx was concerned that industrialized capitalism separated people from the production of the goods they used, and in the process, the good lost its meaning normally gained through involvement in production. Jhally comments that due to this separation, commodities "appear as miraculous products of an invisible process of production" (1989, p. 224). Into this gap, argues Jhally, comes advertising. When we are not involved in the production of goods, or are involved in only a few steps of the process, we as consumers have "little information about them beyond what manufacturers choose to tell us through media advertising or packaging," (p. 219) and therefore, "the function of advertising is to refill the emptied commodity with meaning" (p. 221). Like the *Wizard of Oz*, there is a curtain hiding the real and often ugly mechanizations and mechanisms involved in the goods themselves. Consumers prefer that these remain a mystery, enjoying the visions created by advertisers instead. Furthermore, traditional institutions became weakened during the industrial revolution, and "advertising derives its power from providing meaning not available elsewhere" (p. 222).

Jhally outlines a brief history of advertising in four phases, the names of which have clear religious overtones. First, from 1890–1920, is the *idolatry* stage. During this time "advertising has a strong theme of veneration of products, almost worshipping the fruits of industrial technology. Commodities are idols in early advertising" (1989, p. 222). The techniques in ads include large images of goods towering over the landscape as if from heaven, or the wearing of halos of light and lines, triggering the awe of audiences. Jhally borrows words from Roland Marchand's work *Advertising the American Dream* (1985): "Ads used 'sacred symbolism to transform a product,' producing 'secular revelations' and 'faith in mass consumption.'" During the *iconology* stage, from 1920 to 1940, advertisers left behind the good itself and focused on the meaning of the good. A shift to the consumer, and the good empowering the individual, marked the *narcissism* stage from 1940 to 1960. Finally, from 1960 to present, Jhally says advertising is in the *totemic* stage, where goods are "badges of group membership" that allow an individual access to a consumption community (p. 224).

Christopher Lasch, author of *The Culture of Narcissism* (1979), expresses a dim view of advertising, arguing, like other critical theorists, that the new role of advertising manipulates audiences into a value system of needs and wants—similar to the functions religion previously played in everyday life. He states:

> In a simpler time, advertising merely called attention to the product and extolled its advantages. Now it manufactures a product of its own: the consumer,

> perpetually unsatisfied, restless, anxious, and bored. Advertising serves not so much to advertise products as to promote consumption as a way of life. It "educates" the masses into an unappeasable appetite not only for goods but for new experiences and personal fulfillment. It upholds consumption as the answer to the age-old discontents . . . at the same time it creates new forms of discontent peculiar to the modern age. (p. 72)

Jhally, although also critical of the role of modern advertising, provides a more nuanced view, writing that the real function of advertising "is not to give people information but to make them feel good," to satisfy, and to justify our choices (p. 225). He states:

> It helps us to understand the world and our place in it, and it accomplishes this through integrating people and things within a magical and supernatural sphere. If this function were attributed to an institution in non-capitalist society, we would have no trouble seeing it for what it was—*religion.* (p. 225)

As to what kind of religion, Jhally claims it is fetishism, a nature-based system of belief where objects are "believed to be possessed by some kind of supernatural spirit, which if worshipped and appeased, could have a beneficial influence on the worldly existence of the owner" (p. 226). This is not a total spiritual system, for it lacks, among other things, a ritualized moral core or code.

Jhally ends on a whimsical note (an ending that leaves many subsequent scholars feeling shorted). He quotes Raymond Williams, who likens advertising to a "highly organized and professional system of magical inducements and satisfactions" (226, original 1980, p. 185). But, note Jhally and Williams, although magic reveals amazing things, it also obscures reality. Jhally later narrated two films, *Advertising at the End of the World* (1998) and *Advertising at the Edge of the Apocalypse* (2018), in which he argues that the hedonistic values shown in advertising distract us from the realities of climate change and overconsumption. Williamson, in *Decoding Advertisements* (1978), also gives a nod to the magical properties of advertising and similarly critiques the role of this magic in hiding the means and exploitation involved in production. Products are presented to consumers magically ready-made, and the consumer need only take the minimal action of buying the product to create "a 'magical spell' element: from a little action, we get 'great' results (or are promised them)" (p. 140). Buying a product produces a miracle: "Magic is the production of results disproportionate to the effort put in (a transformation of power—or of impotence *into* power). In this sense, all consumer products offer magic, and all advertisements are spells" (p. 141).

Jhally is not the only one to assert that advertising is a type of religion. For example, Jesuit scholar John Kavanaugh, in *Following Christ in a Consumer Society* (1981), writes: “What is ‘ours,’ what we possess, what we own and consume has become the ultimate criterion against which we measure all other values. As an ultimate, this criterion is our functional god” (p. 26).

NOT QUITE A RELIGION

Whether advertising *is* a religion may best be left to the scholarly, yet the ways in which they overlap are seen in both the images we present in this book and the functions of these institutions. Einstein summarizes a number of the functional overlaps:

> These institutions both rely on storytelling, meaning making, and a willingness of people to believe in what is intellectually unbelievable. Religions create meaning through myths, rituals, and practices; marketing creates meaning through advertising and shopping. Religion is the acceptance of a belief system; marketing is the acceptance of beliefs about a product. Religions have faith communities; marketing has brand communities. Religion has become a product; products have become religion. (2008, p. 78)

In a 2006 book based on her graduate thesis, Tricia Sheffield, an ordained minister with a doctorate in Theological and Religious Studies, questions Jhally’s assertions and expounds at length about why advertising is not a religion, but reports three key dimensions in common with Jhally. Sheffield’s *The Religious Dimensions and Advertising* uses Émile Durkheim’s definition of religion (from *The Elementary Forms of Religious Life*) to posit that advertising is not itself a religion, but it has three main religious characteristics (dimensions). Durkheim posits totemism (rather than the fetishism of Jhally) as the most primitive form of religion. Totems mark people as members of a particular collective or community. Thus, totems formalize a community much like a religion does, whereas fetishism is individual (Sheffield, 2006). In describing how totemism works, Sheffield writes that “society fixates on a thing or idea, which eventually imparts sacredness to it . . . As mentioned before, the thing is not intrinsically sacred, the properties of sacredness are added to it through the collective’s imparting such qualities” (2006, p. 47). Advertising attempts to move an individual “into a ‘consumption-clan’ by admonishing him or her to purchase the totems that will mark the person as a member of a desired clan” (2006, p. 48). This is an example, says Sheffield, of “advertising trying to sell products to the consumer using ‘the promise of magical self-transformation through the ritual of purchase'" (Sheffield, 2006, p. 58; quoting Durkheim, p. 42).

However, argues Sheffield, advertising does not provide a "foundational and steadfast" institution like religion; instead, it is purposefully fleeting, fully intending that objects will become obsolete, replaced by new and better things (2006, p. 16). Sheffield writes:

> In the sense that advertising binds together certain groups of people through class differences, purchasing power, and brand names into a recognizable community through image, language, ritual, and seemingly supernatural powers, it is very much like a religion. (2006, p. 16)

Yet, she argues, it is not a religion itself. She posits that there are three main ways that they overlap: the divine mediator, sacramentality, and the ultimate concern.

The first religious dimension is the divine mediator figure. Sheffield writes that "Advertising is the mediator through which the culture of consumer capitalism and humanity receive 'revelation and reconciliation' . . . advertising mediates the message that consumerism desires to give to humanity" (2006, p. 106). It reveals the message. Reconciliation happens when the divine object is purchased and consumed by a person, so consumerism and the individual are brought together, and the person gains admittance into a consumption clan. Advertising, she concludes, "works by mediating the rituals of collective consumption by coding itself and objects as a type of sacrament" (2006, p. 115). Advertising even mediates messages about rituals of shopping and consuming, such as through special Black Friday and Cyber Monday campaigns. Sheffield quotes Meeks (from *God the Economist,* 1989, p. 173), "Once buying is seen as a way of dealing with guilt, failure, the loss of self-esteem, and the fear of death, it will be elevated to the status of worship" (2006, p. 112). Sheffield provides as examples of other divine mediators, Moses, Siddhartha, Mohammed, and Christ.

The second dimension in advertising is sacramentality. Sheffield says that "objects become symbols of desire through advertising's bestowal of a type of divine grace to the object and then to the individual who possesses it" (2006, p. 116). Her argument is based on Durkeim's theories that an object can be given power by collective agreement and meaning is negotiated and conferred by the community.

The third dimension is the ultimate concern. The culture of consumer capitalism teaches that the way to a better life is through the purchase and owning of the right goods. Einstein describes the fantasy of this ultimate concern, "that men and women might become fulfilled human beings not through spiritual good or through pursuit of the 'eternal' but through the acquisition of 'goods'" (2008, p. 60). The religious desire for salvation or the care and favor of a supreme being, for example, "was now replaced by product desire as individuals were promised the good life through the acquisition of new market products bearing the familiar brand name" (Einstein, 2008, p. 61).

NOT HOLY HYPE: AMERICAN CIVIL RELIGION

The prevalence of religiosity in the United States throughout its history is one reason there is so much overt religious symbolism in advertising. This pervasiveness has also resulted in a unique way of mixing religion and society called civil religion. In this book, we do not consider civil religion to be a part of holy hype. However, it needs to be explained and examples given in order to separate the use of religious imagery and the selling of religion in this sense from our examples and discussions of holy hype.

Notwithstanding well-founded arguments in favor of church-state separation, Bible-related rhetorical devices, mostly Christian symbolism, continue to be recognized as authentic parts of America's "civil religion," a term introduced by political philosopher Jean-Jacques Rousseau in his 1762 book *On the Social Contract:*

> Religion, considered in relation to society, which is either general or particular, may also be divided into two kinds: the religion of man, and that of the citizen. The first is . . . the religion of the Gospel pure and simple, the true theism, what may be called natural divine right or law. The other, which is codified in a single country, gives it its gods, its own tutelary patrons; it has its dogmas, its rites, and its external cult prescribed by law. (n.p.)

Robert N. Bellah,[1] an American sociologist and educator, is perhaps most widely recognized for framing the discipline of religious and moral sociology and for being the first to exhaustively research and describe the phenomenon of civil religion. Bellah expounds on the meaning of "civil religion":

> What we have, then, from the earliest years of the republic is a collection of beliefs, symbols, and rituals with respect to sacred things and institutionalized in a collectivity. This religion—there seems no other word for it—while not antithetical to and indeed sharing much in common with Christianity, was neither sectarian nor in any specific sense Christian. (1967, n.p.)

Bruce Murray quotes the late professor of religious studies Rowland Sherrill in comments about the nature of civil religion: The sociological construct is a set of religious beliefs shared by most citizens about "the sacred nature, the sacred ideals, the sacred character, and sacred meanings of their country—its blessedness by God, and its special place and role in the world and in human history" (n.d., n.p.).

The opportunities and venues for employing the rhetoric of civil religion in speech and in visual symbology are many, and although not all invoke the name of God, most do include words such as "freedom" and "liberty," as well as references to a higher and/or divine authority. In addition to the Pledge of Allegiance, which includes the phrase "under God,"[2] and its concomitant display of the American flag, several familiar examples of civil religious speech are (1) sessions of the House and Senate opening with prayer; (2) "In God We Trust" inscribed on our currency and chiseled into the walls of many of our government buildings; (3) biblical quotations or paraphrased scriptural references appearing in political addresses; (4) the invocation of God on our public monuments; (5) the national anthem and "God Bless America" being sung at public events; (6) the utterance of "So help me God" at the end of the oath one swears before assuming elected office; and (7) the placement of one's hand on the Bible while being sworn in as a testifying witness in a court of law.

Religious rhetoric has been a characteristic of written and oral American political expression since the founding days of our nation. Scripturally laced speech, commonly referred to as "God talk,"[3] especially when used in addresses to "the people" on ceremonial occasions, is one of the strongest threads of the American societal fabric. Indeed, it has been a thoroughly researched and documented aspect of presidential oratory since George Washington's time. President George W. Bush's atypically expansive spoken piety, dovetailing with an extremely high level of "certitude rhetoric,"[4] in conjunction with today's more religiously oriented electorate, has contributed to a widespread public discussion concerning the propriety of religious rhetoric in politics.

While some of our civil religious rhetoric finds its way into the religious conversation we witness every day, holy hype is distinguished from it by its purpose, the framing of its message, the venue and context of its delivery, its targeted audience, and other factors. Civil religion in the United States exists to perpetuate the idea that America is a Christian nation, or at least a God-fearing nation of believers. Civil religious rhetoric serves to advance itself. It does not advertise anything else. It does not even advertise Christianity per se. As an example, Israel uses civil religious rhetoric and behavior to portrayal of itself as a Jewish nation. Its civil religion does not advance Judaism, but that Judaism is the reason for the country's existence. A country's civil religion is an almost invisible protection against anyone or any group attempting to change its nature—even if or when another group becomes the majority of its population. Certain words and images become civil religion's totems, those symbols or emblems that serve as the nation's venerated marks that distinguish it from all others.

Placing one's hand on the Bible while taking an oath of office is another common example of US civil religion. However, members of Congress are sworn into office en masse by the speaker of the House, without the use of a Bible or any other sacred book. Indeed, the Constitution requires that "no religious test shall ever be required as a qualification to any office or public trust under the United States" (US Constitution, Article VI). One senator is known to have placed his left hand on an expanded version of the Bible, which included the Book of Mormon, during his private swearing-in ceremony. Some elected officials, such as Theodore Roosevelt, have opted to use no book at all, and President John Quincy Adams placed his hand on a law book that included the transcript of the Constitution (Lampman, 2006). In a similar vein, the phrase "so help me God" at the end of an oath is recited at the prerogative of the oath taker.

In late 2006, Keith Ellison of Minnesota, the first Muslim elected as a representative to the US Congress, became the focus of a media uproar when he suggested that he would take the oath of office using the Qur'an (formerly "Koran") instead of the customary Christian Bible. Some political conservatives and religious fundamentalists, led in this case by Virginia congressman Virgil Goode and Jewish pundit and talk-show host Dennis Prager, voiced their strong opposition to Ellison's using the Qur'an during the taking of his oath despite the fact that the use of any sacred text is reserved for private ceremonies following the public one (Prager, 2006; Swarns, 2006). In fact, Prager further remarked:

> Insofar as a member of Congress taking an oath to serve America and uphold its values is concerned, America is interested in only one book, the Bible. If you are incapable of taking an oath on that book, don't serve in Congress. (n.p.)

In perhaps the greatest irony of all, the Qur'an that Ellison used once belonged to Thomas Jefferson and is now housed in the rare book and special collections division of the Library of Congress (Fischer, 2007).

Generally, it is the Protestant Christian belief that America was formed as, and should once again be deemed, a Christian nation (Fea, 2016). The leaders of America's extreme Christian right wing, who view the United States as the New Israel, have insinuated that the Bush inauguration was an ordination of a Christian nation's chief representative whose oratorical religiosity is what they would fully expect to hear from the pulpit. Evangelical Christians, who are overtly, and perhaps hyperbolically, the most ardent supporters of President Donald J. Trump, have advanced the notion that Trump has been ordained by God. The president's campaign manager for the 2020 election,

Brad Parscale, disseminated this tweet: "There has never been and probably never will be a movement like this again. Only God could deliver such a savior to our nation. . . . God bless America" (Americans United, 2019, n.p.).

FROM THE PULPIT TO MADISON AVENUE

There is another interesting relationship between religion and advertising, and that is the people who were instrumental in establishing the advertising industry in the United States. These men "embodied a fusion of commerce and Protestantism. In fact, a number of those pioneering agents, either sons of Christian ministers or ministers themselves" were key contributors (Kelso, 2018, p. 24). Sheffield concurs, commenting: "It was no coincidence that advertisers used ultimate language . . . many of the ad agency executives came from a strong affluent Protestant background: Indeed, many of them were the sons of ministers" (2006, p. 61). Historian Jackson Lears writes in *Fables of Abundance: A Cultural History of Advertising in America:*

> By the early 1910s, the most influential agencies with the biggest accounts were staffed by a remarkably similar group of Anglo-Saxon males: College-educated, usually at prestigious Northeastern schools; Protestant, many the sons of Presbyterian or Congregationalist ministers; . . . they were the sons . . . of the liberal Protestant elite . . . they clung to a secularized version of their parents' worldview: A faith in inevitable progress, unfolding as if in accordance with some divine plan. They also had a tendency to cast themselves in a key redemptive role . . . [and] the belief that Christ would return after human beings had created the Kingdom of God on earth. (1994, p. 154)

A few of these whom we now meet are Charles Stelzle, Bruce Barton, George Batten, Francis Wayland Ayer, Artemas Ward, Claude C. Hopkins, John Wanamaker, and Asa Candler. Although their published work sometimes reflected their faith, it was the contribution of their values to the field of advertising that is their legacy. Advertisements were often associated with false claims of the patent medicine vendors, rampant money-making schemes, and general nefarious purposes. These men brought organization, professionalism, and integrity to both the ads they oversaw and the businesses they founded. They brought credibility to their communication with consumers.

Charles Stelzle (1869–1941) was a Presbyterian minister and sociologist who used such techniques as billboards, electric signs, and "other flashy modes of publicity" in preaching the gospel and church advertising (Kelso, 2018, p. 14). He later leveraged his expertise in public relations, handling publicity for the American Red Cross during World War I, and later directing promotional campaigns for religious, patriotic, and community organizations (Prabook, 2020, n.p.). He was a part of the early "social gospel" movement, which sought to close the gap that had opened between workingmen and the church by getting involved in social issues. Stelzle portrayed Jesus as "a union carpenter, a member of the carpenters' guild of his day" (Nash 1970, p. 158), and that unionism was basically a religious phenomenon. He was acclaimed as a "pioneer in the present-day interest of the church in the labor movement, earning the nicknames the 'Apostle to Labor' and 'the workingman's real representative in the church'" (Nash, 1970, p. 151). Stelzle is a strong early example of man who used his talents and faith to bring attention to secular need through advertising and marketing.

Bruce Barton (1886–1967) is one of the most well-known admen of the early twentieth century. He cofounded the Barton, Durstine & Osborn (BDO) advertising agency in 1919 and later merged his company with the George Batten agency (see below) to become Batten, Barton, Durstine & Osborn (BBDO). Barton headed the BBDO agency from 1939 until 1961, where he developed it into one of the major advertising firms operating in the United States (Adbrands, 2020a). This agency had a hand in creating images and campaigns for Betty Crocker, General Motors, and General Electric (Ingham, 1984). Advertisements associated with Barton and his agency include those in figures 3.1c and 3.1f. Barton was the son of a liberal Congregationalist minister. He was influenced by his father: "His style often resembled the sort of sermon he had heard his father preach as a child, full of grand and crusading calls to action and a strong moralistic tone" (Adbrands, 2020a, n.p.). He was "a key figure in the spiritualization of American industry that continues to this day" (Schultze, 2007, 38). Barton authored bestselling books, popular magazine articles, and syndicated newspaper columns. He wrote philosophical and spiritual works, celebrating both Christian beliefs and American values, businesses, and industry leaders. In a fanciful mixing of advertising and religion, Barton's popular (yet also controversial) book, *The Man Nobody Knows* (1925), likens Jesus to a business leader who inspired and maintained the devotion of his team (the Disciples), who "knew how, and taught His followers how, to catch the attention of the indifferent, and translate a great spiritual conception into terms of practical self-concern" (p. 57). This sounds a lot like what Jhally and Sheffield have said about advertising. Jesus is also portrayed by Barton as an advertiser:

> This aspect of Jesus' universal genius may perhaps be best understood by the psychologist and the businessman . . . Jesus was using a method not unlike those used now as the most modern technique of overcoming unreasoning resistance to a helpful idea, service, or product. (pp. 57–58)

Figure 3.1 a) George Batten ad for Warren's Standard Printing Papers (1929). b) Artemas Ward ad for Sapolio Soap (1903). c) Ad for the anti-war group World Placeways by Bruce Barton with art by Herbert Morton Stoops (1935). d) Claude Hopkins ad for Quaker Oats (1930). e) Claude Hopkins ad for Palmolive soap (1920s). f) General Electric ad by Bruce Barton (1920s). g) Advertising postcard supplied by General Electric (1905) to its distributors, imprinted with the seller (Wanamaker) who then sent it to potential customers. h) Wanamaker's store, showing the organ and main shop floor. *Source: a) Reprinted courtesy of Sappi North America, Inc. b) Public domain image retrieved from vintagepaperads.com. c) Public domain image retrieved from Swarthmore College Peace Collection. d) Public domain image retrieved from periodpaper.com. e) Public domain image retrieved from fineartamerica.com. f) Public domain image retrieved from lewsissuffragecollection.omeka.net. g) Public domain image retrieved from oldchristmastreelights.com. h) Image courtesy of Joseph Routen, ©Joseph Routen photography.*

Those methods included the use of parables. Barton writes that "you will find that it is a perfect example of the way in which a new idea may be presented" (p. 77), making Jesus an expert salesman. Jesus's persuasive techniques, as listed by Barton, include (a) condensed stories, told in a few sentences; (b) simple language; (c) sincerity; and (d) repetition. Similarly, in his book *He Upset the World*, Barton set out to demonstrate that St. Paul would have run a large multinational corporation had he lived in the twentieth century (Adbrands, 2020a).

George Batten (1854–1918) was also the son of a minister. He once worked for Ayer (described below), but then opened George Batten Newspaper Advertising Agency in New York and later teamed up with Bruce Barton at BBDO. Batten was known to be "fiercely religious and humorless" (Adbrands 2020b, n.p.). As the son of a minister, Batten espoused strong values of "honesty, decency and truth" and personal dignity, and he is "credited with adding respectability to the ad profession" (Adbrands, 2020a, 2020b, n.p.). It is claimed that Batten "insisted on complete accuracy in all advertising copy, as well as the use of plain, simple type, which he said, 'stands out like a Quaker on Broadway'" (Adbrands, 2020a, n.p.). An example of Batten's copy is in figure 3.1a.

Francis Wayland Ayer (1848–1923) began his career selling advertising for a religious newspaper and later founded N. W. Ayer & Son, where he brought to advertising respectability and stability. He attracted such prominent clients as American Telephone & Telegraph Company, W. K. Kellogg Company, and Steinway & Sons (Encyclopedia Britannica, 2020). As a fervent Baptist, Ayer served as the Superintendent of a Sunday School in Camden, New Jersey, and president of the New Jersey State Convention of Baptists for 25 years (Ingham, 1984). He was described as a "paragon of sobriety, without humor, and a symbol of rectitude" (Kelso, 2018, p. 24). Large companies trusted Ayer's agency to represent them on the basis of the values that stemmed from his faith.

Artemas Ward (1848–1925) was the son of an Episcopal minister and one of the most creative and innovative of the fathers of advertising ("Artemas Ward Dies," 1925). Ward founded the *Philadelphia Grocer*, a trade periodical, which led to an offer to manage advertising for household cleaner Sapolio Soap (Michigan State University, n.d.). Ward made Sapolio one of the most recognized brands of its time, working there from 1885 to 1910 ("Artemas Ward Dies," 1925). An ad for the soap can be seen in figure 3.1b. He used countrywide transit ads that blended fanciful scenes and clever poems and captions; he later negotiated exclusive use of advertising facilities on New York City's elevated railway and subway systems (Michigan State University, n.d.). Like Ayer, Ward's moral reputation helped him connect with businesses and consumers.

Claude C. Hopkins (1903–1984) was descended from a long line of preachers; he even entered and served in the ministry for a short while and believed strongly in the Protestant work ethic (Adbrands, 2020c). He is described as a cautious and prudent person from a deeply religious family (Kelso, 2018). His strict upbringing brought little joy, and Hopkins escaped into sales and later copywriting, becoming one of the first great professional copy writers and the founder of the "Reason-Why" method (to state a fact about a product or service in the headline and then explain why the fact is true in the text). He portrayed an Edenic world of the bright, happy, and attractive (Kelso, 2018). Hopkins "applied the same missionary zeal to his job in advertising as his family had to their church," and brought success to brands including Bissell Carpet Sweeper, Schlitz Beer, Palmolive, Quaker Oats, and Goodyear Tires (Adbrands, 2020c, n.p.). Two ads of Hopkins can be seen in figure 3.1d and figure 3.1e. At the end of the nineteenth century, Quaker Oats broke through by tying its public image to a religiously inspired model of "good quality and honest value," the Quaker himself (The Quaker Oats Company, 2019).

Asa Candler (1851–1929) was an investor in and later owner of Coca-Cola, where he marketed it to national and international fame. The Candler family were Southern Methodists, and Asa's brother became a bishop, factors which influenced Asa; a 2002 biography of him was titled *God's Capitalist* (Kemp, 2002). He was involved in religious and philanthropic work throughout his life and was a key financier for Emory University and its medical school (Ingham, 1983). As with others of his time, his strong Protestant work ethic drove his business decisions just as much as his philanthropy and earned him trust among his contemporaries.

John Wanamaker (1838–1922) was a pioneer in both merchandising and the department store concept. He produced the first copyrighted store advertisement in 1874, and his flagship store, Wanamaker's, opened in Philadelphia, in 1876 (PBS, 2004). The store eventually contained a restaurant, elevators, artwork, and a grand court housing the world's second largest organ (still in use today—see figure 3.1h) (PBS, 2004). Wanamaker was a deeply religious man "firmly established upon the truth of God's Word" (Christian Heritage, 2020, n.p.). He founded Bethany Presbyterian Sunday School, which became one of the largest in the country having 5,000 students, for a time was president of the Young Men's Christian Association, and founded Philadelphia's Presbyterian Hospital (PBS, 2004; Christian Heritage, 2020). In addition, he wrote and published several volumes of prayers (Christian Heritage, 2020). Wanamaker infused "his establishment with what he saw as more moral, and therefore Christian, business practices" (Carroll, 2019, n.p.). He refused to advertise on Sundays and valued truth and frankness in advertising (Advertising Hall of Fame, 2020). An example ad put out by Wanamaker's store is in figure 3.1g. Wanamaker was a moral reformer; his store was designed to look like the interior of a church (figure 3.1h), and he wanted to "evangelize his consumers and employees, creating model middle-class Protestants" (Kirk, 2018, n.p.)

CONCLUSION

Einstein (2008) writes that "there are numerous similarities between marketing and religion, and the line between the two has become increasingly blurred" (p. 92). Whether in the mixing of secular and profane images, in the overlap of conceptual foundations and purpose, or in the faith that drove its pioneers, religion and advertising are intertwined. This chapter considered several perspectives on the intermixing of religion and advertising. We did this to encourage the reader to consider not only the advertisements themselves, but how the larger societal conceptions of religion and advertising are related. The tensions and similarities underlying holy hype lend it more complex and nuanced characteristics and impacts than it may initially seem. We encourage the reader to consider not only the symbols and language of ads when analyzing them with a spiritual lens, but also to note the ways in which ads fulfill human needs for values, experiences, and a universal order. Remember that

> whether we are talking about religions or brands, what we are searching for is a sense of hope, a sense of satisfaction, perhaps even nirvana. Today that sense is as likely to be generated by a product as it is by a preacher. (Einstein, 2008, p. 86)

NOTES

1. A complete biography and list of publications can be found on R. N. Bellah's Website from the Department of Sociology at the University of California, Berkeley, located at http://www.robertbellah.com/
2. "Under God" is a phrase that was inserted into the Pledge of Allegiance at the instigation of the Knights of Columbus in 1954. It was purportedly inspired by the words of Abraham Lincoln from the Gettysburg Address: "This nation, under God, shall have a new birth of freedom" (Lincoln, 1863).
3. The term "God-talk" was coined by John Macquarrie in his God-Talk: An Examination of the Language and Logic of Theology, published in 1967 by Harper & Row, New York. His use of the term can be described as talk or discussion about the nature or meaning of God. The more recent use of this term is the actual mention of any descriptor of God in writing, in casual discussion, or in speeches. Examples of

some of the more common descriptors are the Almighty, the Creator, Providence, a higher power, and Lord

4. "Certitude is a rhetoric 'in which an author writes as if he intentionally wishes to communicate or unintentionally exposes his sureness, confidence, or even dogmatism. The style of certitude is frequently to be found in discussions of religion, politics, and English grammar'" (Kollman, in Huttar & Schrader, 1996, p. 125). As Duhamel expounds, "Interest was focused upon the expression of ideas for which the highest type of certitude was already present, divine testimony" (1949, p. 345).

REFERENCES

Adbrands. (2020a). History of BBDO. www.adbrands.net/us/bbdo-us-p2.htm

Adbrands. (2020b). George Batten. https://adage.com/article/special-report-the-advertising-century/george-batten/140230

Adbrands. (2020c). Lord & Thomas. https://www.adbrands.net/files/us/lord-and-thomas-us.htm

Advertising Hall of Fame. (2020). John Wanamaker. http://advertisinghall.org/members/member_bio.php?memid=814&uflag=w&uyear=

Americans United. (2019). God and Trump: The offensive notion of divine anointment. *Church and State Magazine.* https://www.au.org/church-state/june-2019-church-state-magazine/editorial/god-and-trump-the-offensive-notion-of-divine

Artemas Ward Dies. (1925, March 15). *The New York Times.* https://timesmachine.nytimes.com/timesmachine/1925/03/15/issue.html

Barton, B. (1925). *The man nobody knows.* Read Books.

Bellah, R.N. (1967) Civil religion in America. *Journal of the American Academy of Arts and Sciences 96*(1), 1–21.

Burton, L.A. (1983). Close encounters of a religious kind. *Journal of Popular Culture, 17*(3), 141–145. doi: 10.1111/j.0022-3840.1983.1703_141.x

Caroll, T. (2019, February 5). What a hundred-year-old department store can tell us about the overlap of retail, religion and politics. *Smithsonian.* https://www.smithsonianmag.com/history/what-hundred-year-old-department-store-can-tell-us-about-overlap-retail-religion-and-politics-180971413/

Christian Heritage Ministries. (2020). John Wanamaker (1838–1922): The prayers of John Wanamaker. *Historic Truthopedia.* https://historictruthopedia.com/john-wanamaker-1838-1922/

Einstein, M. (2008). *Brands of faith: Marketing religion in a commercial age.* Routledge.

Encyclopaedia Britannica. (2020). Francis Wayland Ayer. https://www.britannica.com/biography/Francis-Wayland-Ayer

Fea, J. (2016). *Was America founded as a Christian nation?* Westminster John Knox Press.

Fischer, A. (2007, January 4). Jefferson's Quran in the news. *Library of Congress Information Bulletin, 66*(1–2). https://www.loc.gov/loc/lcib/07012/quran.html

Ingham, J. (1983). *Biographical dictionary of American business leaders, Vol. 1.* Greenwood Press.
Jhally, S. (1989). Advertising and religion: The dialectic of technology and magic. In I. Angus & S. Jhally (Eds.), *Cultural politics in contemporary America* (pp. 217–229). Routledge.
Kavanaugh, J. (1981) *Following Christ in a consumer society: The spirituality of cultural resistance.* Orbis Books.
Kelso, T. (2018). Promoting heaven on earth. In *The social impact of advertising: Confessions of an (ex-)advertising man.* Rowman & Littlefield.
Kemp, K.W. (2002). *God's capitalist: Asa Candler of Coca-Cola.* Mercer University Press.
Kirk, N.C. (2018) *Wanamaker's temple: The business of religion in an iconic department store.* NYU Press. [Kindle Edition]
Lampman, J. (2006). At swearing in, congressman wants to carry Koran. Outrage ensues. *The Christian Science Monitor.* https://www.csmonitor.com/2006/1207/p01s03-uspo.html
Lasch, C. (1979). *The culture of narcissism: American life in an age of diminishing expectations.* W.W. Norton and Company.
Lears, J. (1994). *Fables of abundance: A cultural history of advertising in America.* Basic Books.
Marchand, R. (1985). *Advertising the American dream.* University of California Press.
Marx, K. (1887). Capital: Critique of pollical economy. *Volume I Book One: The Process of Production of Capital.* Progress Publishers. https://www.marxists.org/archive/marx/works/download/pdf/Capital-Volume-I.pdf
Michigan State University Libraries. (n.d.) Ward, Artemas. https://d.lib.msu.edu/content/biographies?author_name=Ward%2C+Artemas
Murray, B. (n.d) With 'God on our side?': Following the contours of civil religion in America. *SageLaw.us.* http://websage.us/religion/sherrill.htm
Nash, G.H. (1970). Charles Stelzle: Apostle to labor. *Labor History 11*(2), 151–174. doi: 10.1080/00236567008584114
PBS. (2004) They Made America: John Wanamaker. https://www.pbs.org/wgbh/theymadeamerica/whomade/wanamaker_hi.html
Prabook. (2020). Charles Stelzle. https://prabook.com/web/charles.stelzle/1106610
Prager, D. (2006). America, not Keith Ellison, decides what book a congressman takes his oath on. *Townhall.* https://townhall.com/columnists/dennisprager/2006/11/28/america,-not-keith-ellison,-decides-what-book-a-congressman-takes-his-oath-on-n792991
Rousseau, J. (1762) *The greatest works of Jean-Jacques Rousseau* (B. Foxley, G.D.H. Cole, & S.W. Orson, Trans, 2018). [Kindle Edition]. e-artnow.
Schultze, Q.J. (2007). The man everybody knew: Bruce Barton and the making of modern America [Review of the book by Fried, R.M. & I.H. Dee]. *Christian Century 124*(17), 38–41.
Sheffield, T. (2006). *The religious dimensions of advertising.* Palgrave.
Spitzer, L. (1962). American advertising explained as popular art. In *Essays on English and American literature* (pp. 248–277). Princeton University Press.

Sullivan, P.A. (2011). Theology in 'contact with its own times': Advertising and evangelization. *New Blackfriars 92*(1040), 443–463. doi: 10.1111/j.1741-2005.2010.01371.x

Swarns, R.L. (2006). Congressman criticizes election of Muslim. *The New York Times.*

The Quaker Oats Company. (2020). Our Oat Origins. https://www.quakeroats.com/about-quaker-oats/content/quaker-history.aspx

Williamson, J. (1978). *Decoding advertisements: Ideology and meaning in advertising.* Marion Boyars.

Chapter 4

In the Beginning

At the Intersection of Damascus Road and Madison Avenue

Chapter 3 told the story of how religion was incorporated into modern advertising at the end of the nineteenth and beginning of the twentieth centuries. It also explained who the leading players were in this sometimes unintentional exercise and how religious practice changed the copy and visuals in advertising in many ways. Bruce Fairchild Barton, cofounder of Batten, Barton, Durstine & Osborn, wrote that "if you have anything really valuable to contribute to the world, it will come through the expression of your own personality, that single spark of divinity that sets you off and makes you different from every other living creature" (1920, p. 81). Modern media and communication scholars who study the intersection of religion and advertising (Einstein, 2008; Moore, 1994; Mallia, 2009) have tended to concentrate their research on twentieth- and twenty-first-century advertising approaches that use religious imagery. In contrast to the conventional, contemporary confines of this subject matter, this chapter situates the emergence of holy hype in earlier times, mostly in England. This period of time was ripe for holy hype. In light of high illiteracy at the start of this period and high religiosity throughout the Middle Ages, communication through pictorial signage and illustrated biblical texts assisted in meaning making by a generally uneducated public.

Blair (1996) investigates the possibility of visual argument while admitting there is no doubt that images are capable of affecting attitudes and beliefs. For the purposes of evaluating the strength of persuasion in advertising, though, visuals must be shown to be able to make arguments. In other words, the visuals must make a claim. As in all advertising, and consonant with a condensation of Blair's list of argument properties: (a) the ad makes a claim for which there is a reason; (b) the reason supports whatever is to be believed, chosen, or done; (c) the claim and reason are linguistically explicable; (d) there is an intended message or claim recipient who is addressed by both; and (e) "it is the intention of the 'user' [message producer] to bring the recipient to accept the claim on the basis of the reason(s) offered" (n.p.). Messaris expounds on the persuasive job of the visual in the argument:

> When we look at the world, we are strongly predisposed to attend to certain kinds of objects or situations and to react in certain kinds of ways. . . . In short, real-world vision comes with a set of built-in response tendencies. Consequently, to the extent that a picture can reproduce the significant visual features of real-world experience, it may also be able to exploit the response tendencies that are associated with those features. (p. 4)

Visual persuasion particularly using sacred images becomes an issue in and of itself during this span of time in history. Through the discussion of the "iconoclast debate," we demonstrate the gradual movement of religious visuals into church prayer, personal home prayer, and the broader culture, paving the way for secular holy hype.

Although all forms of holy hype have been featured in advertising communications during the past 135 years, especially in American and British print and outdoor media, the evidence of their premodern roots is incontrovertible yet sparsely represented in the literature. In this chapter, we explore the Late Middle Ages and the early Renaissance as the periods during which the forerunner to modern secular holy hype emerged after centuries of religious holy hype. In effect, we summarize the evolution of holy hype from the convergence of pivotal socioreligious, industrial, and economic dynamics unique to those times. We explain several significant forces, including (a) the pervasiveness of religious practice and identification with it through religious holy hype, (b) the invention of the printing press, and (c) the rise of commerce.

DEVELOPMENT OF HOLY HYPE

When we trace the development of holy hype, we are looking at a unique communication phenomenon which has persisted for almost 800 years. Advertising in written form probably originated 5,000 years ago, when the Sumerians invented cuneiform writing (Kramer, 1981). Prehistoric people were already trading with each other and using special verbal techniques to barter their crafts for food and clothing. Presbrey (1929) writes about humanity's early tribes:

> As men discovered that they could get food and clothing by trading their own specialties for these necessities, the arts began to develop. Skill in making things grew, and each craftsman's output increased. When a man found rivals in his

> line it became necessary to do some "selling," to persuade, and he evolved a selling talk. This, incidentally, gave a decided impetus to language. (p. 1)

Later, the use of religious holy hype was sometimes dictated by the church and the ruling class. The use of sacred images in certain circumstances has not always been accepted, and its history has a long and contentious past. The argument over the use of religious symbols is termed the "iconoclast debate," and this controversy helped shape religious holy hype into what it is today. The iconoclast debate began with a conflict in the eighth century CE under the emperors Leo III and Constantine V. The Second Council of Nicea met in 787 CE and addressed the issue of iconoclasm, defined as "the destruction of images or hostility toward visual representations in general," in this case, religious images, which were removed from churches and destroyed ("Iconoclastic controversies," n.d.).

The council ruled in favor of the use of icons. This did not end the debate, though, and it reemerged in the early ninth century, with the Byzantine emperors supporting iconoclasts (those against the use of religious images in worship) and the Papacy supporting the iconodules or iconophiles (those in support of the use of religious images in worship). The iconoclast debate did not come to a head until 843 CE, when the use of religious images was approved by the Papal States and King Charlemagne (Besançon, 2000; Martin, 1978; Bradlaugh & Gillespie, 1872). The use of religious imagery during worship was publicly approved by the ruling class as well as the Catholic leaders, and this formal sanction paved the way for an increase in "advertisements," or advocacy, for the church in the form of images.

The debate about the use of sacred images for worship in church, and eventually in one's home, resumed in the late fourteenth century and continued into the sixteenth century as a tipping point that would contribute to the Protestant Reformation. According to White (1989), the Catholic Church was comfortable with widespread use of these symbols, especially the images and statues of saints and the veneration of the eucharist, but the Protestants were not. Non-Catholic churches began to purge what they perceived as idols, reducing these images to "the mandatory tablets (Decalogue, Creed, and Lord's Prayer)" (p. 106). Despite the resumption of this controversy, sacred images and their spiritual meanings were already embedded in the cultural consciousness. Religious holy hype became a staple of architecture, art, and personal adornment in the Middle Ages and the Renaissance. Its inescapable frequency in all aspects of society was perhaps responsible for diminishing its faith-related significance to the masses.

Whereas the Roman Catholic clergy emphasized the power of the cross symbol to defend against evil, the Hebrew Scriptures did not assign to the Jews' mezuzah a mystical or protective purpose. During the Middle Ages, however, Christians were suspicious yet desirous of the mezuzah and its suspected magical powers. Likely influenced by the fear of another destructive plague of disease, Christians of higher classes and greater economic means in the decades following the Black Death saw nothing wrong in doubly protecting themselves by using the Jewish symbol as well as the cross on their own doorposts (Trachtenberg, 1939). Trachtenberg, an American rabbi and scholar, described such an occurrence:

> Toward the end of the fourteenth century the Bishop of Salzburg asked a Jew to give him a mezuzah to attach to the gate of his castle, but the rabbinic authority to whom this Jew turned for advice refused to countenance so outrageous a prostitution of a distinctively religious symbol. (p. 4)

What would need to occur for secular holy hype to materialize? One prerequisite was that aspects of the secular domain be inculcated into or at least tolerated in the sacred realm and vice versa. This coexistence would necessitate a variety of things: (a) church sermons, prayer books, and biblical texts must be accessible to the masses in the vernacular; (b) an increase in literacy among the common people must be fostered; and (c) secular activities conducted within the abbey and deemed important to the mission of the monastery must be seen as almost sacred in the secular domain. A few other factors instrumental in the development of secular holy hype would be the freedom of individual religious choice, the acceptance and universal understanding of religious symbols by a visually and aurally oriented culture, the invention of the printing press as the means of disseminating information and advertising to a mass audience, and a healthy, competitive marketplace free of religious interference or regulation.

MEDIEVAL HOLY HYPE

Although secular holy hype did not fully manifest itself until the late fifteenth and early sixteenth centuries, the factors contributing to its complete emergence as a singular phenomenon, independent of religious holy hype, appeared as early as the middle of the fourteenth century though without the mass dissemination made possible by the printing press. Numerous attitudes, events, and revolutionary ideas came together to lay the foundation for the use and manipulation of sacred or biblical images and themes in the advertising of consumer goods and secular enterprise. By way of setting the scene, we must first take a brief look at the depth and breadth of medieval religious expression.

Medieval art was highly allegorical (Stern, 1988) and provided a rich canvas for religious promotion, or holy hype. In figure 4.1a, seven annotations

Figure 4.1 a) "The Mystic Marriage of St. Catherine," painted by Lucas the Elder Cranach, c. 1516 with annotations by Dr. Richard Stracke. b) "Court of the Ladies of Queen Anne of Brittany" (early sixteenth century, cropped). The lady in waiting, third from left in the right-hand half of the illustration, is wearing a cross pendant. c) Silver Apostle spoons from London, 1536–1537 C L to R-Andrew, Bartholomew, Mathew, Thomas. d) A 1425 CE Manuscript Illustration of a Medieval German Beer Brewer Standing in Front of his Guild Sign, a Hexagram, which Hangs from a Horizontal Pole. e) House Logo of the Aldine Press, Designed by the Publisher, Aldus Manutius. *Source: a) Reprinted courtesy of Dr. Richard Stracke. b) Image from manuscript of the "Epistres Envoyées au Roi" (Sixteenth Century), obtained by the Coislin Fund for the Library of St. Germain des Pres in Paris, now in the Library of St. Petersburg. Retrieved from Project Gutenberg. c) Photo retrieved from Wikimedia Commons user Hoppyh. d) Public domain image retrieved from annmarieackermann.com. e) Image retrieved from University of Waterloo archives.*

have been added to the painting to explain what these items stand for. For example, in the top and largest text balloon, the act of the child giving St. Catherine a ring is described as representing Catherine's refusal of "the evil emperor Maxentius, saying Christ was her only spouse." Another is the grapes being handled by the Virgin Mary, who is holding the baby. The image states: "grapes refer to the Eucharist." In addition to public displays of holy hype in the form of architecture and artwork, personal holy hype was also quite common. People would display sacred images and objects in small shrines in their own homes to facilitate personal, private worship. As proof of certain early uses of self-identification, a miniature derived from a painting produced in the Middle Ages, "Court of the Ladies of Queen Anne of Brittany" (figure 4.1b), depicts a lady in waiting wearing a cross around her neck. Monks and nuns, too, often wore crosses on chains from their necks or waists (see Chapter 6 for more modern examples). As Morse (2007) tells us, the sacred goods in the Renaissance Venetian household were used for a variety of purposes including fostering devotion, functioning as a protective device, providing an aid for religious development, and serving as an outward expression of the family's "devoutness and honourable reputation" (p. 2).

The Middle Ages were a time of fervent religious practice, with almost all aspects of life revolving around religion in some way. Indeed, Huizinga (1954) points out that in the Middle Ages, every action and object was in some way correlated with Christ or salvation. As he explains, much of the art and architecture, as well as personal adornment, can be seen as religious holy hype, but the focus on religion went much deeper than that. Religion, Christ, and the quest for salvation were not merely symbols or decoration, but a way of thinking and behaving. The focus on salvation permeated all facets of life, and therefore it is not surprising that religious images became prominent in secular as well as sacred practices. This universality of religion created a society in which government, marketing, commerce, family, and community activities were all imbued with religion. In the Middle Ages, this environment provided the backdrop to the movement from solely religious holy hype to secular holy hype.

We will now explain the medieval dynamics that came together within a religious context to make the fusion of religious faith and the profit motive not only possible but indeed the next logical step in the development of holy hype. It must be noted that there is considerable overlap in the temporality of the factors discussed herein. The complex evolution of secular holy hype in medieval and Renaissance Europe was not linear and not seen as unnatural in an environment steeped in such fervent religiosity.

THE BLACK DEATH

Our examination of secular holy hype's stimuli will begin with the most unlikely of forces for the establishment of *any* widespread *cultural* phenomenon—the Black Death[1]—the only contributing factor not attributable to human thought or behavior. Throughout the plague, well-educated and experienced priests who faithfully performed their duty of reciting the Last Rites to those who lay dying were likely to contract the fatal illness as well. The subsequent death of a disproportionately large number of clerics and the attendant loss of academicians and physicians compelled the expeditious recruitment of less-qualified substitutes into those essential posts. Latin, and occasionally French, had been the *linguae francae* in ecclesiastical and educational milieus, but now, most of the novitiates in the church and university were fluent in neither language. Thus, for the replacements to perform with a modicum of competence in their new professions, they would have to be instructed in a language they could read and write. This dire situation called for an increase in the production of manuscripts written in the vernacular, both sacred and secular (Byrne, 2004). The laity's consequent perception of a link between religious thought and the vernacular, without the stigma of sacrilege, was the first step in accommodating a confluence of the sacred and secular worlds.

PROTESTANTISM AND THE INVENTION OF THE PRINTING PRESS

John Mirk was a late fouteenth- and early fifteenth-century English author of sermons and other publications written to aid the new group of pastors substituting for the clerics lost to the Black Plague. Barr and Miller (2018) state:

> Mirk's orthodoxy stood at the forefront of the religious movements of his time, and both his pastoral manuals and his sermons reflect innovative approaches to pastoral care and gender. Thus, John Mirk, himself a product of late medieval reforms, is one of the key individuals who also drove reform and helped to teach the practice of piety to clergy and ordinary parishioners alike. (n.p.)

But before Mirk's writings, there was a new movement brewing that would have a profound effect on religion throughout the world for centuries to come.

Much of the basic thought that grew into an alternative to Roman Catholicism during the Middle Ages can be attributed to John Wyclif (1328–1384) and the Lollard movement, precursor to the Protestant Reformation. Wyclif's vernacular Bible and subsequent modifications would not attain widespread dissemination before 1538, when the first printed English Bibles appeared in England. Of course, Gutenberg's German Bible was published in 1466 on his new invention, the printing press (Maas, 1912). Not only would Gutenberg's device revolutionize the propagation of information, but it would also spawn the new secular profession of publishing. The publishing world would produce the first examples of religious themes and images used to advertise consumer products and services. Publishers would unabashedly promote their religious books directly from the pages of those books.

The religious roots of publishing are firmly situated in the medieval monastery, where publishing became an art in the illuminated manuscripts produced by monks. Thus, another condition for secular holy hype had been fulfilled, the development of a mass medium for the spreading of promotional messages. One more element of the construct remained, and that was the maturation and expansion of a capitalistic consumer marketplace.

RISE OF COMMERCE

Clegg and Reed (1994) characterize the church in the Middle Ages as a commercial enterprise, "a firm which sold two products: religious services and social services" (p. 262). Up until about 1350, the monastery flourished, but during the next 200 years, corruption became widespread, eroding the reputation of this branch of the church. Continuing the business metaphor, Clegg and Reed claim that the monastery arm had gradually lost "its market share to private charitable foundations, the state, and Protestant religions" (p. 262) until King Henry VIII officially dissolved it in 1536. It should be noted that by this time, the abbey had also lost two more of its revenue streams, beer and manuscript sales, to secular commercial establishments that could produce a greater quantity of both, faster and much less expensively.

The guild system was established during the Middle Ages for religious and commercial purposes. Traditional analyses of the guilds hold that these organizations were monopolistic in theory and practice, and yet there is a growing body of work that contradicts, or at least serves to substantially diminish, the anti-competitive goals or effects of the merchant and crafts guilds (Hirshler, 1954; Hickson & Thompson, 1991; Greif et al., 1994; Favier, 1998; Richardson, 2004). Clearly, without substantial competition and a profit motive, there was little need for advertising. However, in the Middle Ages, competition between cities and countries increased as travel over long distances became easier and more cost effective (Favier, 1998). Indeed, as urban centers continued to increase in population into the Renaissance, competition between local merchants grew as well, despite "legally enforced egalitarianism" (Favier, 1998, p. 95), and not just on the basis of product price. Quality of merchandise was of utmost concern in the medieval market. Fraud was an ongoing concern (Kranton, 2003; Favier, 1998). Guild regulations and municipal statutes encouraged high quality by requiring craftsmen to put identifying marks on their work. In this way, for example, one cobbler's shoe could be distinguished from another cobbler's shoe, allowing substandard workmanship or price gouging to be tied to its negligent manufacturer (Wilkins, 1994). The mark served in much the same way that trademarks do in commerce today. The artisan's good name and surviving mark was his brand. To preserve his valuable brand, he delivered only the best product or service, whether it was bread, books, tableware, or tailoring.

As trade became heavier and more competitive,[2] merchants and craftsmen became more dependent on effective promotional efforts to grow their profits. As it is today, in the Late Middle Ages and the early Renaissance period, it was most important for the seller's messages to project reliability and high quality. In a time of pervasive religiosity and faith, relating to the potential customer through a common ethic, such as pride in one's work, could persuade the message recipient of the product's quality or the maker's honesty.

EMERGENCE OF SECULAR HOLY HYPE

With the economic, religious, and social climates all concurrently favorable, the use of sacred motifs in secular contexts for commercial identification began to manifest itself through the ancient medium of signboards. Industrial production of alcoholic beverages, particularly beer, in the larger villages and cities was replacing monastery output as the cost of brewing equipment for mass quantities became prohibitive for money-conscious church institutions. The most prevalent signs in the Middle Ages were signboards affixed to the taverns, inns, and public houses (pubs) to distinguish them from abutting cottages. These were identified by the sign of the "bush," a broomlike device representative of "a clump of ivy and vine-leaves symbolical of Bacchus" (Burke, 1930, p. 23), the mythical Roman god of wine, revelry, and intoxication (Gill, 2009). By medieval and modern standards, signs were not considered advertising in a strict sense. In fact, guilds prohibited advertising to control yet not prevent competition (Favier, 1998; Henning, 2005), but encouraged signs for enabling townspeople to distinguish one business from another. The lack of vigorous competition in certain areas and the high level of illiteracy generally made it practically useless anyway to supplement images with text for the purpose of promotion.

Seals, signboards, and heraldry were omnipresent in medieval England. Emblematic elements, similar in purpose to today's corporate logos, were displayed above residential door lintels and on signs attached to shop buildings. For example, to help a villager or visitor find him, the gravedigger showed symbols of his tools, a pickaxe and lamp, on his sign; for the cobbler a shoe, and for the tailor a scissors (Larwood & Hotten, 1866). The guilds themselves employed symbols as logos. Interestingly, the beer brewers' guild identified itself by the image of a hexagram, a six-pointed star, identical to a Star of

David. Brewers hung their guild symbol outside on a long pole (figure 4.1d), and taverns hung out the sign of the bush. A researcher might understandably jump to the faulty conclusion that there was a link between Judaism and the production of beer. However, a six-pointed star, eventually called the Star of David, did not signify Judaism until the nineteenth century (Ronen, 2009).

More germane to secular holy hype per se were visual representations associated with the type of product sold or even the kind of customer preferred. Larwood and Hotten (1866) explain that "certain devices would doubtless be adopted to attract the attention of the different classes of wayfarers, as the Cross for the Christian customer, and the Sun or the Moon for the pagan" (p. 4). Eventually, the use of symbols not literally illustrative of a unique product or service would represent still another step in the development of secular holy hype. It would lead to the depiction of the qualities of a product or a service by associating them with other objects connoting those qualities. In a society that placed a premium on cultivating a good memory due to the inability to read or write, the memorability of a symbol was of paramount concern. Clanchy (1979) expounds:

> Twentieth-century advertising uses a comparable technique in imprinting on the mind's eye the symbolic shell of Shell Oil or the tiger associated with Esso. Because the symbolic image is memorable in itself, it cues the memory, which then recalls the information required about the particular knight or brand of oil. This is the process, which Hugh of St. Victor describes as "exciting the memory" (*ad memoriam excitandum*). (p. 174)

APOSTLE SPOONS

In a culture steeped in religion, what image could be more recognizable or more memorable than that of Jesus or one of his Apostles? One of the earliest consumer items to incorporate a sacred image in its construction was the medieval spoon. As early as the thirteenth century, spoons began to be used in English households. The hostess did not furnish them due to concerns about hygiene. Consequently, each guest carried his or her own spoon when dining out. The first spoons were fashioned simply as a bowl, slender handle, and small knob at the end. Soon, craftsmen began designing them in keeping with personal aesthetic sensibilities, finishing each spoon handle with a decorative flourish, such as an acorn. Not long thereafter, individual spoons began to appear with the likeness of one of Jesus's Apostles or the Virgin Mary affixed to the distal end of the handle (Addison, 1908).

As these so-called Apostle spoons (figure 4.1c) became increasingly popular, they became the gift of choice from the sponsors at a baptism. Most children of humble origins would receive one, or sometimes two, Apostle spoons, but a child of wealthy parents or godparents would receive a set of 12, each spoon of the dozen adorned with a different one of the 12 Apostles. Occasionally, sets of 13 spoons were presented at baptism. The 13th, or Master, spoon would frequently be adorned with Jesus as the Good Shepherd. The material of which one's Apostle spoon was constructed would determine one's seating during a meal at the host's residence. As an indicator of class membership, a silver Apostle spoon would place the spoon's owner at the table on the dais, with tin spoon owners at the next lower level of seating, and wood spoon owners at the farthest seating from the main table (Addison, 1908; Murphy, 1921).

SECULAR HOLY HYPE GOES TO PRESS

Although Sarapin (2008) clearly considers signage and consumer products, such as Apostle spoons, as legitimate conveyances for holy hype of all types, the key to a rapid growth of secular holy hype into the Renaissance and beyond would be the availability of a medium designed to affordably disseminate advertising messages to a mass audience. As already mentioned, Gutenberg's printing press would satisfy that precondition. As it did with so many other phenomena and ideas, the printing press gave secular holy hype currency in the Late Middle Ages and early Renaissance. Secular holy hype was no longer an aberration and no longer a unique statement by one individual. People began to use sacred imagery, text, and themes specifically for the purpose of selling things, such as books and high-quality craftsmanship, to a mass audience. In the late fifteenth century, secular holy hype earned authenticity as an advertising technique.

We still see remnants of mass-produced holy hype first observed in the colophons of late fifteenth-century books. In an article about the history of title pages in books, Gilchrist (1947) expounds on the concept of a colophon, which was originally an inscription at the end of a book giving the title or subject, the names of the author and publisher, and the date and location of publication. The first machine-printed colophon appears in 1457 in the *Mainz Psalter* (Jeske, 2004). In their "printer's advertisement," as Gilchrist calls it, Fust and Schoeffer make the undeniable connection between the worship of God and their ability to complete the publication:

> The present copy of the Psalms, adorned with beauty of capital letters, and sufficiently marked with rubrics, has been thus fashioned by an ingenious invention of printing and stamping without any driving of the pen, and to the worship of God has been brought to completion by Johann Fust, a citizen of Mainz, and

> Peter Schoeffer of Gernsheim in the year of the Lord 1457 on the vigil of the feast of the Assumption. (Fust & Schoeffer, 1457, n.p., as cited in Jeske, 2004)

By 1500, the practice of including a colophon, often incorporating a publishing house logo amid the text, had become common practice.

Venetian publisher Aldus Manutius (1450–1515) is credited with moving the colophon to the front of the book, a practice that became standard in European printing by 1520. On the title page, Manutius displays his well-known Aldine Press logo (figure 4.1e), which consists of a dolphin wrapped around an anchor (Jeske, 2004). It is posited here that his logo was an expression of religious faith through the use of two ancient symbols of Christianity. The anchor symbolizes the hope of receiving everything that God promises (Hassett, 1907; Dilasser et al., 1999). In addition, the ancients believed "dolphins brought souls to their goal safe and sound" (Dilasser et al., 1999, p. 39). Barnes (1909) explains:

> With an anchor the dolphin occurs frequently on early Christian rings, representing the attachment of the Christian to Christ crucified. Speaking generally, the dolphin is the symbol of the individual Christian, rather than of Christ Himself, though in some instances the dolphin with the anchor seems to be intended as a representation of Christ upon the Cross. (n.p.)

Manutius considered his profession a sacred personal mission blessed by God, and he advertised it as such.

One of the outstanding exemplars of secular holy hype offered here for consideration is a full-page display advertisement, published in 1683 in London, which told the story of a market fair held on the frozen Thames River during the "Violent Frost" from the beginning of December to the following 12th of February. The top portion of the display (figure 4.2a) includes a headline, illustration, and legend. The lower half of the page is a poetic narrative of all the wares, crafts demonstrations, and other activities found at the huge event. All of the merchants were identified by their crafts or services. The headline, "God's Works Is the Worlds [*sic*] Wonder," makes salient the link between the work of God's hands and the work of man's hands.

In the Renaissance period, secular holy hype became more like what would emerge as one common style of nineteenth- and twentieth-century advertising. Sir Hugh Plat wrote a gardening book in 1654, which he titled *The Garden of Eden or, an accurate description of all flowers and fruits now growing in England, with particular rules how to enhance their nature and growth, as well as seeds and herbs, as the secret ordering of trees and plants* (figure 4.2b). The book took advantage of the biblical story from Genesis, in which the first two humans, Adam and Eve, lived in a beautiful garden created by

Figure 4.2 a) Newspaper broadside following the London Fair in 1683. "God's works is the world's wonder." It boasts of the successful market to convince the powers that be to hold a similar event the following year. b) Newspaper advertisement for the book *The Garden of Eden* by Sir Hugh Plat in 1660. c) Labels of some of today's most respected breweries, one of which, Leffe, claims to have been brewing since 1240 CE Abbot Ale has been in production since the 1950s (the Greene King Brewery dates back to 1799) and Franziskaner Weissbier since 1363. La Trappe is an "Authentic Trappist Product" according to the International Trappist Association. *Source: a) Public domain image retrieved from the British Museum collection. b) Public domain image retrieved from dominicwinter.co.uk. c) Images courtesy of AB InBev, Greene King Brewery, and La Trappe.*

God. The allusion to this story was used to entice as well as relate to the highly religious intended audience. The title reflects the use of secular holy hype.

OF BEER, LIQUEUR, AND THE CHURCH WHEN MODERN GOES MEDIEVAL

Moving to a product-specific perspective, beer is one commodity of modern times that has maintained its religious connotative ties to the Middle Ages. And for that reason, it makes the strongest case for the origin of secular holy hype during that period of time. Unger (2004) verifies this proposition:

> As late as the twentieth century in Norway, brewing was approached with a certain religious earnestness and a belief that the brewing process had to be protected from potentially dangerous forces, such as the little people. Various signs and symbols, such as the sign of the cross on barrels, showed up in parts of northern Europe in an attempt to keep evil magic from contaminating the beer. (p. 39)

The cachet of medieval beer brewing extends into the twenty-first century through an assortment of beers hoping to ride the coattails of the monks' robes. Beers and ales are marketed to take full advantage of the prestige and traditions psychologically associated with the monastic version. Abbey beers, those not Trappist sanctioned, abound in today's market with names such as Father Theodore's Stout, Monty Python's Holy Grail, Brother Dan's Double, and Monks Habit.

The mental picture of a monk toiling away at the painstaking task of illuminating a manuscript is certainly a common one. Perhaps a less familiar but no less prevalent picture is of the men of the abbey brewing beer. The cloistered Roman Catholic clergy did not invent the process, but were engaged in it for centuries. Beer brewing became a high art in the monastery, and the product was enjoyed by the general population in monastery pubs. The church's public houses, which were given tax-free status, were closed when they began to represent too much competition for the privately owned taverns and beerhouses (Unger, 2004). However, the monks continued to brew high-quality beer for their own consumption and for that of wayfarers. Good beer was so prized that it was deemed acceptable for the tithe, which was mandatory (Clegg & Reed, 1994). Beer was such an important commodity in daily life that images of beer barrels were often pictured with the god Bacchus, thus representing beer's otherworldly characteristics.

Figure 4.2c shows labels of the so-called abbey beers, which are products similar in style or presentation to monastic beers and use monastic imagery in marketing their products. Leffe®, a Belgian ale, claims to have been brewing since 1240 CE, but is no longer produced in an abbey. Abbot Ale (from Greene King® brewery) is a nod to the history of the brewery's location, Bury St Edmunds in Suffolk, which is well-known for the remains of its former abbey. Franzikaner® is a Bavarian brew, and its label features a Franciscan friar holding a malt shovel. On the other hand, La Trappe®, a Dutch ale, is an Authentic Trappist Product according to the International Trappist Association, brewed within the walls of the Koningshoeven abbey walls.

CONCLUSION

We know that secular holy hype emerged gradually as the Late Middle Ages were transitioning into the Renaissance and in the midst of integral social, economic, and political forces in the shadows of a cataclysmic plague of disease. Ironically, what we have come to understand is that secular holy hype was in fact arising from two requisite secular activities, publishing and beer production, conducted under full ecclesiastical authority, direction, and supervision within the very walls of a medieval religious institution, the monastery. As we have seen, at least one of these segments of the market (beer) continues to find its earliest advertising archetype salient for current potential customers.

Whatever the qualities embodied, there is something undeniably compelling about motifs from the Middle Ages and the Renaissance. It is now left to scholars to more deeply explore the secular holy hype that we experience today. Is it telling us about religion, spirituality, culture, or clever salesmanship? What happens when a religion's time-honored and sacred symbols are appropriated for secular purposes to such a degree that their religious significance is transformed into something antithetical or, worse, profane? Chapter 5, in all three "verses," introduces the advertising student, scholar/instructor, or fascinated observer to a wide range of examples of holy hype from about 22 decades of published designs implemented in a variety of industries for all types of targeted audiences. Arranged alphabetically, the reader may select categories of special interest, such as devils, angels, sin in general, sin by type, the Christian cross, the Jesus pose, and dozens more.

NOTES

1. There is continuing scholarly debate about the extent to which the Black Death influenced the development of the commercial system and social and economic processes in medieval England (Hatcher, 1994; Byrne, 2004; Herlihy & Cohn, 1997). The propositions and arguments in this paper are independent of the outcome of this controversy.
2. Max Weber's theory about the Protestant Ethic being the primary cause of the rise of modern capitalism in the Middle Ages and Renaissance is debated to this day (Kim, 2007). For this reason, and because it is not within our purview to explain the rise of capitalism, but only to verify that it did happen, we chose to omit discussion of this argument.

REFERENCES

Addison, J. D. G. (1908). *Arts and crafts in the Middle Ages*. The Page Company.

Augusta State University. (2009). Christian iconography. http://www.aug.edu/augusta/iconography/

Barnes, A. (1909). Dolphin. In *The Catholic Encyclopedia*. Robert Appleton Company. http://www.newadvent.org/cathen/05100a.htm

Barr, B. A., & Miller, L. J. (2018). John Mirk. *Oxford Bibliographies.* https://www.oxfordbibliographies.com/view/document/obo-9780195396584/obo-9780195396584-0259.xml

Barton, B. F. (1920). "They say" has made many a good man good. In *It's a good old world.* The Century Company.

Besançon, A. (2000). *The forbidden image: An intellectual history of iconoclasm.* University of Chicago Press.

Blair, J. A. (1996). The possibility and actuality of visual arguments. In *Groundwork in the Theory of Argumentation*, 205–223. Springer.

Bradlaugh, C., & Gillespie, W. H. (1872). *Atheism or Theism? Debate between Iconoclast, the accredited champion of British atheists, and others, and William Honyman Gillespie.* Houlston.

Burke, T. (1930). *The English inn.* Longmans, Green & Co.

Byrne, J. P. (2004). *The black death.* Greenwood Publishing Group.

Clanchy, M. T. (1979). *From memory to written record: England 1066–1307.* Harvard University Press.

Clegg, N. W. & Reed, C. G. (1994). The economic decline of the Church in medieval England. *Explorations in Economic History, 31*(2), 261–280. doi: 10.1006/exeh.1994.1011

Connelly, A. (n.d.). Photograph from personal blog. http://www.adrianconnelly.com/wp-content/uploads/2009/05/exhibit07.jpg

"Court of the Ladies of Queen Anne of Brittany." Wikimedia Commons. https://commons.wikimedia.org/wiki/File:Court_of_the_Ladies_of_Queen_Anne_of_Brittany_Miniature_representing_this_lady_weeping_on_account_of_the_absence_of_her_husband_during_the_Italian_war.png

Dilasser, M., Durkin, M. C., Morson, C., & Beaumont, M. M. (1999). *The symbols of the church.* The Liturgical Press.

Einstein, M. (2008). *Brands of faith: Marketing religion in a commercial age.* Routledge.

Favier, J. (1998). *Gold and spices: The rise of commerce in the Middle Ages* (C. Higgitt, Trans.). Holmes & Meier.

Gilchrist, D. B. (1947). Title pages: A footnote to the history of printing. *University of Rochester Library Bulletin, 3*(1). https://rbscp.lib.rochester.edu/2441

Gill, N. S. (2009). Dionysus or Bacchus—God of wine. *About.com.* http://ancienthistory.about.com/od/godsmyth/ig/Gods-and-Goddesses/Dionysus-or-Bacchus.htm

Greif, A., Milgrom, P., & Weingast, B. R. (1994). Coordination, commitment, and enforcement: The case of the merchant guild. *The Journal of Political Economy, 102*(4), 745–776. doi: 10.1086/261953

Hassett, M. (1907). The anchor (as Symbol). In C. G. Herberman, E. A. Pace, C. B. Pallen, T. J. Shahan, & J. J. Wynne (Eds.), *The Catholic Encyclopedia.* Robert Appleton Company.

Hatcher, J. (1994). England in the aftermath of the black death. *Past & Present,* (144), 3–35.

Henning, J. (2005). Bar associations, law firms, and other medieval guilds. *Litigation, 32*(1), 17–21.

Herlihy, D. & Cohn, S. K. (1997). *The Black Death and the transformation of the west*. Harvard University Press.
Hickson, C. R., & Thompson, E. A. (1991). A new theory of guilds and European economic development. *Explorations in Economic History*, *28*(2), 127–168.
Hirshler, E. E. (1954). Medieval economic competition. *The Journal of Economic History, 14*(1), 52–58.
Huizinga, J. (1954). *The waning of the Middle Ages: A study of the forms of life, thought, and art in France and the Netherlands in the XIVth and XVth centuries*. Doubleday & Co.
Iconoclastic controversies. (n.d.). Khan Academy. https://www.khanacademy.org/humanities/medieval-world/byzantine1/beginners-guide-byzantine/a/iconoclastic-controversies
Jeske, J. (2004). *Storied words: The writer's vocabulary and its origins*. iUniverse, Inc.
Kim, K. (2007). *Concepts of development in the Christian traditions: A religions and development background paper*. RAD Working Papers Series. http://epapers.bham.ac.uk/1497/
Kramer, S. N. (1981). *History begins at Sumer: Thirty-nine firsts in recorded history* (3rd Edition). University of Pennsylvania Press.
Kranton, R. E. (2003). Competition and the incentive to produce high quality. *Economica, 70*(279), 385–404. doi: 10.1111/1468-0335.t01-1-00289
Larwood, J. & Hotten, J. C. (1866). *The history of signboards from the earliest times to the present day*. Piccadilly.
Maas, A. (1912). Versions of the Bible. In C. G. Herberman, E. A. Pace, C. B. Pallen, T. J. Shahan, & J. J. Wynne (Eds.), *The Catholic Encyclopedia*. Robert Appleton Company.
Mallia, K. L. (2009). From the sacred to the profane: A critical analysis of the changing nature of religious imagery in advertising. *Journal of Media and Religion*, *8*(3), 172–190.
Martin, E. J. (1978). *A history of the iconoclastic controversy*. AMS Press.
Messaris, P. P. (1996). *Visual persuasion: The role of images in advertising*. SAGE Publications, Inc.
Moore, R. L. (1994). *Selling God: American religion in the marketplace of culture*. Oxford University Press.
Morse, M. A. (2007). Creating sacred space: The religious visual culture of the Renaissance Venetian casa. *Renaissance Studies*, *21*(2), 151–184. doi: 10.1111/j.1477-4658.2007.00357.x
Murphy, C. Q. (1921). *The history of the art of tablesetting: Ancient and modern*. [Author published].
Presbrey, F. (1929). *History and development of advertising*. Doubleday, Doran & Company.
Richardson, G. (2004). Guilds, laws, and markets for manufactured merchandise in late-medieval England. *Explorations in Economic History, 41*(1), 1–25. doi: 10.1016/S0014-4983(03)00045-7
Ronen, M. (2009, May 3). Magen David: From mystical talisman to Zionist symbol. *Jewish World*. http://www.ynetnews.com/articles/0,7340,L-3709939,00.html

Sarapin, S. H. (2008). Holy hype goes unconventional: Shock and awe at the intersection of Madison Avenue and Damascus Road. Unpublished paper presented at the 2008 National Communication Association Conference.

Stern, B. B. (1988). Medieval allegory: Roots of advertising strategy for the mass market. *The Journal of Marketing, 52*(3), 84–94. doi: 10.1177/002224298805200308

Trachtenberg, J. (1939). *Jewish magic and superstition: A study in folk religion.* Behrman's Jewish Book House

Unger, R. W. (2004). *Beer in the Middle Ages and the Renaissance*. University of Pennsylvania Press.

White, J. F. (1989). *Protestant worship*. Westminster John Knox Press.

Wilkins, M. (1994). When and why brand names in food and drink? In G. Jones & N. Morgan, (Eds.), *Adding value: Brands and marketing in food and drink* (pp. 15–40). Routledge.

Chapter 5

Selling the Goods Amidst the Good News

VERSE 1

Artist Paul Klee wrote that "art does not reproduce the visible but makes visible" (Klee, 1961, p. 76). In this chapter, we present ads that make religion visible amid the trappings of consumer culture. Many creatives in the ad business, art directors and copywriters alike, find that the Bible contains the answers to all of humankind's dilemmas because they have found, among many other things: (a) solutions to vermin infestation at The Last Supper; (b) the best choice for the "mass" transit of a large group of nuns in a Volkswagen bus; (c) the remedy for ending up in baggage hell at American airports in Samsonite luggage's path to baggage heaven; and (d) the solution to the problem of inheriting the Earth even if you are *not* meek—in leather, atop a Harley. There are answers from both the Old (the Hebrew scriptures or Tanakh) and the New Testaments, the Quran, the Book of Mormon, and other sacred texts; hence, secular holy hype is non-sectarian and non-discriminatory. Interestingly, even atheists use holy hype to score points in their ad messages because they truly understand their targeted audience. In 1909, J. Walter Thompson, creator of one of the world's most enduring and revered worldwide advertising agencies, remarked, "America is the advertiser's Promised Land, turned into reality" (Laird, 1998). New consumers, new products, new institutions, and new ways of life present thousands of opportunities to incorporate this method of delivering just about any kind of message. With our target audience squarely in mind, the supreme question we must ask is this: Is this a proper approach to use to create or intensify a positive attitude toward the ad's message—to build or reinforce a positive attitude toward the product or brand, and to effect intentions to purchase?

Cultural norms change to the point that behaviors or products that were once taboo or rarely mentioned in mixed company are today proudly advertised to the masses. For example, think about the history of body art. There have been periods during which tattoos were worn by those in high society. Then, they went out of style and favor about 60–70 years ago, when it seemed as though the only people wearing them were sailors, prostitutes, and gang members. Then, of course, after World War II and the Nazi tattooing of concentration camp residents with identification numbers, Jews did not adorn their bodies with these symbols of the Holocaust. Today, tattoos are socially acceptable in all segments of society. Think about how the connotations of tattoos have changed throughout history and how the advertising for these services has changed over time. References to the biblical text are conspicuous, comprehensible, accessible, and unambiguous, if not personally meaningful, for almost all Americans and to a large part of the world outside the United States as well.

This chapter executes a deep dive into the most visible category of holy hype by illustrating it with graphic examples dating back to the late nineteenth century. The main focus here is on the type of holy hype that is considered most representative of modern advertising principles, secular holy hype. Examples of secular holy hype are commonly seen in our culture, and are now becoming prevalent, if not always acceptable, in Brazil, Italy, England, and other areas outside the United States.

This type of holy hype, as seen in modern times, would have to have started when advertising became necessary. Gone were the days when every commodity sold in the general stores was generic. The Industrial Revolution gave rise to mass production, which led to an oversupply of certain goods. Advertising was seen as a way to drive consumer demand for particular "brands" so as to sell off the surfeit. Brands were novel, and generic goods were seen as poorer in quality. No longer did customers grab a few bars of soap from a large wooden barrel. Beginning in 1879, there was a choice in most general stores. Decorated, paper-wrapped, consistently sized bars of Ivory soap were available as well in neat tabletop displays. And each bar of Ivory boasted some astounding claims about its features and benefits. No such claims could be found anywhere about the raw cakes of soap. Ivory could float, for heaven's sake! And, it was 99 and 44/100% pure! There was the early American belief that "cleanliness is next to godliness." The phrase actually came from a sermon delivered by John Wesley in 1778, and yet it took the soap companies' advertising to bring the saying into a whole new dimension of fame and meaning. In fact, Ivory Soap, for example, took its very name from Psalm 45, which reads: "All thy garments smell of myrrh and aloes and cassia out of *ivory* palaces whereby they have made thee glad." It came as a revelation to Harley Procter, the founder's son, one Sunday in church as he was skimming the Bible. This sentiment and the understanding that the majority of US customers were Protestant led the soap manufacturers to use religiously nuanced language or art in their advertisements to appeal to that Christian audience (Akh, 2019; Procter & Gamble, 2006) (figure 5.1a).

It was Quaker Oats' logo that gave the company its religious bent. It was the very first registered trademark for a breakfast cereal brand. On the registration form, the company owners described it as "a figure of a man in 'Quaker' garb" (Quaker, 2020). At the end of the nineteenth century, Quaker Oats broke through all of the other advertising at the time by tying its public image to a religiously inspired model of "good quality and honest value," the Quaker himself (Quaker, 2020) (figure 5.1b). Between 1877 and 2020, the Quaker company changed its spokesperson's appearance many times. Sometimes the alteration was minor and barely noticeable—a friendlier look on his face, perhaps, or some small adjustment to his collar or hair. In subsequent decades, the man evolved from a full figure to just a head-and-shoulders view of the religious fellow. The ads were never religious or spiritual per se except for the use of "thee" and "thou" in messages to the consumer from the Quaker and the use of the line "Warms your heart and soul." In addition,

Figure 5.1 a) Ivory hired artist Leyendecker to paint this ad in 1900. It is a monk drawing closer to God through cleanliness. b) This is the original Quaker man, registered in 1877 as the first of many versions of the Quaker Oats logo through the decades. *Source*: *a) Public domain image retrieved from Arthur, the digital museum at arthur.io/art/j-c-leyendecker/ivory-soap-advertisement. b) Public domain image retrieved from an advertisement sold on ebay.com.*

the Quaker carried a document stamped "pure." As we will discover, the use of religious symbols in logos is actually quite common and always has been.

As explained in Chapter 2, secular holy hype is forthrightly commercial in the selling of consumer products. Looking at thousands of examples of this genre, it becomes instantly obvious that several industries are particularly well-represented among them, such as cars, liquor, and food, which tend to find commonality between the experience of using their products and some religious sensibility. In addition to the frequently appearing sectors of business are the conspicuous thematic categories. The common themes are usually more pronounced than are the industries for which they speak. For this reason, we alphabetically arrange our examples according to the religious motifs that are most evident. We will begin with the category of Adam and Eve, which is a perennial go-to theme in advertising. And it should be. This is where the Jewish and Christian theological stories began in the Garden of Eden, in the beginning.

ADAM AND EVE AND CREATION

The story of Adam and Eve in the Bible is believed to be the truth by about 40% of Americans (Brenan, 2019). Despite 60% adhering to the opposite view, it is probably one of the most recognized parables in the entire Jewish scriptures—by all people, whether religious or unaffiliated. Even if people are unaware of all of the details, they are most likely familiar with the gist of the story. This would suggest that references to Adam and Eve in advertising are identifiable and understandable for a large part of the global public.

Adam and Eve frequently appear in ads together as the pair we meet first in the Bible's Garden of Eden. Either could present alone without the other and still be recognizable due to their environment and clothing, or lack thereof. Together, they tell a story of creation, disobedience, and a fall from grace. It is a story of great substance, and therefore it is a story that lends itself well to a variety of advertising contexts. A few of these are illustrated in figure 5.2. Considering all of Eve's behavior in Eden that was not compliant with God's commands, Eve ends up representing temptation and sin, so she could work very well in ads for just about anything people perceive as immoral, bad, or sinful in some way (figures 5.2a and 5.2b). In figure 5.2a, somehow it seems that Eve could not resist Altoids, "the curiously strong sours," and so she offered them to Adam. They look shocked and in fear of God's wrath because they are aware of their sin. The next ad, which features Eve alone (figure 5.2b), gives us PETA's impression of a sin to be wary of—eating meat—in the group's promotion of vegetarianism. The vines wrapped around Eve's, no, Angela Simmons's, body serve as the serpent, and her long locks

Figure 5.2 a) Eve and Adam simply cannot resist "the curiously strong sours." The phrase "forbidden fruit" comes from Genesis 3:3 of the Bible. b) PETA pro-animal ad advocating for vegetarianism. Angela Simmons teaches us what sin is. c) 1985 ad for Coty Musk and Wild Musk for men. "The essence of animal attraction." d) 1928 ad for Bird's Custard. "and Eve said unto Adam, 'Where's the Bird's Custard!'"*Source*: *a) Ad by Leo Burnett, © Altoids.com. Screenshot retrieved from ebay.com listing. b) Image courtesy of People for the Ethical Treatment of Animals (PETA). c) © Coty. Screenshot retrieved from listing on ebay.com. d) Public domain image retrieved from ebay.com listing.*

hide her nude body. And still, with her "come hither" look, she is tempting us with her apple, which is forbidden fruit. The term, "forbidden fruit" comes to us from Genesis 3:3 of the Bible. Over the centuries, we have envisioned this fruit as an apple, when rabbis have opined that it was really one of these: a fig; tomato; grapes or wine; wheat; a lemon; or a nut (Shurpin, n.d., n.p.). Shurpin explains how it might have come to be seen as an apple:

> As for apples, the modern consensus seems to be that the source of this misconception is that the Latin word *malum* (with short *a*), meaning "evil," was associated with *malum* (with long *a*), another Latin word, borrowed from the Greek, meaning "apple." (Shurpin, n.d., n.p.)

A secular holy hype ad using the Adam and Eve motif can creatively change up the story by substituting something else for the forbidden fruit, but it must be done thoughtfully. The alternative item must be relevant to the ad narrative. In figure 5.2a, the apple is now a round tin of Altoids; in figure 5.2c, bottles of musk cologne, the essence of animal attraction. Figure 5.2d is an example of Eve doubly tempting Adam—once with the apple and again by asking for the perfect apple accompaniment, Bird's Custard. The text of the ad informs us that no matter how people cook their apples, "they are never so delicious as when served with Bird's Custard." There is the slightest implication that this custard may be so good that when paired with the apple, it becomes even more forbidden.

Adam is almost never the sole character in ads. A glaring exception to that would be the category of secular holy hype that involves stories related to the topic of Adam's creation. In an unscientific reckoning of the frequency of these ads, we find that Adam, in take-offs of Michelangelo's painting on the ceiling of Rome's Sistine Chapel, "Creation of Adam," is one of the most recognizable.

The layout of the original painting of God and Adam is such that caricature and satire are compelling responses. God, positioned on the right and surrounded by angels, extends His finger out to Adam's finger in an act of creation. There is a small space between the two fingers, and Adam's position lower than God's is an invitation to play with the power differentials manifested by the space each one takes up. In almost all ads constructed to make use of this particular configuration and painting, the owner of the finger on the right is in control. When using satire or caricature, it is critical to retain at least a couple of the most prominent attributes of the original. This maintains the resonance and salience of the referent. If the reproduction veers too far away from the relationships in the original, the connection to the original can be lost, resulting in a failed message. Figures 5.3a, c, d, and e are successful at making meaning despite the omission of God and Adam because the primary relationship in Michelangelo's painting is the focus on the two index fingers. Our minds see that relationship in the ads and then jump to the original image to which the ads allude, mentally filling in the blanks. The more difficult the designer makes any such connotation for the ad viewer to "get" or to perceive, the less likely the message will be received as intended. In figure 5.3a, the pizza slice, which makes up a "slice of time" in the company logo, is being passed from God to Adam. Figure 5.3c recreates Michelangelo's

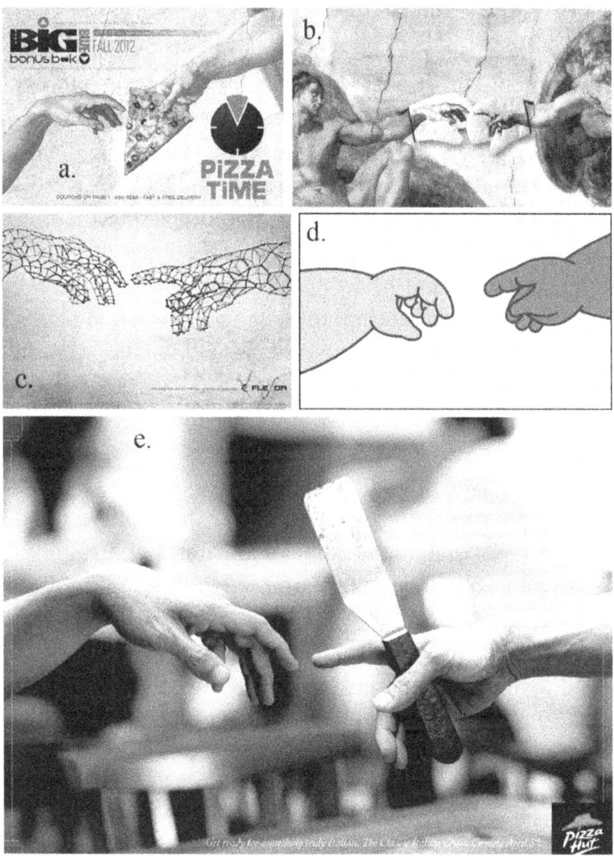

Figure 5.3 a) Pizza Time ad. b) "Creation of Adam" oven mitts by i3Lab. c) Ad for Flexor. "The construction system for all kinds of creations." d) This stock illustration is unusual in that it provides the artist with a method of changing the power dynamics by implying that God is a being of color. e) God is giving Adam the tool for enjoyable living—a pizza spatula. *Source: a) © Pizza Time, photo courtesy of owner of Bellingham Pizza Time, Peter Allen. b) i3Lab; no longer in business. c) Flexor; no longer in business. d) © iStockphoto artist Paladjai. e) © Pizza Hut, image courtesy of Gavin Simpson, art director.*

religious painting using Flexor® parts, figure 5.3d provides only the slightest sense of the original by using the cartoonish hand and arm of Adam and a brown cartoonish hand of God implying a power dynamic rarely illustrated, and in figure 5.3e, Gavin Simpson has designed an ad for Pizza Hut in which God passes the spatula to Adam, creating his ability to obtain his own slice.

In a widely reproduced photograph, Dr. Kim, a plastic surgeon in Beverly Hills, CA, is offering some very special ways for people to be "born again" on the third floor of his office building. God even points the way to the elevator button for "up." Unfortunately, we are unable to show this excellent exemplar of holy hype here because we were not able to connect with the doctor to get permission, but you should look this one up on the internet. It is worth the time to do so. Adding "Be born again" to the mural refers to the effect of undergoing plastic surgery as well as alluding to the evangelical concept of a rebirth in Christ. Imputing a religious attribute to Dr. Kim's proficiency with those words embeds another dimension of holy hype into the image. Another aspect not as obvious as "born again" is that one must go "up" to reach the office. God, the heavens, and perfection are above us, figuratively. The best cosmetic surgeons are often referred to as "gods." To wit, a plastic surgeon in Florida, Leonard Hochstein, is nicknamed the "Boob God" (Palmer, 2019). In response to some fundamentalist Christians, who insist that cosmetic surgery is a sin, Dr. K. O. Paulose, a surgeon at a Christian mission hospital serving the poor says, "God is using me as an instrument of His healing ministry to fulfill His purpose" (Nsenduluka, 2015).

Figure 5.4 continues showing ads that feature the creation of Adam. Figure 5.4a is a hand-painted statement that demonstrates the highly competitive English football league—so competitive, in fact, that the team players out of Manchester, England, called the Manchester United Red Devils, tout their very creation as coming directly from God. Although not the first club formed in England and Wales, it is the best according to its fans. The "handwriting on the wall" (Daniel 5:5–30) is bold enough to profess that Manchester was created as God's last act before resting on the seventh day. In figure 5.4b, we see a child's arm and fist at left actually defying God's attempt to make the child an angel. The child is defying cancer, too, and has decided she is not ready to be an angel in heaven yet. This ad is soliciting financial contributions for the Kids Cancer Project in Alexandria, New South Wales, Australia, and its copy asserts, "New treatments will bring new hope. Help us get in front of cancer. Donate today."

In a bus ad we could not show, Epic Burger® in Chicago asserts that a conspicuous horizontal hand of God in the cooks' creation could be just the thing. Epic Burger explains that its burger is also more mindful because it is made with divine help as indicated in these bus and subway ads. What could make their burgers epic? They are made using all-natural and non-processed ingredients, so consumers can think more about their health and happiness and the health of our planet as well.

Mindfulness is an important buzzword these days, and buzzwords can be used effectively in advertising if not overused. A buzzword is jargon or slang that eases its way into the vernacular and into vogue. Before the internet, the uptake of buzzwords used to be rather slow, but, today, it can happen virally, within hours even. These words or phrases come from industry in general, particular professions, marketing, or fields of study and practice. Sometimes

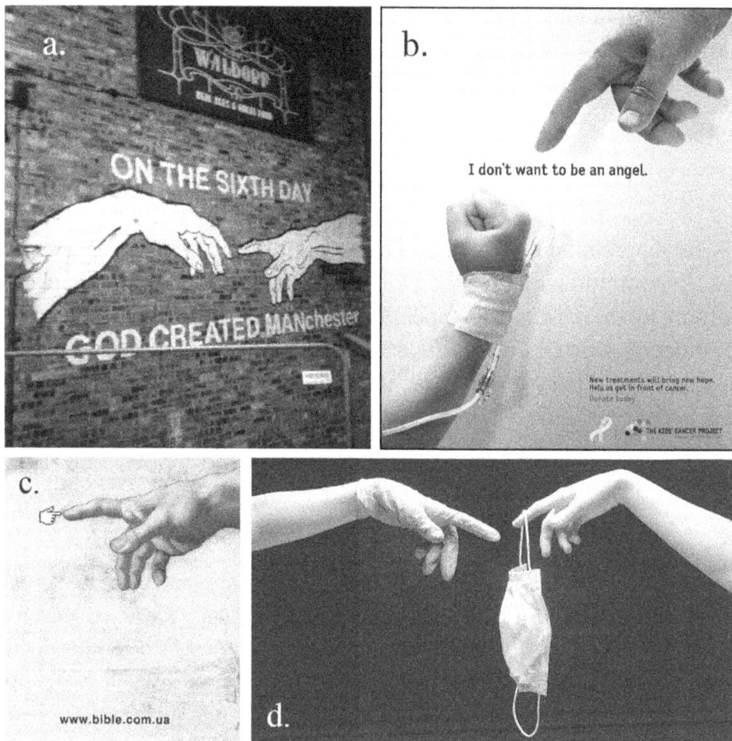

Figure 5.4 a) "On the sixth day, God created Manchester." b) The Kids' Cancer Project ad, "I don't want to be an angel." c) Ad for www.bible.com.ua. d) Illustrative of a pandemic like COVID-19. *Source: a) Painting by Trafford Parsons, photo anonymous. Image retrieved from flickriver.com. b) © The Kids' Cancer Project. Image courtesy Saatchi & Saatchi Sydney and Jennie Smiedt of The Kid's Cancer Project. Creative directors: Piero Ruzzen & Flavio Fonseca. Strategy director: Peter Pippen. c) Bible Online; no longer in business. d) Image © iStockphoto photographer nycshooter, created by Stanislav Chegleev.*

they go out of style and then return to popular usage decades later. Some of today's more common buzzwords are: big data, low-hanging fruit, wheelhouse, above my pay grade, boots on the ground, hard stop, close the loop, line in the sand, move the needle, and—you get the picture. A buzzword or a play on a buzzword can be the inspiration for an ad's art direction and often is.

In figure 5.4c, we see an old ad for a company trying to connect site visitors with God by offering the Bible online. In place of Adam's hand on the left, the advertisement uses a familiar computer icon of a pointing hand. This could have led the way to numerous takes on this digitized version of the holy book. Figure 5.4d is a perfect illustrative scenario to be employed during the coronavirus pandemic. God and Adam are shown touching with the assistance of face masks and gloves because actually making contact would be tantamount to spreading a spark of COVID-19.

ANGELS

Angels are a perennial favorite of so many people and companies for so many reasons. In common parlance, the word is often used as a term of endearment. In addition to their frequent appearances in ads, these good beings, either whole or deconstructed into wings, halos, and harps are common in corporate names and logos. They are first mentioned at the moment of creation in the Hebrew Scriptures at Genesis 1:26, when God says, "Let us make humankind in our image, in the likeness of ourselves" (Complete Jewish Bible, 1998, n.p.; Fried, 2017, n.p.). "Who is *us*?" Rabbi Fried asks. Expounding, the Rabbi says:

> The classical commentator Rashi explains that God presented the question of the creation of man to His heavenly court of angels. (This, Rashi explains, is to teach us humility, that one should always consult with one's underlings before making a decision that will affect them.)

The angel is considered to be a messenger of God. Beginning in the Book of Daniel, angels are called by name—in this case, Gabriel and Michael ("Do Jews believe in Angels?", 2020). Jews, Christians, Muslims (Hameed, 2018), Hindus (Hopler, 2018), and adherents of the Bahá'í and Zoroastrian faiths all believe in the existence of angels in a sacred, supernatural, or religious way. Other minority faiths may also claim some association of angels with faith; however, angels are most important in the three Abrahamic religions—Judaism, Christianity, and Islam. So, despite the differing beliefs about angels, they are easily recognized in ads as holy hype. Meanings of religious symbols must be understood in the language and knowledge base of the common public, especially if your target audience is the general public. Obscure significance will not be appreciated or comprehended by average people viewing an ad, and, thus, the message of the advertisement may be totally lost on them. If you must explain the meaning of an ad *in the ad*, you have just lost. If your holy hype message is a joke, it should not be an inside joke.

When the name of a company includes the word "angel" or "angels," it is probable that a halo or wings, if not an entire angel, will be included in the company's logotype. Angels are sweet, innocent, winged, caring, pure, ethereal, childlike, spiritual, and cute and pudgy or sophisticated and wispy—and all things good—except when they are used in ads not properly thought through. Many people do not think of the angel as religious because it has become famously symbolic of concepts more secular, such as the performance of good deeds or love. However, angels, or cherubs, are placed by God at the gates of the Garden of Eden in Genesis 3:24. Some renditions may be used sexually on purpose, and some ads with angel impersonators can be inadvertently sexual. This would apply to a Target ad showing an attractive young woman in winter clothing splayed on a rug emblazoned with the Target logo with no snow in sight (ad not shown due to indecency). The positioning of the woman on the target symbol allows the viewer to reach some vulgar conclusions (Falls & Deckers, 2012). On a more wholesome note, angels can even be saviors (see the Tappan fix-it man in figure 5.21d). They are almost always heaven-sent unless they are the kind that ride Harley-Davidson® motorcycles as members of the Hell's Angels® or of the very earthly Guardian Angels®, who make up a nonprofit group of unarmed volunteers engaged in crime prevention.

The angel is a universal icon belonging to all of us, except when it is a unique, copyright-protected angel, like the Angel Moroni, a sacred figure in the Book of Mormon from the Church of Jesus Christ of Latter-day Saints. He is reportedly the last Nephite prophet, who appeared in a vision to Joseph Smith, founder of the church (The Church of Jesus Christ of Latter-day Saints, 2020). In 2007, an ad in the forms of a T-shirt and greeting card created for a small coffee shop in Taylorsville, Utah, became a point of contention between the store owner, Ed Beazer, and Church officials. Not only was the use of Moroni's image in the design an issue of copyright violation, but it was also a slap in the face, despite the humorous intention, to the religion's doctrines and gospel regarding physical health; Mormons do not drink hot, caffeinated coffee or tea. In the artwork, a carafe of coffee is being manipulated by God's hand coming down from the heavens to pour the hot beverage into the bent horn in Moroni's mouth. When notified of the copyright concern, Beazer pulled the items.

Figure 5.5 is a collection of four ads in which the angel is the featured figure or essence around which the copy is written. That is, the angels are integral to the ad's message. Figure 5.5a comes from 1970 for Banlon® socks. A trio of identical male angels sits on a cloud while one serenades them all with his harp, an angel's instrument. They look down, astounded that they have risen to such great heights, but they are thrilled that their socks have stayed up, too. The PETA® ad in figure 5.5b pushes every moral button. Joanna Krupa asks you to be an angel just like she is. Adopt your little puppies; don't buy them from breeders. So many of them need a home. The nudity and position of the cross may be extremely offensive, but the animal advocacy organization has never shied away from shock or what some would call outright blasphemy. Could this have been as attention getting or as effective in persuading people

Figure 5.5 a) Banlon Socks from 1970. "No matter how high up you go, your socks should stay up with you." Even in heaven. b) Joanna Krupa as a sexy angel. PETA asks you to: "Be an angel for animals. Always adopt. Never buy." c) Ad for the 1960 Chevy Impala. "Nobody takes such tender, lovin' care of you as a Chevrolet." Ad features little girls dressed as angels going into the church. d) 1956 Betty Crocker angel food cake ad. "7 good ways to be an angel." *Source: a) Public domain image retrieved from ebay.com listing. b) Courtesy of PETA, © People for the Ethical Treatment of Animals. c) © Chevrolet, public domain image retrieved from ebay.com listing. d) © Betty Crocker, public domain image retrieved from ebay.com listing.*

to adopt their pets using the angel metaphor without the unmitigated sexuality and religious irreverence? Only PETA knows how successful this ad was. We are not privy to the dollar amount of total contributions coming in as a result of exposure to this ad.

Figure 5.5c is an ad for the Chevy Impala from 1960. If you read the text carefully, you will notice there is not one mention of angels. The headline is: "Nobody takes such tender, lovin' care of you as Chevrolet." So, why have the designers used angels in the ad? We often call our children angels, and the children in this ad are actually dressed as angels for a church production. We always want to take tender, lovin' care of our little angels, so when we want them to be safe, we drive them around in the safest cars, like the Chevy Impala. It is just that today, 60 years later, we would not consider a convertible with the top down the safest way to transport our children. Additionally, it was not until 1984, almost 25 years after this ad was published, that seatbelts began to be mandatory in some states. We offer one more example, figure 5.5d, which is an ad from 1956 for Betty Crocker angel food cake mix, titled "7 good ways to be an angel." The angel atop the finished cake is a mix between an angel and a fairy with her magic wand. A second part of the ad provides seven different cake recipes made with Betty's cake mix. The ad ends with this: "Bake one today, why don't you? Then just wait! Somebody's sure to say it—'You're an angel!'" With just a wave of the wand, you can turn this mix into something new and wonderful while turning yourself into an angel for doing it.

Not all ads depicting angels are particularly religious—or religious at all. However, the mere inclusion of these beings qualifies them as holy hype. And, even some of these ads display the essence of angels without using explicit images of angels. One especially nostalgic use of angels in ads makes use of them as angels in snow. The key to making a snow angel irresistible in an ad is making the angel essential to the persuasive point. The copy and images must work hand in glove in relating the story of the ad. One snow angel ad that is truly exemplary and effective in telling its tale without the use of an angel illustration, is an ad for Finlandia Vodka by St. Louis ad firm, Boxing Clever (figure 5.6a). Residents of Norway live in a place that is about as far north as civilization goes on earth. Finlandia, the vodka, on the other hand, pinpoints *its* location by telling us it is "somewhere between heaven and earth (but a little closer to heaven)," "where the ordinary world drops away." At the end, we learn that drinking Finlandia just might be a supernatural experience because it is "vodka from above." Have *we* become angels? After all, we have left no footprints. Finlandia is heaven-sent, but it somehow feels like home—one adventure in most humans' attempts to create for themselves their heaven on earth.

Poor uses of snow angels in ads for consumer products are ubiquitous, but there are two more excellent examples that are definitely deserving of representation in this category (figure 5.6b and figure 5.6c). Figure 5.6b is a stock photo that can be turned into an ad for a Christmas event or food with just the right copy. The snow and the red and green buttons on the gingerbread man say "Christmas." This little man made from cookie dough is making a snow angel. After all, anything with arms and legs can make a snow angel. Figure 5.6c is a brilliant conceptual ad by Brad Connell of Canada. He imagines a snow angel made by someone who does not have 100% use of his or

Figure 5.6 a) A "feel-good" ad for a hallmark product of Finland. "Vodka from above." b) Gingerbread man as a snow angel. c) Snow angel ad for a chiropractor, who heals people with limbs and backs that don't operate perfectly. A person with a bum left arm is not going to make an ideal snow angel. "If it hurts, see a chiropractor." *Source: a) © Finlandia Vodka. Design by Boxing Clever, St. Louis, MO. Courtesy of Dallas Cheatham and Finlandia. b) Image downloaded from Shutterstock on May 29, 2021. Created by Kolpakova, Svetlana. c) © Brad Connell.*

her limbs. Obviously, the creator of this snow angel is having some issues with his or her left "wing." It is difficult to imagine a better way to get the message out that it is time to see the chiropractor. The advertiser, the Alberta College and Association of Chiropractors, would like you to know that there are medical professionals, who heal people with limbs and backs that don't operate perfectly. A person with a bum left arm is not going to make an ideal snow angel. "If it hurts, see a chiropractor."

Another example you may run into on the internet or in magazines is one for Iams®, a popular brand of pet food. Unable to receive a response to our e-mail requests for permission to show the ad in this book, we speak about it because it is such a great example of holy hype. It demonstrates just how well Iams®'s advertising agency understands its customers and their love of their pets. A happy, well-nourished dog is getting his snow angel on, now that his immune system is improved. He feels like a puppy again! This is another ad that is worth your time to search for on the internet. And, one more of the few non-humans, or superhumans, we have seen creating a snow angel is the Jolly Green Giant. In a current TV commercial representing his long-awaited return to the small screen, the Green Giant is situated next to a tiny human figure—both of whom are making snow angels. This part takes up a few seconds at the end of the commercial; however, its purpose is something of a mystery. The main message is that it is easy to get children to eat vegetables when they are as tasty as these. It seems that the Giant making snow angels is to introduce this fella to a whole new generation of folks while appealing once again to today's grandparents who became fond of him in the 1950s and 1960s. Advertisers are making a return to vintage mascots that were successful brand promoters decades ago.

Our exploration of snow angels in advertising uncovered many fun and interesting images of snow angels. But is there something about the snow angel that conveys the story of the product being sold, or is the message being forced to correspond to the snow angel? A couple of automobile manufacturers, most notably Mini® and Volkswagen®, have employed a similar concept separately in two of their ads. Using an aerial view, the car is either in the act of making a snow angel by having opened and closed the doors to move the snow into wing-like impressions, or the car has created a snow angel in the same way, but has driven away from the angel, leaving the image about 10–15 feet behind it. The photography and art direction are gorgeous, but one wonders how these ads differentiate their autos in the marketplace.

The snow angel theme is so popular that we have provided three more excellent examples in figure 5.7. The first ad at figure 5.7a is one for Old Spice®, a well-established men's fragrance company that had assigned its advertising agency a "simple" greeting-type ad. Designer Shawn Gauthier explains his goal of creating a holiday ad in the style he prefers, one which would definitely satisfy the ad parameters—images without words. He titled this one, "Two people. One snow angel." The footprints lead us to believe we have witnessed the aftermath of a man and a woman leaving a snow angel they made together. They were not together when they began, but they leave the angel together. In a potent message for the brand, we are left to assume that the man's scent attracted the female in the first place and then was alluring enough to keep her close. In figure 5.7b, another stock photograph wants to help designers, who create ads for companies that manufacture products associated with beaches and summertime, such as sunscreen. Consequently,

Figure 5.7 a) An Old Spice ad featuring a perfectly formed snow angel. b) A snow angel made in the sand. c) An ad for Toyota advertising the new heated seats in the RAV4. *Source: a) © Old Spice, image provided courtesy of designer Shawn Gauthier. b) © iStockphoto.com/nycshooter. c) © Toyota, image provided courtesy of Toyota.*

this woman is making her "snow" angel in the sand instead. Banana Boat® has tried this approach for its sunscreen that allows the "sun worshipper" to "Fall in love with sand all over again." With the lotion's ability to brush away the sand and moisturize the lady's skin at the same time, the sunscreen will keep the sand from interfering with her tan. In another masterful application of the snow angel theme (figure 5.7c), and as an answer to the issue of identification in the marketplace, Toyota® cannily uses two human-engineered snow angels instead of implying the angels themselves were truly sent from heaven. This is the point that gives meaning to the use of snow angels made by actual, living people. The people have left the scene, and where their buttocks had touched the snow, the grass underneath is showing through, indicating that their hind ends had been warmer than the rest of their bodies, warm enough to melt the snow underneath. This makes perfect sense because, in this ad, Toyota is promoting the Rav4's new seat-warming capability.

BIBLICAL SAYINGS AND RELIGION-RELATED WORDS

There are so many religious expressions we use when we speak colloquially that many people have forgotten or never even knew that these idioms and clichés originated in the Bible. Many are obvious, such as phrases like "love thy neighbor" or "in the beginning"—other sayings, not so much. Jones (2015) captivates us with 18 sayings that most people cannot connect to scripture. These include "at the eleventh hour" and "at your wit's end." Then there are those like "eat, drink, and be merry," which many of us believe was a Shakespearean invention in Hamlet. Sorry, but that phrase appeared first in the Book of Ecclesiastes (8:15), "man hath no better thing under the sun, than to eat, and to drink, and to be merry." Some are slightly modified to accord with our modern use of language, like "a leopard cannot change its spots" from "Can the Ethiopian change his skin, or the leopard his spots?" (Jeremiah 13:23). Then, there are words that connote religious belief, such as grace, mercy, spirit, sanctuary, glory, amen, sin, devil, born again, divine, resurrection, hallelujah, and dozens more. Here is an illustrated sample of those frequently used in advertising.

Born again, or Rebirth. "Born again," regeneration, and conversion are fairly common terms among Evangelical Christians, although there is no definition that satisfies everyone's perspective on the experience. Regeneration or conversion is a concept that is central to Christianity. According to the New Testament, particularly John 3:3, being born again is the only way an individual can see the Kingdom of God. Foubert et al. (2012) explain four different types of conversion by way of "illustrating the variance in conversion experiences, maintaining that most experiences of transformation include elements of each type of conversion" (p. 216). Whether an exceptional one-time event or a process, the four dimensions that combine to create unique wisdom-gaining and consciousness-raising as a spiritual rebirth for each in his or her relationship with Jesus are: (a) progressive or step-by-step; (b) aesthetic; (c) intellectual; and (d) ethical or moral. No matter how these attributes are distributed throughout one's born-again experience, "becoming born again, [is] an act of individual choice to take up the Christian faith and to follow the teachings of Christ as presented through Scripture" (Foubert et al., 2012, p. 217).

Figure 5.8 a) Rebirth on a Harley— "experience rebirth on two wheels." b) Cannon towel ad from 1943. c) 1983 Toyota Corolla redesign—the Corolla is redesigned, and thus, reborn. *Source: a) Screenshot of the Harley Davidson company home page. b) Image retrieved from ebay.com listing by The Jumping Frog. c) © Toyota.*

It is obvious, through the ads displayed in figure 5.8, that this highly emotional and personal experience is seen in a much more literal than spiritual way when promoting secular goods. In the advertising sense, owning or consuming certain products transforms our relationship with the world's materiality. In one of the better examples of holy hype, Coloria® promotes its ability to assist its customers in their efforts to convert their jeans to a born-again condition. The old denim skin is shed to show the born-again pair. No headline is necessary.

In figure 5.8a, Harley-Davidson® reminds us that the company and its products are all about the adventure—perhaps even a life-changing adventure for its devoted followers. If someone is searching a store for just the right motorcycle, leaving on a Hog® is an experience of rebirth, but not like other rebirths. This one is on two wheels. Figure 5.8b from 1942 tells the story of how Cannon® towels can create born-again experiences through a "glorious, tingling rubdown." With these absorbent, fluffy towels, you will "rub up your morale." You will feel like a new person at a time of giving "more in strength, and time, and sacrifices," during World War II. The ad even subtly recommends that consumers buy war bonds in the small, white handwriting on the frame of the photo at upper left. In figure 5.8c, the 1983 Toyota Corolla has been redesigned, or "reborn" as the advertiser reminds us in large yellow letters against a black background. The message is hard to miss.

Commandments. The Ten Commandments should be easily recognized, yet they are actually quite slippery when we try to name them. It seems that the public is well aware of the "thou shalt not" part, but when it comes to the rest of the divine rules, we go blank. In 2010, the Pew Research Center conducted a poll of American adults and how much they know about religion. Professor Stephen Prothero, a prominent scholar of religion, lamented the sparse data on religious knowledge as opposed to religious practice. In one of his books, he "argued that Americans are both deeply religious and profoundly ignorant about religion" (Pew Research Center, 2010, n.p.). It should tell us something that 3% of the respondents thought Mother Teresa was Jewish. Who knew? Only a little more than half the participants knew that the Golden Rule is not one of the Ten Commandments. Most surprising among this sample of Americans, 75% of whom profess affiliation with a religion, is that 60% of them cannot name five of the Ten Commandments (Cureton, n.d.). If recognition of "thou shalt not" were less frequent than it actually is, then perhaps using the commandments in the text of advertising would be riskier.

The four ads shown in figure 5.9 take advantage of Ten Commandments verbiage, specifically the part "Thou shalt not," in constructing publicly disseminated messages. Figures 5.9a and 5.9d belong to the same campaign for the Fresh Awards advertising competition. Instructions for these contests are usually written as positive steps to take in entering submissions, but these posters use the negative, making sure ad agencies avoid these mistakes. Figure 5.9a admonishes contestants to avoid sexual relations with judges, which makes perfect sense to us. This behavior could sway a judge one way (or the other) in evaluating one's work. Figure 5.9d warns submitters not to steal the ideas of others—be original. In a photo by Minya of the Curious Uptowner blog, the sign in figure 5.9b is a message for dogs (and their owners) from The Cathedral Church of Saint John the Divine in New York City. People coming to or leaving church do not like stepping in a canine's waste material. There cannot be any clearer message from God than "Thou shalt not poop." The ad in figure 5.9c depicts a hamburger as evil by adding red horns and a pointed devil's tail. The tail is directing the eye to the headline: "Thou shalt not judge—(mind your own food)."

Figure 5.9 a) Advertisement for Fresh Awards, "Thou shalt not commit adultery with thy judges." b) "Thou shalt not poop" sign owned by The Cathedral Church of Saint John the Divine. c) "Thou shalt not judge. (Mind your own food.)" d) Advertisement for Fresh Awards, "Thou shalt not steal from annuals." *Source: a) Image courtesy of Fresh Awards and Jack Kramer, creative director. b) © The Curious Uptowner Blog, image provided courtesy of Minya. c) A conceptual ad. Image courtesy of the rights holder. d) Image courtesy of Fresh Awards and Jack Kramer, creative director.*

DIVINE, SANCTUARY, SOUL, RESURRECTION, AND SAINT

Next, we feature five words among many terms associated with religion in general that are frequently seen in secular holy hype (see figure 5.10). The divine, in the religious sense, refers to a higher power, a god or the Supreme Being. It can also refer to something as having come from a god or the God, heavenly, godlike, or superhuman—all totally aside from the earthlier meaning as in marvelous or wonderful. Figure 5.10a is the new angle on the Lincoln® Aviator®, which was launched in December 2019. Ford calls it a "serene approach . . . and a new twist on ice fishing" (Lincoln Motor

Figure 5.10 a) "Your sanctuary awaits" with Lincoln. b) Resurrection beer advertisement. c) "Mr. Jack Daniel was no saint, but he did start something of a religion." *Source: a) © Lincoln, screenshot retrieved from company website. b) © The Brewer's Art. Image provided courtesy of Volker Stewart. c) Image provided courtesy of the rights holder.*

Company Media Center, 2019). The viewer watches the popular Matthew McConaughey find his piece of heaven on earth, his temple, his holy, or his sacred place—a place that protects him from the outside world. The whole time the actor watches his ice hole dug in the frigid cold, he sits inside the automobile, where the heat is running. His roomy, "luxurious, sanctuary-like" Aviator, keeps him safe and toasty warm even with the hatch open—his "shelter from the elements"—while he awaits the signal that informs him there is a fish on the line (Lincoln Motor Company Media Center, 2019). The viewer of the commercial can appreciate this as a soulful, religious or spiritual experience. The marketing crew explains, "It's about being at ease, about being your best self, about finding your own piece of sanctuary in a stressful world." Generally, the soul is the essence of a person or a thing, separate from the body. Soul certainly can be a religious concept, but in advertising, it is most commonly used in terms of the object's transcendent quality, more of a spiritual approach. Other times, soul is used as part of an idiomatic expression. For example, in 1965, Van Raalte, a lingerie manufacturer, ran a lovely advertisement for its short chemisette slip. The headline was: "Brevity is the soul of fit," a play on the idiom "brevity is the soul of wit." Today, we commonly see ads using "body and soul," "heart and soul," and "soul food."

A religious word that is almost always associated with Christianity and Jesus is "resurrection" even though it is a concept in Judaism as well (Moffic, 2016). Here, though, in 5.10b, we see it as the name of an ale by The Brewer's Art®. The brewpub-restaurant has a divine back story, of course, for its choice of product name. Volker Stewart, one of the principals, explained it just like this:

> The first time we brewed this beer it did not have a name, and we were agonizing over one. As it would happen, the yeast we selected for this beer was one that was super-slow . . . and then stopped fermenting altogether! The brewer at the time used some tricks that brought it back to life (Resurrected it, if you will)—to complete the fermentation process. When all of this happened (1997) we had no idea that this beer (a Belgian Dubbel) would become a cult beer in Baltimore, and our flagship brand.

The image in the ad seems to indicate that God had a "hand" in the creation of this beverage as He can be seen reaching down from the heavens to pop the top off a can of this blessed brew. This establishment also offers a winter warmer beer called St. Festivus, celebrating the secular holiday of the same name, which was invented in 1966 by author Daniel O'Keefe as a pushback against the pressure and commercialism of the Christmas holidays and is observed on December 23. The holiday was brought into greater cultural awareness through an episode of *Seinfeld* written by O'Keefe's son (Burns & Schildhause, 2018).

The final ad in this array, figure 5.10c, is an ad for Jack Daniel's® Old No. 7 whiskey, one of the best-selling sour mash whiskeys in the world. Lynchburg, Tennessee is known for this product, and its advertising evokes thoughts of this historical town and its Jack Daniel narrative. There was a real Jack Daniel, and there is real religion behind his story (Furman, 2012, n.p.). Born around 1849, Jasper Newton Daniel, nicknamed Jack, "the boy distiller," left home at about 15. Luckily, he turned up at the home of the Rev. Dan Call, a Lutheran preacher, owner of a general store, and a whiskey distiller. This is possibly the Protestant version of the medieval monk brewing beer. Call took the lad in, and with the help of an enslaved man named Nathan "Nearest" Green, young Jack learned the craft of making whiskey. Jack opened the Jack Daniel Distillery, with Nearest as the head distiller. Its first product, Old No. 7, became a renowned whiskey, winning the first of its seven gold medals at the 1904 World's Fair. Mr. Jack was a natural at marketing. He dressed flamboyantly, so people would remember him, and when he was shown the first square-shaped bottle, he adopted it as his product's packaging because he knew it would stand out among its rivals. Furman states, "the square look reinforced the idea that Jack was a square dealer who put honest work and high standards first" (2012, n.p.).

And so, as the advertisement's story tells us, Mr. Jack Daniel, quite the bon vivant and ladies' man, was no saint, but for discriminating imbibers all over the world, drinking his whiskey has become something of a religion.

We have also become aware of an ad in which we are being sold on the fact that pulling on a pair of Levi's will take us from mere human beings to god-like beings. The man in the ad, who probably was unable to perform a back flip before wearing Levi's, is now radiating a divine aura as he executes one. An older ad from 1971 is a promotion for Crown Royal Canadian whisky. The headline is: "To hoard Crown Royal is human; to pour it freely is divine." The advertiser is separating the secular from the religious, the profane from the sacred. If people keep it all to themselves, that is definitely blasphemous. However, if people share it, especially liberally, they have entered into godliness.

Clergy and Church (Nuns, Monks, Catholic and Buddhist Priests, and Rabbis)

Clergy from all denominations have been appearing in ads since the late 1800s. Catholic monks and nuns were the first to be known for promoting consumer products, and nuns continue to be the most frequently employed ad fodder for all manner of products. From 1893, there is an ad for Cherry Blossom "presentation cases" for holding toilet powder and soap, which features an illustrated lattice frame covered in cherry blossoms within which sits a beautiful nun (see figure 5.12e). The words "nun nicer" are printed under her image. In the midst of those of Quaker Oats and a few other companies, this is undoubtedly one of the earliest published slogans for a product or company.

We have seen a Xerox copier ad from the 1970s (figure 2.1d), and an example of a monk in an Ivory soap secular holy hype ad from 1922 (figure 5.1a). During the Middle Ages, Franciscan and Trappist monks all over Europe were the primary brewers of beer and some specially made liqueurs, highly regarded and commonly drunk beverages at the time (Louviere, 2020). And until the introduction of the printing press in the mid-1400s, they were also the producers of illustrated texts for the church. Therefore, it is no surprise that monks show up frequently in advertising, especially for beers and ales. In a conceptual piece (figure 5.11a) for Frangelico® hazelnut liqueur, a professional photographer working in London, England, Phil Sills of Stills & Motion, tells us that he felt inspired one day to artistically take Frangelico liqueur to its logical place on earth, dropped down from heaven and glowing in a divine aura.

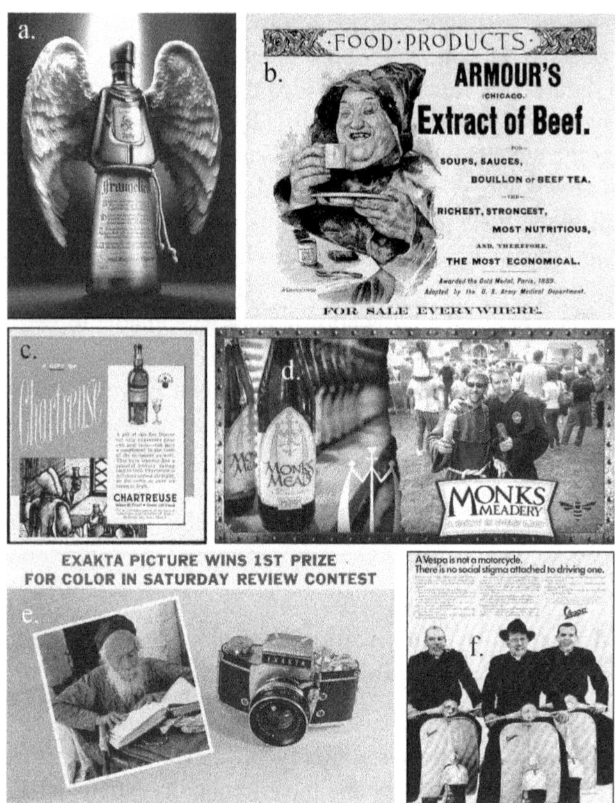

Figure 5.11 a) Conceptual ad featuring a liqueur bottle with wings. b) Armour's ad for "Extract of Beef." c) Chartreuse liqueur ad from 1960. This liqueur is made by Carthusian monks. d) Ad for Monks Meadery. "A story in every drop." The company's focus on the making of mead takes the viewer back to the Middle Ages. e) 1959 Exakta camera. Photo of Yemenite rabbi wins the first prize in the *Saturday Review* magazine photography contest. f) Priests riding Vespas from 1965. "A Vespa is not a motorcycle. There is no social stigma attached to riding one." *Source: a) © Phil Sills, Image courtesy of Stills & Motion. b) Public domain image from 1891. c) Public domain image retrieved from ebay.com listing. d) © Monks Meadery, image provided courtesy of Justin Schoendorf of Monks Meadery. e) Public domain image. f) Public domain image retrieved from ebay.com listing.*

This is an excellent exemplar of the representation of the essence of angels or the divine without using explicit images of angels, and it appears on the front cover of this book. The monk, himself, is physically absent, but is implied by the bottle shape, a purposeful design by the Frangelico owners. The bottle is shaped like a Franciscan monk's silhouette, right down to the detail of the rope belt, a cincture, which the monk wears around the waist of his tunic, knotted as a signifier of his commitment and of the ropes that bound Jesus among other vows such as poverty, chastity, and obedience (Keller, 2020).

The Frangelico story is an old one, developed by the company for its launch in 1978. Frangelico's owners and marketers not only set the cordial's roots firmly in the seventeenth century, when alcoholic recipes and production methods were crafted by men of God in dark monasteries (Louviere, 2020). In 1891, Chicago's Armour & Company® advertised its canned extract of beef using a particularly unattractive monk, who is labeled "a connoisseur" (see figure 5.11b). There seems to be no sound justification for using a toothless monk in the ad—certainly not one who would make the product look so unappetizing, but somebody thought it was a good idea.

Figure 5.11c is another sales message, this one appearing in 1960. Once again, the monk makes an appearance but for good reason. Chartreuse is a liqueur that has been made by Carthusian monks since 1764. The liqueur's provenance is not medieval yet it was and is still made according to the medieval instructions from François Annibal d'Estrées in 1605. There was quite a lot going on in the Middle Ages, which set the stage for the more culturally awake era of the Renaissance.

Figure 5.11d shows another example of clergy associated with a beverage. This facility is in the business of fermenting honey to create mead, an alcoholic drink known as the "nectar of the gods," which predates both beer and wine by about 40,000 years. Monks Meadery® is the first of its kind in Georgia, the brainchild of Justin Schoendorf and Martin Key of Atlanta. They were two young college grads who found themselves in an unenviable predicament—relatively poor and, at the same time, insatiably thirsty for craft beer, in a state that did not allow the sale of beer above 6% ABV (alcohol by volume). So, as they say, necessity is the mother of invention. They dove right into the home beer-making business. Upon learning about mead, they began producing that product, sometimes creating a variety with upward of 15% ABV. Schoendorf and Key continued experimenting with recipes and finally arrived at one to which their friends gave the enthusiastic thumbs up. The next step was going public and commercial. As they explain on their website, they chose the name of

> Monks Meadery because of the historical significance of monasteries related to mead production (and the loss of the popularity of mead in England). Monks were the main keepers of bees to harvest the wax used in religious ceremonies. Since there was not a large demand for honey, they would make mead to earn extra income for their monastery. During the English Reformation, Henry the VIII dissolved all the monasteries and destroyed most of the hives—as the honey disappeared, so did the mead. Justin and Martin thought it would be

suitable for "Monks" to usher in the comeback of a once-popular beverage . . . either that or they just like the sound of the name.

Schoendorf truly enjoys the marketing part: selecting the names of the different concoctions, designing the labels, and researching the process and the history of religious iconography are just part of this aspect of the business. For example, Monks offers "Stigmata," "Monks Mead," and "Abstinence in the Abbey," all of which get the holy hype creative copy juices flowing.

The ad positioned at figure 5.11e is a promotion for the 1959 Exakta camera. A photo of a Yemenite rabbi has won the first prize in the *Saturday Review* magazine photography contest. This demonstrates that the only connection between the rabbi and the selling of the camera is that he is the subject of the winning photograph. This might be considered by others as holy hype, but it is not. The winning photo could have just as easily been a great shot of an otter doing tricks in the water. This ad is included for exactly this purpose—to show how a religious image in an ad is not always holy hype. Figure 5.11f is a vintage Vespa® ad from 1965, featuring three Catholic priests on motor scooters with the headline, "A Vespa is not a motorcycle. There is no social stigma attached to driving one." One must decide whether there is a hidden agenda or code in the last sentence. Whereas this probably means to say something about the respectful appearances Catholic priests aim to make in public, it could also refer to the Christian sense of stigmata, which are scars or bodily marks showing up in the same places as the wounds did on Jesus. Perhaps we are reading something into this, but maybe not.

Rabbis appear infrequently in secular holy hype ads. That is probably due to such a small percentage of Jews in American society, estimated at between 1.5% and 2.0%. In 2020, it is approximately 1.7% of US population with a real number of about 5.7 million ("Vital Statistics," 2020). Outside of large metropolitan areas, rabbis are probably not as well recognized as other clergypersons.

The examples we display in figure 5.12 are five more that are representative of how clergypersons can be incorporated into advertisements. The ad in figure 5.12a from 1981 features two nuns out for a drive on a rainy day, when they spot the Goodyear® blimp in their rearview mirrors. The headline of this ad for Goodyear radial tires is: "When the heavens open and the curves are slick, it helps to have the blimp behind you." Adding to the holy hype verbiage, the driver remarks, "It's good to have friends in high places." The best way to make it possible to use this language is to have two immediately recognizable religious figures doing the driving. Figure 5.12b is an ad for Gingiss, which used to be a company in the business of renting and selling tuxedos for men. This ad from 1971 is a take-off of the old joke that begins something like this: "A rabbi, a Protestant minister, and a Catholic priest walk into a bar." It exemplifies high-quality copy writing. Pastors do not wear

Figure 5.12 a) Goodyear ad from 1981—"When the heavens open and the curves are slick, it helps to have the blimp behind you." b) Gingiss men's formalwear ad from 1971—"Rabbi Goldman, Father O'Connel and Reverend Henry won't endorse our formalwear for your wedding. But they give it their blessings." c) Bell & Howell ad from the 1950s—"Bell & Howell brings out the expert in you." d) Polaroid ad from 1968 featuring excited nuns. e) 1893 Cherry Blossom ad—"Nun nicer." *Source: a) © Goodyear, public domain image retrieved from ebay.com listing. b) © Gingiss Formalwear, no longer in business. c) Public domain image retrieved from ebay.com listing. Bell & Howell is no longer in business as a photographic equipment manufacturer. d) Public domain image retrieved from ebay.com. e) Public domain image retrieved from ebay.com listing by BarrelOrgan.*

tuxedos to weddings; they wear their ministerial garb. So, obviously, as the headline informs us, they will not endorse Gingiss's formal menswear. They are honest men who do not bear false witness and could not recommend a product they do not use. However, as the headline continues, they *are* willing to "give it their blessings." What a nice turn of phrase. It is a phrase like this that will take a ho-hum promotion and convert it into a truly memorable one.

Figures 5.12c and 5.12d depict a common behavior for nuns at large gatherings—taking pictures. The ad for Bell & Howell from the 1950s, figure 5.12c, shows a nun directing traffic for the best photograph. Move a little over there, please. The small caption under the nun's photo states, "The picture must be perfect or she can't push the button." So, the headline and copy inform the viewer that this camera is full of automatic mechanisms for under $100: "Bell & Howell brings out the expert in you (automatically!)." In the next ad, figure 5.12d, Polaroid takes a bite of the same apple in 1968. A decade or more later, this camera delivers color photos on the spot in 60 seconds for just $50. We viewers are supposed to believe this is a modern-day miracle! At the time, it really seemed as though it was. There is no doubt the Polaroid was the answer to the ancient dilemma of finding a way to turn a scene we view with our eyes into a durable finished product through photographic means. Polaroid went many steps further, combining focusing, exposing, sloshing the paper through several chemical solutions, and drying into one step—pushing the button. And, to make it all the more supernatural, Polaroid accomplished this feat automatically in a minute.

This vintage Cherry Blossom ad for presentation boxes is one from 1893, and it rounds out our presentation of religious figures (figure 5.12e). The play on "nun-none" is a common one, but it can still be effective after more than a century of use. Arctic Cat® Bikes takes a hint from the Vespa priest ads of the 1960s and the Cherry Blossom ad to put a sister on its motorized bike, veil wafting in the breeze. It is not displayed here, but its message is that there is "Nun like it." This particular pun is considered overdone, and, thankfully, makes infrequent appearances these days. At times, the mere presence of a nun or other type of recognizable clergyperson in an ad will make the point.

VERSE 2

Crosses and the Jesus Pose

The cross is probably the most recognized icon of Christianity, and it is a shape around which thousands of ads and logos have been designed, even if the cross is merely alluded to. Inserting the cross into so many different contexts has embedded it with a myriad of meanings. It can imbue a person, object, or theme with an aura of godliness or divinity. The cross can evoke religious or spiritual feelings about life, death, health, struggle, achievement, and any other realm or dimension of human existence (see figure 5.13). Images of the crucifix, of course, are more specifically about Jesus and are significative of Jesus's principles, goodness, and sacrifice. They are recognized, if not always appreciated, even by those who are unaffiliated with the Christian religion or are members of other religions. This difference between the cross alone and the crucifix, which includes the figure of Jesus, is likely a contributing variable in the consumer reaction to an ad in which either one is shown. This reaction would be in terms of both emotion and the formation of an intent to purchase or not to purchase the product, and the ad is often considered offensive and sacrilegious when the cross is used to sell goods (Mallia, 2009; Sarapin & Morris, 2020). Mallia (2009) explains that much of what makes one such ad acceptable while another offensive is the difference between a spiritual connotation and a religious connotation of the symbols used. As maintained by the British association that monitors this type of advertising in England, the distinction lies in the "dismissive or irreverent depiction of sacred figures, symbols, texts, and places—for example, images of the crucifixion, 'especially if that depiction could be construed as mocking'" (Advertising Standards Authority, 2004, as cited in Mallia, 2009, p. 185).

Our montage of cross-related ads is our figure 5.13. The first one, figure 5.13a, is what we feel is a successful admonishment about smoking, a celebration of World No Tobacco Day. In a cemetery of dozens of crosses indicating the burial sites of non-identified people, there is a small section absent of crosses or graves. In this spot is the phrase, "non smoking [*sic*] area." Think about it—those who do not smoke did not die of lung cancer. Thus, there are no graves there. Outside that small area is the large area full of the graves of smokers—the so-called smoking section. It is a broad-brush approach, but it certainly gets the message across. This ad is a production of the World Health Organization (WHO).

Figure 5.13b belongs to an organization, CPH Vision, that no longer exists. It used to put on trade shows, such as this one for "those obsessed with fashion" from 2004. These people are so obsessed, in fact, that they eat, live, and even dream fashion, and fashion has become their god. Instead of a cross or a crucifix hanging in a familiar place above one's bed, we see it replaced by a seamstress's scissors positioned to resemble a cross. Had this been disseminated in the United States, we believe there would have been an outcry, but this was an ad published in Denmark, a much less religiously devout country. Pew tells us that a 2014 survey reported that 68% of Americans pray daily, but only 12% in Denmark pray each day (Pew FactTank, 2018). Figure 5.13c, an ad by Duval Guillaume, an agency from Bruxelles, Belgium,

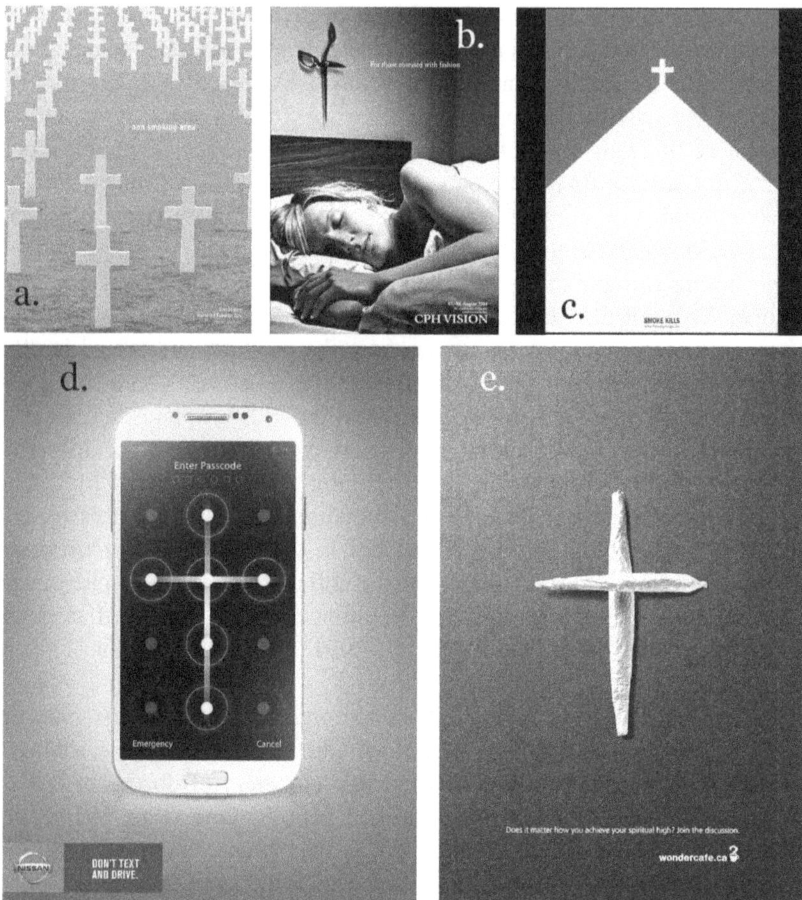

Figure 5.13 a) Ad for World No Tobacco Day. The area devoid of crosses is designated the "no smoking area." b) A pair of scissors is attached to the wall in the shape of a cross. "For those obsessed with fashion." c) "Smoke kills"—a conceptual ad for a nonexistent company called "Free My Lungs." d) Nissan ad—"Do not text and drive." e) An ad for a now-defunct online religious discussion group. Two marijuana joints are arranged in a cross—"does it matter how you achieve your spiritual high?" *Source: a) © World No Tobacco Day, created by the World Health Organization for public dissemination. b) © CPH Vision 2004 for the Scandinavian Design and Streetwear Exhibition. Organization no longer exists. c) Conceptual ad created by Duval Guillaume agency. Image retrieved from adforum.com. d) © Nissan, courtesy of Nissan. e) ©Wonder Cafe of Canada, originally run by The United Church of Canada. Exists in a revised form, Wondercafe2, under different ownership. Image retrieved from adforum.com.*

could serve in the funeral category as well as this category. The cross is quite noticeable despite its small size atop what looks like the sloped roof of a church. The brief headline for this ad for the defunct Free My Lungs informs us that "Smoke kills." From afar, the red-and-white shapes resemble a highly recognizable cigarette box design for popular Marlboro cigarettes. The artist has employed only the most basic of graphic elements of the Marlboro box, but that is all that is needed to convey "cigarettes" to the viewer. We do not need to see an actual cigarette nor do we need to see smoke. This is brilliant design—a scarcity of visuals combined with a scarcity of words. This is what designers mean by "less is more."

Nissan presents its warning about texting and driving in a unique and compelling way (figure 5.13d). That is the trick of holy hype—or any advertising approach, for that matter. It is just that holy hype can become monotonous if the same images or themes are used persistently without creativity. It does not work just because it is. Innovation is the key to using holy hype effectively—employing common pictures and words in uncommon ways. Nissan has taken the image of the "killer device" in this situation, the phone, and turned it into the prophet with the message for those who insist on texting and driving. The cross is what everyone will see on your grave after the crash you are going to have while not paying attention to the road and traffic. It is a jarring image. You might see this ad on a billboard. Nissan hopes you will immediately throw your phone down or into the glovebox.

Wonder Café of Canada, a blog for "cool people" who like to discuss religion with other cool people, advertises itself as a place online inhabited by laid-back people from everywhere. In figure 5.13e, it asks, "Does it matter how you achieve your spiritual high? Join the discussion." The cross is constructed of two marijuana cigarettes running perpendicular to each other. If you partake in the smoking of weed, you will not be judged. Your conversation contributions are as valuable as anyone else's. This pun on the word "high" and the cross made of reefers are what give this ad its ingenious slant.

A corollary to the crucifix is not a new phenomenon, but it has taken off in popularity and frequency recently. It is called the T-pose (see figure 5.14 for three examples). One we do not show is an ad for a Brazilian rum using a Jesus lookalike striking a T-pose with the help of a pool cue. This ad was ranked the most offensive among 15 ads presented for evaluation in a survey we ran in 2020 (Sarapin & Morris, 2020). The ads shown in the survey encompassed a broad range of holy hype from very mildly religious to overwhelmingly religious, but all were ads promoting a consumer product. As to offensiveness, the Jesus pose ad set in a billiards hall selling alcohol was found to beat the Sweet Jesus ice cream ad that uses a logo in which the "t" in "sweet" is positioned upside down, and the "immaculately conceived" Federici Italian gelato ad featuring a pregnant nun.

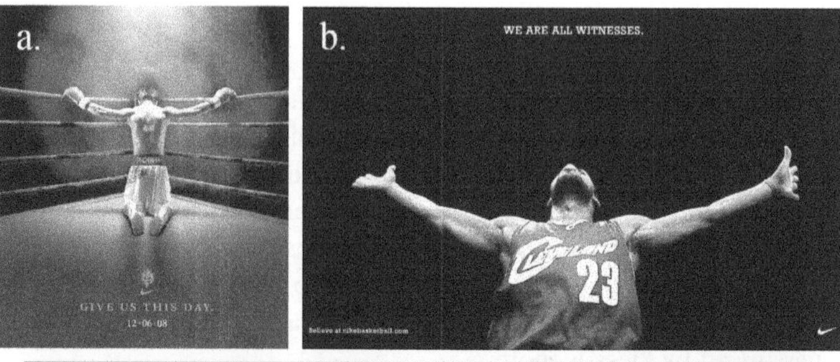

Figure 5.14 a) Nike poster featuring Manny Pacquiao. "Give us this day." b) Nike poster featuring LeBron James. "We are all witnesses." c) Conceptual ad for ESPN Classic showing a Jesus lookalike with halo in an outstanding performance on the rings. Title under logo states "Where men become gods." *Source: a) © Nike, Image provided courtesy of Nike. b) © Nike, Image provided courtesy of Nike. c) © Diego Rionda, courtesy of designer Diego Rionda, diegorionda.com.*

The T-pose occurs when a person strikes a posture imitating Jesus on the cross—arms extended out from the sides of the body and slightly uplifted and, perhaps in addition, legs crossed at the ankles. Images suggestive of the cross are potent for the Christian viewer. The T-pose was considered the best meme of 2018 (Feldman, 2018, n.p.). Originating as a software glitch and operating as the default stance for 3-D characters in animation, people assume the position for all sorts of reasons, even for demonstrating authority over the less powerful at school, a sort of bullying behavior to establish seniority or dominance (Feldman, 2018, n.p.; Hathaway, 2018). Zellman (n.d., n.p.) calls it the "new sieg heil of White America" and asserts it should be stopped.

Yet actual opposition to this image is minimal. In fact, there is a T-shirt on the market, imprinted with an illustration of Jesus in the T-pose along with the saying, "Jesus T-posed for our sins." A thorough internet search for any references to the T-pose and its relationship to Jesus on the cross results in one theme: Jesus himself originated the T-pose along with a direct reference to the Christ the Redeemer statue in Rio de Janeiro. According to Zachary Huelsing, architect and frequent traveler to Brazil, Brazilians are proud of this statue and strike the pose in reverence when in its presence. Boorstein (2016) explains: "Some see it as a tribute to Catholicism while others consider it a salvo against secularism. Still others in the rapidly diversifying country consider it a general symbol of welcome, with arms open wide" (n.p.). Tourists find this a necessary stop on visits to the South American country, Huelsing remarks, and posing in sync with the statue is de rigueur. Other than that, most commentary on the T-pose does not mention any similarity to Jesus on the cross.

Nike has used the Christ-like figure quite frequently in its sports ads. Figures 5.14a and 5.14b are representative of that application. In figure 5.14a, Manny Pacquiao, a champion boxer, is shown on his knees in the ring in front of a corner post, possibly in prayer before a bout, arms spread out from his body each grabbing a rope. In a very dark room, he is bathed in a divine light shining from above. His head is bowed, and the post extends upward above his head, completing the image of the crucified Christ he resembles from behind. The headline? "Give us this day." There is absolutely no doubt what Nike's message is here. Pacquiao is one of the athletes in their stable. Let us pray for him to win this fight. Figure 5.14b is the other Nike ad in this array. LeBron James is another of Nike's prime athlete-endorsers. Sometimes called King James, he is often shown in a religious perspective. In this ad, James strikes a common posture, arms outstretched as in the Jesus pose, head held upward as though looking toward God. The statement at the top of the design is "We are all witnesses." At bottom left, we see the words "Believe at nikebasketball.com." The word "witness" is part of the Christian vernacular. Christians are commanded to witness to others about their belief that Jesus is their savior, all in the attempt to convert as many people to Christianity as possible. Of course, another interpretation of this headline is that we are all witnesses of James's miraculous talents on the court, but that explanation would be a way to deny the religious dimensions of the company's advertising. It is clearly holy hype.

The third ad in this display, figure 5.14c, is a rendition of Jesus as gymnast. This is a conceptual ad for the ESPN Classic designed by Diego Rionda. It shows a Jesus lookalike with ahalo in an outstanding performance on the rings in an old, ornate sanctuary. The title under the logo states: "Where men become gods."

In another ad (not shown), we see a Jesus lookalike strapped to a table in readiness for his imminent execution. The fingers on his hands are positioned in one of the ways Jesus gestures with his hands in the sign of benediction in many old paintings, sculptures, and illustrations. This may or may not be the ordained placement of his fingers as paintings vary on this, but it is clear in this image that the man about to be put to death is holding the fingers of both hands in the same way, and that way is not what we would anticipate as a natural gesture. This ad promotes the International Society for Human Rights, the IGFM in Bulgaria, a secular group that advocates for an end to capital punishment. This use of holy hype is tremendously appropriate in so many ways despite the secular nature of the organization. Most religions take a stance on capital punishment, for or against, and that allows—no, strongly suggests—a religious treatment of the topic. The image of the Jesus-like prisoner harks back to the tenet that Jesus has already died for Christians' sins. Why should he need to go through this crucifixion again? Why should anyone have to undergo this punishment if Jesus has already done it for us? There is so much more to this ad than what we see at first. It requires contemplation and a real search of one's soul. If you search for this ad on the internet, you will see that it accentuates the Jesus figure in that his ankles are crossed.

DEVIL AND EVIL

This category of secular holy hype imagery, devils and evil, is the opposite of angels, but just as prominent, or perhaps even more so at times. The devil is a flexible signifier, which makes it available for use in numerous scenarios. The devil is used as a counterweight at times when using an angel, reminiscent of the angel on one shoulder and the devil on the other, each weighing in with an opinion in the face of temptation. The angel represents heaven and goodness, and the devil inhabits the domain of hell and sinfulness so there is some overlap in advertisements. Frequently, in ads emphasizing hell, we are almost as likely to see angels as devils, and in ads featuring heaven, devils almost as likely as angels.

Apple has consistently used the angel/devil couplet in its advertising. During the years of the company's Apple versus PC television commercials and print ads, the character representing "PC" was advised by a clone of himself dressed all in white and a clone dressed all in red, the common color scheme for the angel (white) and the devil (red). Apple continues in this vein in a recent ad that poses the question "Should I buy Apple Airpods?" The white angel resides on the character's right shoulder, and the red devil on the left shoulder. This implies another long-standing controversy about left versus right—one, left, being bad or evil, and the other, right, being good or divine. Casasanto says it concisely: "Idioms in English associate good with right but not with left" (2009, p. 351). Years of experience in the design and communication fields tell us that such a placement is a designer's or writer's purposeful move, believing that these two abstract concepts (good and evil) are perceived in this way by the audience. However, Casasanto's experiment demonstrates that left-handed people see it in the opposite way—left is good, and right is evil.

Levine (2004) informs us about the origins of the angel/devil metaphor, explaining that it could have begun with an Escher painting of white angels alternating with black devils. Depending on the focus of the viewer's attention, either the angel is perceived or the devil is perceived, with one as the presence of figure and the other as absence of figure or "ground." Levine asks, "So what are the brain's analogs of angels and devils? They are the brain's decisions about what classes of behaviors to enhance or suppress" (p. 2).

Not surprisingly, in drama and comedy, good is dressed in white, and bad is dressed in black, as in good versus evil. In the old westerns, the good guys wore white or light hats, and the bad guys wore black or very dark or dirty hats. This was done so, at the first appearance of a person on screen, the viewer would know immediately whether the individual was a good guy or a bad guy. It must be noted, though, that in the early days of mass media, color was not a part of the equation. Print pieces were published in black and white; television began as black and white; movies were first shown in black and white. When color came into the picture, literally, the devil became red. Coming from hell, a fiery place, the devil has absorbed the color of red-hot flames. In an example of topic overlap, the ad in figure 5.9c admonishes us to abstain from judging. In this sense, the burger is viewed by many as a bad food, and here it goes a step further. The burger is represented as a devil with the devil's red horns and the devil's curvy red tail. Figure 5.15 is an array of ads featuring a devil. Sealtest devil mint ice cream is the advertiser in 5.15a. In this illustration, the childlike devils could easily be angels except for their horns and tails. They are actually cute, just mischievous, and in this ad, they represent temptation. And yet, the temptation is for something definitely not evil. Interestingly, these immature devils are not red. They are "mint" green. The ad is printed in a four-color process, so printing the devils in red, just as the Sealtest logo is, would not have been an issue. The choice to print them in green was a conscious one. One devil says, "What a combination! Extra-special Sealtest Chocolate laced through with zippy green Peppermint!" Another little devil urges you to give in to the allurement, saying "Taste it! Try it!" In this conception, we are once again confronted by a color issue. Peppermint is almost always represented as red, spearmint as green. It is indeed odd to see "zippy green peppermint." If only Sealtest were still in business, we could ask the ad designers what they had in mind.

We have spoken of the Sapolio company in Chapter 3. Figure 5.15b is an early ad from this company, dated 1887. The devil is labeled "dirt," so it appears to be a premonition for Dirt Devil products. Sapolio soap will get rid of the most wicked kinds of dirt, so you will not have to use dynamite. Figure 5.15c, a 1958 print ad for Snider's catsup, moves us into the twentieth century. This condiment with the chili-pepper taste is deservedly presented by a devil—it is "for those who like it HOTTER." And, of course, devils come from the hottest part of the universe.

In figure 5.15d, we see one of those angel-devil combos, a rare 1942 ad for the J. Walter Thompson advertising agency. The man pictured sports horns and a halo. As the headline tells us, we can turn horns into halos. The text tells a story about this man, the insurance agent. The public and business owners think of him as an expensive imposition—a devil, as it were. If you are the owner of that insurance company or an agent of same, you need a way to convince the public that you are really an angel. How do you do that? You hire the J. Walter Thompson agency to prepare advertising materials for you to change that bad impression and make you a hero to your clients. The clincher of the ad is this: "With business men who suspect that their detractors can't quite see their halos, we shall be happy to discuss a number of ways and means of *changing people's thinking*."

Figure 5.15e is the next ad that shows the use of the devil from 1951. Sinclair Oil Corporation is going to tell us how it "helps NEW CAR OWNERS 'Beat the Devil.'" What in the devil is the company talking about? It's rust, what Sinclair calls the red devil, in the gasoline station fuel pumps and in your car's entire fuel system. Using Sinclair Oil prevents this evil thing from happening. The Sinclair people have developed RD-119, the "amazing new gasoline ingredient that covers metal surfaces with an invisible rust-proof coating." Next, from 1963, we have figure 5.15f, an ad for Underwood Deviled Ham. In the ad, a devil stands behind our everyman, who is eating a deviled ham sandwich. The sign is imprinted with "That bit of devil in a man should be Underwood Deviled Ham (sandwiches)." The company asserts, "There's a *devilicious* change of pace to a submarine sandwich made with Underwood Deviled Ham." So, a company that began offering deviled ham spread in a can in 1868 had to wait until 1926 to advertise it to be used on a submarine sandwich, which is when they were first introduced to the American public. By the time this ad came out, the company certainly knew what it was talking about.

Alcoholic beverage companies have been using the devil in advertising for years. From 1968, we see still another one playing a role in Smirnoff's vodka martini. A she-devil makes an appearance in figure 5.15g. She is suggesting

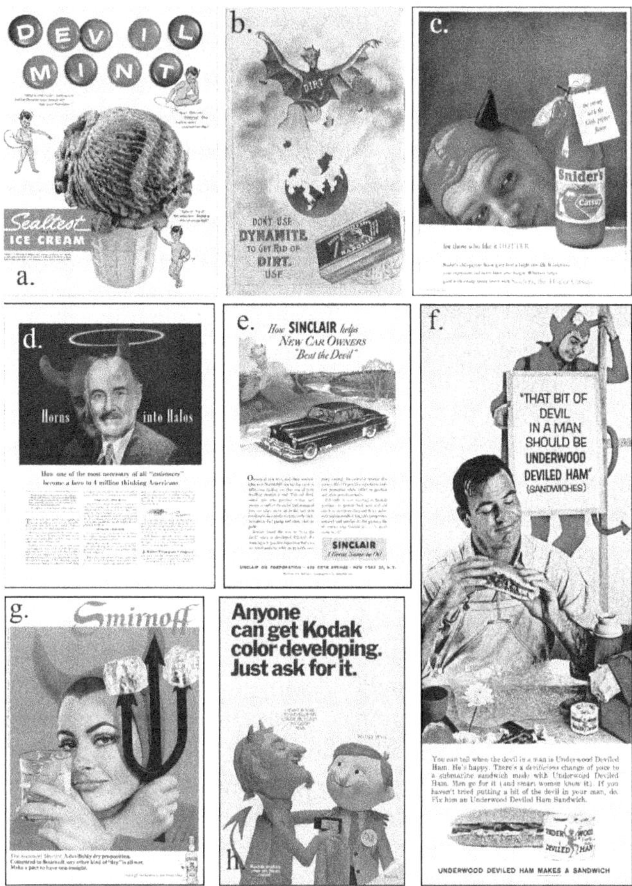

Figure 5.15 a) Sealtest ad for "Devil Mint" ice cream. b) "Don't use dynamite to get rid of dirt. Use Sapolio." c) Snider's chili pepper catsup ad from 1958. "For those who like it hotter." d) 1942 ad for J. Walter Thompson Group advertising agency, claiming to turn "horns into halos." e) Sinclar Oil Corporation ad from 1951. f) Underwood Deviled Ham ad from 1963. "That bit of devil in a man should be Underwood Deviled Ham." g) Smirnoff Vodka ad from 1968. "The Smirnoff Martini. A devilishly dry proposition." h) 1971 Kodak ad. "I want Kodak to develop my color pictures, my good man." "You sly devil." *Source: a) © Sealtest, no longer in business. Public domain image retrieved from ebay.com listing. b) © Sapolio and Intradevco Industrial SA. Public domain image retrieved from abebooks.com. c) © Snider's, no longer in business. Public domain image. d) © J. Walter Thompson Group. Public domain image retrieved from ebay.com listing. e) © Sinclair Oil Corporation. Public domain image retrieved from ebay.com listing. f) © Underwood®. Public domain image retrieved from ebay.com listing. g) © Smirnoff, public domain image. h) © Kodak. Public domain image retrieved from ebay.com listing.*

"a devilishly dry proposition. Compared to using the "vodka [that] leaves you breathless . . . any other kind of 'dry' is all wet." Rounding out this figure, we move into the 1970s to be exposed to Kodak assuring us that *anyone*—even a devil—can get Kodak color developing. "Just ask for it." The friendly photo dealer in this 1971 ad says to his customer, "You sly devil." You would be correct for wondering why a devil was used in this ad. It was not necessary. He certainly is "anyone," and he makes way for the "sly devil" comment, but, other than that, it could have been a wicked-looking, old West villain or any other less-than-respectable or undeserving person.

Two other advertisements that have created a stir using the devil is one of Benetton's most disputed ads ever and an extremely creative, thought-provoking, and possibly offensive ad from Dirt Devil. Let's first examine Benetton's "Ebony and Ivory" from 1981, a photo of a Black child (made up as a devil) and a White child (the angel) in a friendly embrace. It is iconic and is easily found on the internet. As George Floros tells us in his exposé on what he considers the 10 most controversial of Benetton's ads, the company's marketing focus changes when Mr. Benetton meets photographer Oliviero Toscano, "who shows him that a focus of message over product could be more effective" (Floros, 2020, n.p.). In this one, though, Floros opines that in contrast to the White girl on the left, the Black girl "has her hair spiked up like devil horns and resists a smile. Although attempting a 'uniting' effect, the ad fails in its racist shortcomings, separating colors into good and evil." There is another way to look at it, though, and it is possible that a uniting effect is not what Toscano was striving for. Perhaps Toscano wanted us to see the imbalance of real life, in bold white and black—that this is what we see in media, but it is time to change. Floros is evaluating this 1960s-era ad with the sensibilities of a man living in 2020 during a widening effect of Black Lives Matter and broadly disseminated rhetoric in support of White supremacy and the American Confederacy. Societal context is so important in advertising. It must never be discounted because it is the agar plate, or growth medium, within which political views either proliferate or fail to thrive.

The other truly original ad, this one from 2000, must be one of the most distinct, creative, and memorable Dirt Devil print ads in the company's history. The ad designers from Scholz & Friends Group must have been asking themselves in their brainstorming sessions, "What situation could possibly show how clean Dirt Devil leaves a carpet?" Clean enough for what? Whoever came up with the answer, "Clean enough for a pope in his white robes to kneel on and kiss," had eaten his berries, dark chocolate, and green tea for breakfast. Everything must be pure and perfectly clean for the Pope. Also, the Pope juxtaposed with the name of a vacuum cleaner with the word devil in it is certainly attention getting. And showing the Dirt Devil vacuum is not even necessary. It is implied. In 2011, Dirt Devil ventured into holy hype area again with a commercial take on the movie *The Exorcist*. The woman apparently in need of exorcism is thrashing against the ceiling and screaming as a Roman Catholic priest watches her, mouth agape. As the camera pans upward to the apartment above the one we have just viewed, we see the reason for the possessed lady position against the ceiling—above her, an elderly woman is vacuuming with a Dirt Devil, and the suction is simply too great for the presumably possessed woman to settle back down firmly on the floor.

Now we turn our attention to a somewhat surprising thematic category of holy hype—funerals.

FUNERALS AND IMMORTALITY

Funerals are usually religious rites that help living people celebrate the lives of their righteous loved ones and send them off to a life of everlasting peace. Each religion has its own customs regarding the funeral and burial activities, but for visual purposes, they can be pared down to their common visual essentials, which customarily include: (a) the presence of a body in an open coffin, a closed coffin, or ashes in an urn; (b) a clergyperson, religious representative, or other leader; (c) one mourner or a group of mourners, some of whom are crying; and (d) flowers. The scene of a funeral can be outside at graveside or inside a church or funeral home. In real life, it is a fairly humor*less* event except for mourners gathering to share funny stories about the deceased or retelling them as personal eulogies, and yet in advertising, the scene can become uniquely memorable by using wry humor, irony, or satire. If a creative designer can find a way to think outside the "box," an ad about funerals or death can be hilarious and unforgettable and can drive home a good lesson to boot. Once the coronavirus pandemic has been brought under control, it is likely that most of these ritualistic characteristics will return to reality from the virtual. Immortality is quite a different story—can we show life after death? That is where the designer's creativity is really put to the test.

Figure 5.16 is a montage of four great examples of holy hype dealing with death and the afterlife. At top left, in figure 5.16a, is an unusual Cadillac Superline Victoria funeral coach ad from 1962. This is what is called a B-to-B ad, that is, business-to-business—a limo manufacturer selling to the funeral home industry. In the largest type, we notice the words "We believe," which we think is catchy and right on as far as meaning goes. People who are religious are called believers by some religions. It would require quite a bit of research to discover the first business that referred to itself as the kind of company one should keep, but in 1962, this seems to be an early example of it. The entire headline is "We believe . . . honor and integrity are judged by the company you keep." So, if you do business with the Cadillac company, you are in good company indeed. Another funeral reference is the ad seen in figure 5.16b from 1945. A war theme was definitely apt for ads during World War II, and this scene captured by someone with a handy camera and film was a familiar one among soldiers. For Ansco Films & Cameras, the message is clearly that we must always have a camera nearby because one never knows when a loved one will no longer be among us. Take pictures while you can because "the dead can't change their minds."

An ad we wanted to display but could not is one for ANCAP, an Australasian nonprofit that employs crash testing as a method of discovering weaknesses of automobiles so as to rank the safety of a wide range of vehicles in the Australian and New Zealand markets. These ratings help car buyers in selecting safe automobiles and manufacturers in improving their designs. Its mission is the elimination of road trauma. Of course, the worst road trauma is death, and this funeral for crash dummies and the stand-in, imitation crash dummy minister leading it say good-bye to those dummies who have sacrificed their lives to reduce deaths of *real people*. It is a striking visual turnabout, and sends a precise message that does not have to be analyzed to death.

Another ad in this category is an extremely clever example of imagining an absurd funerary scenario to bring attention to a fairly well-known organization, Toastmasters International. The group's raison d'etre is alleviating people's number-one fear, which is glossophobia, the fear of public speaking. The group meets to make it possible for people to practice delivering speeches in front of audiences. So, the microphone in this clever ad hovers over the deceased one's head in the casket, just to capture any last words in case the fear was so great, that the prospective public speaker died. The headline: "If the thought of public speaking scares you to death, visit toastmasters.org."

The ad for Olmeca Tequila, 5.16c, challenges us to imagine a drink that turns one night into an event that lives forever. It is just one of two ads in this book that speaks specifically about immortality. The art is showing motion in a still format. People are dancing while "embrac[ing] the Olmeca spirit." The experience is transcendent, going beyond the limits of reality, wafting past the universe toward a space not attainable in human, earthbound experience. That's a tall order for an alcoholic beverage, but Josh Tenser of TBWA/WFH London, The Disruption® Company, pulls it off for Olmeca. According to an e-mail from Tenser, this was the conceptualization behind the advertisement:

> We wanted to make a story out of the name and the branding; the bottle itself even looks like an Olmec temple. We did some reading on Olmec culture and

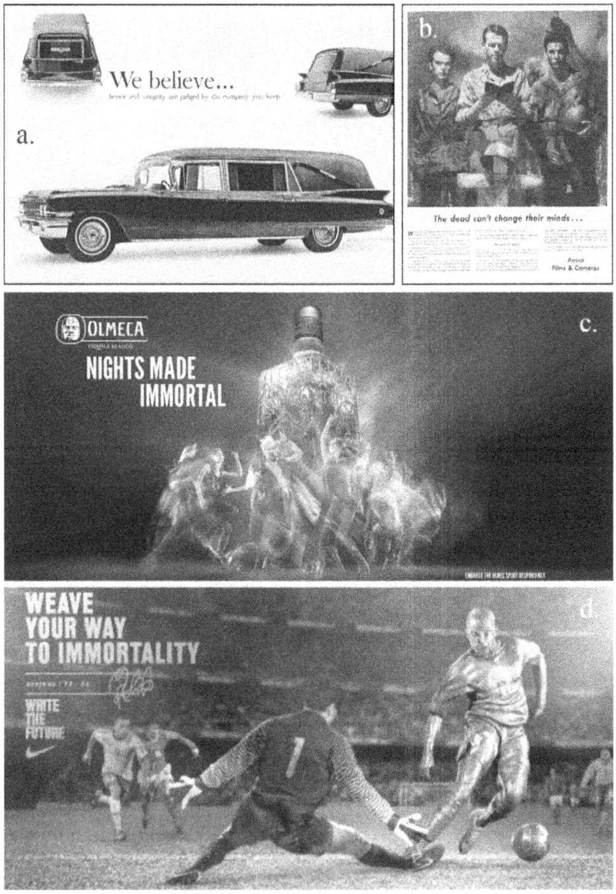

Figure 5.16 a) Cadillac Superline Victoria funeral coach ad from 1962. "We believe . . . honor and integrity are judged by the company you keep." b) 1945 ad for Ansco Films & Cameras. "The dead can't change their minds." c) Olmeca tequila ad. "Nights made immortal." d) Nike ad. "Weave your way to immortality." *Source: a) © Cadillac, public domain image retrieved from ebay.com listing. b) © Ansco, no longer in business. Public domain image retrieved from ebay.com listing. c) © Olmeca, image provided courtesy of Josh Tenser. d) © Nike, image provided courtesy of Nike.*

their shamanism/belief in higher powers at play within the natural world and used that as inspiration when writing the ad. It worked for us because of the parallels with the use of tequila. It is a bit of a ritual (shots, mates, lemons, salt—not just a drink) and it's used to take the night out up a level in energy. We also shot it so the bottle looked like a giant monolith emitting some kind of positive energy. So, yeah, I'd say there were definite deliberate references to mysticism in the approach.

Figure 5.16d is the second ad referring to immortality, which, of course, occurs after death. The question of the "existence" of immortality or eternal life after death is one answered by some religions. This one in a series of ads from Nike uses the ethereal likenesses or ghosts of past great athletes and shows them interacting with current great athletes on today's fields of competition. It may be eerie, but it is inspirational and ethereal at the same time.

GOD AND JESUS

When speaking of religion, there are not many words that are more frequently used than "God" or "god(s)." And that is manifest in advertising, too. Colloquially, people around the world use the lowercase "god" to signify a male who embodies qualities that make him superior to other men, or a man to whom inordinate attention or reverence is given, making him into an idol. The female version is a goddess. In Roseanne Barr's first TV stand-up performance, she referred to herself as a "domestic goddess." It was hilarious and enough to give her an almost supernatural start to her long-running, successful career. At times, the term "god" applies to things instead of people, such as a Heath bar being a toffee god. Some more fundamental religionists are likely to believe that the use of the word "God" in circumstances other than prayer or the reading aloud of the scriptures is a violation of the commandment in Exodus 20:7: "Thou shalt not take the name of the Lord thy God in vain."

In fact, even the impression that one is referring to god or implying God or a god in anything less than a reverent way is abhorrent to many. Hence, they would take great offense at seeing the word in ads. Even saying the phrase, "Oh, my God," is viewed by many fundamental practitioners of any religion as taking the Lord's name in vain. Secular holy hype is a small fraction of all advertising, about 2.5%, so this is usually not a great concern except for the vehement vocal and written repudiation these people exhibit in some countries with strong advertising standards organizations. England and Italy are especially energetic at censoring what they determine to be anti-religious or sacrilegious ads.

One example of this type of censorship occurred in Romania in early 2020 (figure 5.17a). As a result of the coronavirus pandemic, doctors and nurses were hailed all over the world as heroes in their willingness to directly expose themselves to the serious virus to render aid to infected and presumably contagious patients. They have been called saints and gods and are portrayed and promoted as such in publicly displayed, illustrated posters. This particular effort was initiated by an advertising agency, and some of the art by Wanda

Hutira is a fusion of Christian Orthodox iconography and Japanese anime. Other posters represent Buddhist and Hindu deities. The Orthodox response was responsible for a request issued by the PR office for the Romanian Patriarchy for the removal of the posters, claiming the posters were blasphemous, Satanist, and *offensive to doctors*. In Hutira's rendition of the revered doctor, we see the medical professional's head positioned directly in front of a crown of light rays or halo often seen as a backdrop to the head of Jesus and other holy persons in old medieval or post-Renaissance paintings. Franklin (2018) explains that the halo makes its earliest appearance in Egyptian art dating back to 3000 BCE. In Christian art, the halo is seen first around, on, or behind Jesus's head in about the fourth century CE, "only to evolve from a gilded floating disk to a modest hair-thin ring by the 1400s, which we now see today on the heads of angels on drug store greeting cards" (pp. 16–17). Continuing her exposition, Franklin turns from the halo's physical attributes to the importance of its underlying significance:

> The halo has a complicated history and goes by many names—the nimbus, aura, aureole, glory, *corona* [emphasis added]. In its iterations, what seems to matter less is the exact visual object; whether it comes as a disk, a sphere, a ray of light, or a cloud, it seems that the concept of it has more weight than the thing itself. (p. 17)

The halo was a method of identifying saints, angels, and even famous or powerful people in paintings and on statues "at least until the 17th century, when Pope Urban III strictly forbid the representation of still living and not yet beatified men with halos on their heads" (Holyblog, 2016, n.p.). The authors of the site explain its meaning: "It has been used in sacred art as [a] figurative feature since the beginning in many civilizations and cultures to state the divinity, power and regality of a character, and later, in a Christian setting, sanctity" (n.p.). If the viewer looks at this "corona" or crown of light carefully, it resembles a graphic representation of the coronavirus, typically shown as a circle with short, club-like projections extending outward from its body. These are the protuberances that stem from the viral membrane. The CDC (Centers for Disease Control) explains how the coronavirus got its name, stating concisely, "Coronaviruses derive their name from the fact that under electron microscopic examination, each virion is surrounded by a 'corona,' or halo. This is due to the presence of viral spike peplomers emanating from each proteinaceous envelope" (2020, n.p.). In response to the Romanian government's censure of Hutira's art, the sponsoring agency agreed to take down the Christian-related imagery, but left the others in place (Erizanu, 2020). So far, there is no similar reaction from adherents of the other religions represented.

Figure 5.17 a) Poster by artist Hutira displayed on a public street in Bucharest, Romania. b) 1979 ad for Sorels. "Thank God for Sorels." c) Absolut ad, "In an Absolut world." It would be the ultimate world if only the oceans were made of vodka and God was in charge of bringing the ice cubes to the party. d) Lexical ad, "Rock is religion. Speak the language of gods." John Lennon sports a halo and appears before stained glass. He once said, "The Beatles are more popular than Jesus." e) 1970 ad for Leilani Hawaiian Rum. "An act of the gods made this the best tasting rum in the world." f) Memorex ad from 1987. "Everybody knows God loves the blues more than anything else but there's always been a debate over how He listens to them." g) Ad for the Episcopal Church by Fallon McElligott agency. "Unfortunately, this is as close as some people ever get to a sense of God." *Source: a) Image courtesy of AP Photo/Vadim Ghirda. b) © Sorels, public domain image retrieved from ebay .com listing. c) © Absolut, image provided courtesy of Absolut. d) © Lexical, no longer in business. Public domain image. e) © Leilani Hawaiian Rum, public domain image retrieved from ebay.com listing. f) Memorex, no longer in business. Public domain image retrieved from ebay.com listing. g) Image provided courtesy of Father George Martin.*

The second ad in this montage, figure 5.17b, says it right out there in large bold type: "Thank God for Sorels." There is no hiding one's light under a bushel here, and that's good for holy hype because it is a proverb that comes from Jesus's Sermon on the Mount. The ad ran in 1979 for Sorels by Kaufman. The Canadian footwear company was founded in 1908, but filed for bankruptcy in 2000. At that time, Columbia Sportswear bought the Sorel boot trademark.

Absolut vodka, internationally known for its long-running ad campaign using its iconic bottle as inspiration, strayed from this perspective in the ad at figure 5.17c. In 1981, the company, through the efforts of a much smaller TBWA agency, came up with a simple two-word campaign—"Absolut [Something]"—using visual puns based simply on the design of the bottle (AdAge, 2003, n.p.). The first attempt was "Absolut Perfection." Ironically, it was an example of secular holy hype. The bottle was depicted with a halo hovering over the top. The brain trust behind this design included Geoff Hayes, Graham Turner, and Carole Ann Fine. Four years later, Andy Warhol created his unique design for an Absolut ad, and "this effort would mark the beginning of Absolut's long, spectacular, often entertaining and occasionally pompous series of diversions into the realm of art, fashion, geography, design, furniture, cartoons and Christmas greetings" (AdAge, 2003, n.p.). It is considered one of the best print campaigns in the history of advertising. The ad shown here in figure 5.17c does not mention God or gods, and it is not an offshoot from its Absolut [Something] campaign, but it does exemplify holy hype, and it does use a God theme. This ad, "In an Absolut world," shows us what vodka drinkers would imagine as heaven on earth—the Almighty's hands extending downward from the heavens to deliver ice cubes to an ocean on earth, an ocean of Absolut vodka. Now, this would be a perfect world.

Figure 5.17d is a nod to John Lennon of The Beatles. The irony is that Lennon, the atheist, is framed in stained glass, the medium of religion, as a Christ-like character. His right hand is painted in the Jesus gesture, but his atheism is hinted at by the tag coming off his left shoulder, imprinted with the name of his anti-religion song, "Imagine." In addition, the blue glass behind him is adorned with pale-white peace symbols. The text in the black box states: "Rock is religion. Speak the language of Gods." The paradoxical nature of the art and copy grabs our attention immediately. The fifth example in this array is figure 5.17e, a 1970 ad for Leilani Hawaiian Rum, more from the alcoholic beverage industry that would like us to believe that liqueur and other "spirits" in a bottle come to us like manna from heaven. The headline repeats this for us, lest we forget who bestows us with this awesome (in the original non-slang sense) elixir: "An act of the gods made this the best tasting (*sic*) rum in the world." The advertiser explains that according to legend, this rum is created with the help of three gods: (a) the god of Volcanoes; (b) the god of Sun; and (c) the god of Rain. The image represents these gods by placing the wet bottle on a ground of steamy lava rocks with the sun shining down upon the scene. The text ends with this: "Thanks, gods."

Until now, we have seen ads that refer to God, but the one at figure 5.17f dares to picture God. In that regard, it is extremely rare. We have seen very few ads that take this step, which, to a devout, Orthodox Jew or Christian, is a violation of the Second Commandment as written in Exodus 20: 3–4: "[3]You are to have no other gods before me. [4]You are not to make for yourselves a carved image or *any kind of representation of anything in heaven above* (emphasis added), on the earth beneath or in the water below the shoreline." When He *is* illustrated, He resembles the common visualizations of Moses—white hair, long white beard, flowing cloak, or simlah, of wool or linen. However, unlike Moses, God is shown sitting on a soft cloud, lording it over everyone on earth but not pretentiously so. In the Memorex ad, figure 5.17f, God is actually shown holding a packaged Memorex tape. He has become a salesman, much like adman Bruce Barton's Jesus in his book, *The Man Nobody Knows* (1925).

Tom McElligott rounds out this figure with another ad, figure 5.17g, in his campaign for The Episcopal Church. We see the unmistakable front end of a Mercedes Benz sedan with its iconic hood ornament. Owning a car of this brand, for some, comes close to a religious experience. He could have used any of several other automobile brands that compel covetousness, but this brand seems to work perfectly. Even the inimitable Janis Joplin released a self-authored song in 1971 about this car and the materialistic quest for the finest of worldly goods. In her husky, Southern Comfort-influenced voice, she belted out these words:

Oh Lord, won't you buy me a Mercedes Benz?
My friends all drive Porsches, I must make amends
Worked hard all my lifetime, no help from my friends
So Lord, won't you buy me a Mercedes Benz?

It is easy to guess that this concept likely inspired McElligott and led to this ad. His intent is obvious in the brilliant headline and copy: "Unfortunately, this is as close as some people ever get to a sense of God." It continues: "If you believe there should be more to life than the worship of objects, come and join us in the joy and fellowship of God in the Episcopal Church."

As in other categories of secular holy hype, there are other fine examples to discuss, but we could not reproduce them here. One is a compelling graphic sales pitch for Scrabble, the board game made by Milton Bradley. A dog is pictured in the center, emerging from that heavenly white light from which God comes forth, or sometimes "materializes." Floating in the sky are three

Scrabble letter tiles, G, D, and O, which, when arranged in one particular way spell "dog" and arranged another way, spell "God." No further explanation is necessary.

Havas London, an advertising agency in the United Kingdom, created an excellent ad for a special product sold by VO5. We see the back of the head of a person with long hair. We see only beautiful, flowing locks of dark brown hair. Across the hair, only three words are printed in white—"Oh. My. God." It is an example of the use of "God" in an ad in a different treatment of the colloquial OMG in text messages, shorthand for "Oh, my God," a phrase that conservative Christians might find off-putting. So, VO5 pushes the limits here a bit on behalf of its "one-minute wonder," the hot oil.

There is a completely different artistic treatment of the subject for the 1978 ARP Guitars ad for its ARP Avatar. Video games were first introduced in 1971 (Tyson, 2021). Remember that another aspect of attention getting is the style of art—or just using art instead of photography and text. In this modern illustration, which replicates a combination Medieval-Renaissance-style art and can be located online, "painted" on a parchment background, truly stands out against the Tom McElligott-style treatment in figure 5.17g. The man steering the Roman chariot could remind us of Charlton Heston as Ben-Hur in the eponymous movie from 1959. The chariot driver has been imagined as a god of sorts, his head enveloped in a celestial light. He is suspended with his horses high in the air above a huge crowd of admiring followers. It appears as though this god has descended from the heavens as would the "real" God, in an aura. He is holding the product being advertised. In a possible reference to people who steal software, the headline states: "Stolen from the gods of the keyboard. Bestowed on the disciples of the guitar."

Our final discussion of an ad using the word God, is an ad for Dukes Bread in North Carolina. This is one from a campaign conceived and developed by BooneOakley agency. As far as we have determined, this is the only ad in the campaign that is God-related, but another one is also designed in the holy hype vein. This particular one reads: "God never said, give us this day our daily kale." As such, we see a biblical justification for choosing bread over kale, a come-on which should appeal to the religiously affiliated or just anyone with a sense of humor. The other example of holy hype in this campaign is an ad showing a loaf of bread, stating, "No one gets together to break salad," the clear implication being that we get together to break bread, an expression whose etymology is argued and the practice of which predates the Torah in a variety of cultures (Tennent, 2014).

As we have seen in the T-pose discussion, the image of Jesus specifically is treated differently from images or representations of God or gods. In order to visually demonstrate this, we offer figure 5.18. We have read about how Benetton, ever the agent provocateur, believes in helping us expand our

Figure 5.18 a) United Colors of Benetton ad featuring David Kirby, a man dying from AIDS. Kirby wanted the photo to be seen by everyone to expose the truth of AIDS. b) Viewer of Wonder Café is asked to check the right box: Funny or Ticket to hell? c) Ad for LOGIN: the conference for future insights. "What will we worship next?" d) 1971 Jesus Jeans ad. "Thou shalt not have any other jeans but me." e) Image from postcard sent to prospective members of Damascus Road Church. Jesus will be your buddy. *Source: a) Photo by Therese Frare, ad by Benetton. The image is free to be reproduced according to both photographer and subject. b) © Wonder Café, no longer in business. c) © LOGIN: The conference for future insights. Image courtesy of LOGIN. Creative/copywriter: Žygimantas Kudirka; Art director: Dovydas Stonkus; Illustration: Džiugas Valančiauskas. d) © Jesus Jeans, public domain image retrieved from ebay.com listing. e) Damascus Road Church is no longer in existence.*

minds, to think about the world in new ways. The company certainly accomplishes this in figure 5.18a. In 2014, journalist Ben Cosgrove called the image in this ad "The photo that changed the face of AIDS." During the height of the AIDS pandemic, a journalism student, Therese Frare, who had been volunteering at a hospice facility for AIDS patients, accompanied another caregiver to be present as David Kirby was slipping away toward death. Kirby's mother asked her to take photographs of visitors saying good-bye to her son. David assented to the photos as long as Therese promised not to make any money from them, but rather to find a way to get as many people as possible to see the devastating effects of the disease. *LIFE* magazine published this photo in 1990, and Cosgrove claimed it had been seen by about 1 billion people at the time of his article. It has become iconic of the AIDS disaster. This is not to say that the photo has not caused controversy. In 1992, Benetton colorized the photo and published it in the ad format seen in figure 5.18a. Cosgrove explains the pushback:

> Individuals and groups ranging from Roman Catholics (who felt the picture mocked classical imagery of Mary cradling Christ after his crucifixion) to AIDS activists (furious at what they saw as corporate exploitation of death in order to sell T-shirts) voiced outrage. (Cosgrove, 2014, n.p.)

But Bill Kirby, the dying man's father, comforted a discouraged young photographer with these words: "Listen, Therese. Benetton didn't use us, or exploit us. We used them. Because of them, your photo was seen all over the world, and that's exactly what David wanted" (Cosgrove, 2014, n.p.).

Ads 5.18b and c are renditions of what is perceived to be the real Jesus, but not in a realistic style. In 5.18b, we see Jesus as a dashboard bobblehead for an ad from Wonder Café, trying to turn Jesus into a buddy, and posing the question for discussion—is this ad funny or a ticket to hell? And in figure 5.18c, Jesus appears on the cross, which is constructed from the Facebook "f" logo, implying that social media have become our new idols. This was conceived for LOGIN and was designed by the following people: Creative/copywriter: Žygimantas Kudirka; Art Director: Dovydas Stonkus; and Illustration: Džiugas Valančiauskas.

Figure 5.18d shows the viewer an ad for a company that uses "Jesus" in its brand's name—Jesus Jeans. It comes to us from 1971, in an era that was more audacious in just about every category of culture than the current one. If you are too young to remember hot pants, platform shoes, leisure suits, "Have a nice day" imprinted on everything, bell-bottom pants, the Afro hair style, disco music, roller skates, mood rings, and the CB radio, we recommend you go to the internet and check out this unforgettable, shameless decade. It is definitely worth the trip because you know what they say: Don't throw anything away. It will come back in style in a few decades. The ad for Jesus Jeans overlaps some of our categories. With a headline like "Thou shalt not have any other jeans but me," it could be shown in the Ten Commandments category. For the defunct Damascus Road Church that advertised in outrageous postcards, figure 5.18e is the image that was used in one of its mailings. We were unable to locate the whole postcard because the church's postcards have been gradually deleted from any online places in which it might have appeared years ago. There are other churches by that name, but the one that disseminated the novel postcards cannot be found. The church that did use quirky, unconventional marketing tools had a mission to reach people of all social strata, including those who believed they were not good enough or dressed well enough to attend church on a moment's notice. You can see a complete postcard from this institution in Chapter 2 at figure 2.3c. In another one that is not shown here, the church showed a public men's restroom with the caption, "Church for people who pee."

We have more ads that represent this category about the Jesus theme that we would like to discuss here. The first is a controversial ad by Ogilvy for the Chapel Bar & Bistro in Auckland, New Zealand. Aside from the substitution of a cross for the ampersand in the name, in honor of the establishment's seventh anniversary, we see a tuckered-out but happy Jesus sharing a bed with his apparent sexual partner, Mary Magdalene, who is appropriately curled up at the foot end of the bed in subservience to "the Lord." We cannot begin to show our readers all of the ways that Chapel takes off on its satire of Christianity. Even the building's second-story windows are designed to look like stained glass. If you have religious objections to the ad (easily found online), then we can predict that you likely will not enjoy an evening at Chapel. However, the reviews of the food and staff are consistently excellent. The team responsible for this creative effort was composed of Angus Hennah as executive creative director, creatives Steve Hansen and Paul Kim, photographer Troy Goodall, designer James Showler, and account managers Jessica Short and Paul Manning.

In yet another striking image of a Jesus-like figure tied to a table, is an ad in which a man is depicted attached to wires and tubes in readiness for execution. The ad is from IGFM of Denmark, a group that advocates the end of the death penalty. The message is certainly not that prisoners on death row are like Jesus in the way they have lived their lives. They are similar to Jesus in that they are humans being *sacrificed* in the name of justice and atonement. It is an image that is simultaneously hard to look at and hard to turn away from. The allusion to Jesus is an attempt to get the audience to see the inhumanity of execution. This image is also an example of the Jesus T-pose.

Another ad in this category, one we were unable to show, is a cleverly executed and humorous ad for an advertising agency, McCann Erickson. The designers have set the scene—Jesus has come to them for their expertise in corporate identity. Showing him several designs, he seems to prefer the "target symbol" for his Christian identity. The admen are trying to persuade him to choose the cross. The narrative is a pun on the unfortunate situation that often ensues when ad creatives say to themselves, "Let's give the client some really bad designs along with the one great one we think he should use. Obviously, he'll select the good one." It is a common rookie mistake in the advertising business. As it usually turns out, the client chooses a bad idea, and it becomes extremely difficult to move him or her off of that choice.

HEAVEN AND HELL

This category of secular holy hype is the corollary to angels and devils, and it is closely associated with good and evil. Especially for Christians, these are significant and salient religious constructs. There are hundreds of conceptions of these two otherworldly places, but for those who believe they exist and that we are eventually transported to one or the other after death, there are some characteristics of heaven and hell that are shared among different religious traditions. We may disagree about how and by whom the decision is made where we end up after we leave this earth, but through movies, novels, narratives about near-death experiences, cartoons, and ads, we see the same popularly disseminated perceptions of heaven and hell. To wit, hell is hot—very hot—red-hot, and it smells like sulfur, that is, rotten eggs. Heaven's weather, on the other hand, is rarely discussed, but when we see artists' renditions of it, it is full of fluffy clouds and yet bright with sunshine. The angels rest on the clouds, and often, God's chair is situated on a cloud. The temperature in heaven is perfect. Hell is crowded and cramped, often rocky and cave-like, but heaven is composed of mostly wide-open spaces and blue skies. There is a lot of anger and fear in hell, but we see supreme happiness in heaven. Heaven is up, and hell is down, a set-in-stone principle that can restrict certain design ideas and control where photos and/or text are placed. When using these concepts in ads, an art director or copywriter should think first about the traits of each place so as to portray them in the visual terms that will make them salient and visceral for the potential viewers and buyers. Also, remember that other words for the same concept could spark a brilliant idea that "heaven" or "hell" do not. Alternate words for heaven include paradise, Promised Land, immortality, utopia, upstairs, eternity, and Shangri-la, and these words are used frequently in advertisements. Substitutes for hell are inferno, Dante's inferno, Hades, great abyss, fire and brimstone, eternal damnation, and perdition. Keep Roget's Thesaurus nearby when brainstorming.

Heaven

Another word for heaven is nirvana, a term that comes from Buddhism and Hinduism. In those religions, nirvana is the ultimate goal—the best endpoint for all living beings. It is a place of perfect happiness and peace, and it is a state of being that must be achieved by complete religious enlightenment in Buddhism and Hinduism. More specifically, "Achieving nirvana is to make earthly feelings like suffering and desire disappear. It's often used casually to mean any place of happiness, like if you love chocolate, going to Hershey's Park would be nirvana" (Vocabulary.com, n.d., n.p.). We often see this colloquial use in advertising. For example, a company established in 2012, Carvana, uses a logo of a halo suspended over a car. The "vana" in the name implies nirvana. Carvana is meant to be a disruptor in the used car-buying industry, offering a much more pleasurable experience for the buyer by eliminating the traditional automobile dealership haggling model. It turns a stressful, high-pressure, person-to-person game into a blissful online adventure.

In order to create a truly memorable ad using a heaven motif, do as Taco Bell did when its marketers created the "Think outside the bun" slogan. Thinking outside the box, or unconventionally, is actually a tenet of all great advertising. Turn the concept inside out or upside down. Look at the situation from a new perspective. The Nike display at 5.19a speaks of heaven as that purely enjoyable experience in life on earth. Vince Lombardi exposes his innermost space of paradise as he says, "Football. It's about as close to heaven as you can get. I should know." To those who are fans of football, Lombardi's silhouette is unmistakable. Lombardi goes with football like ouzo goes with Greece.

The ad at figure 5.19b is the way Tropical Tobacco would like to be viewed in heaven. This company conceptualizes heaven as a place that makes space for only the best things that we enjoy on earth. In other words, you will not have to give up the pleasure of smoking this brand of cigars in your physical life because you can find them in heaven's smoking section. The cigars are so precious that one must be allowed in by a caretaker who can unlatch the velvet cord entry. Figure 5.19c takes us back to the advertising so common during World War II. In 1943's "Devils from heaven," we see a portrayal of our fighting men using Joyce Aviation parachute and belt hardware after jumping from airplanes in anticipation of confrontation with the enemy. The soldiers come down from heaven and become devils for our side upon landing on a battle site. From the same era, in 1945, comes an ad for Webster Cigars in figure 5.19d. The proud father, who is a soldier, is handing out cigars as is traditional upon seeing his "bundle from heaven." This is a ritual that calls for only the finest cigars, and Webster fills the bill. This is a particularly special moment because the baby is preordained as "another Marine." It is a "fitting occasion for a great cigar—a *Webster!*" Back in the 1940s, smoking in hospitals was not forbidden, so this would have not been deemed inappropriate. Even doctors smoked.

Next, 5.19e, an ad for Hypo, reveals its ad creators from Noah's Ark full-service marketing firm of Lagos, Nigeria, have a perception of heaven similar to that of Tropical Tobacco's take on the hereafter. Hypo is a product that removes stains. All of us have committed sins which have stained our

Figure 5.19 a) Nike ad. Vince Lombardi thinks football is heaven. b) Tropical Tobacco ad—"Welcome to heaven. The smoking section." c) 1943 ad for Joyce parachute equipment company—"Devils from heaven." d) 1945 ad for Webster Cigars. Back in the forties, hospitals thought it was okay for visitors, patients, and employees to smoke inside the building. "Bundle from heaven." e) Hypo stain remover ad designed by Noah's Ark Agency in Lagos for Hypo Homecare Product Limited, a division of the Tolaran Group. The stain of sin shows up on our bodies only. "Wipe your stains away. Happy Easter." f) Ad for Wrigley Field and the Cubs designed by Jones. When we get to heaven, all ballparks will be modeled after Wrigley Field. *Source: a) © Nike, image provided courtesy of Nike. b) © Tropical Tobacco, no longer in business. c) © Joyce, public domain image. d) © Webster Cigars, public domain image. e) Image courtesy of Noah's Ark Agency. f) © Wrigley Field & the Cubs. Image courtesy of MLB (Major League Baseball).*

personhood. We must be stain-free to live in heaven, and Hypo has removed the actual physical body of the harpist so the pure soul can live there in harmony with the righteous environment. Our "normal" vision of heaven may be a place of floating human bodies. Hypo's ad turns that notion inside out. It asks us to think.

Every baseball fan knows that Cub fans are some of the most faithful team supporters in the game. Gee, after winning the World Series in 1907 and 1908, these people waited 108 years for their third World Series championship! Now, that's devotion, exceeded only by pious adoration of God. And until the walls come tumbling down and the ivy withers from lack of rain, Wrigley Field is their heaven on earth. As a matter of fact, when they get to the real heaven, the ballfield there will be modeled after Wrigley. So says figure 5.19f.

Hell and Sin

Hell, like heaven, can be a place of eternal residence, a place or situation on earth, or even a state of mind. It depends on one's relationship with religion and how that relationship manifests itself on the piety scale. Fundamentalists consider the utterance of the word "hell" a transgression when used as an expletive or exclamation, similar to the use of other words such as "damn," "oh, my God," and "Jesus Christ." And, no matter what, do not tell anyone to go there. These words and phrases are quite often replaced by "heck," "darn," and "oh, my gosh," but the substitutes do not ordinarily convey the speaker's actual depth of emotion. The mild oaths can come across as insincere and a bit holier-than-thou in attitude as some of our 2020 survey participants recounted. Bruce Gerencser, a former Evangelical pastor and former Christian, *swears* by cursing. Gerencser says, "I know firsthand that cursing can, and does, have a cathartic effect on a person. While certainly those who swear must be aware of proper social conventions, swearing at the referee on TV who just hosed your favorite football team can be emotionally satisfying, and I highly recommend it" (Gerencser, 2020). What he means is that there is a time and place for it. Just remember that when used in ads, these "bad" words can turn off religiously devout consumers. Most people understand that the choice of text in ads is indeed purposeful. The former preacher offers these acceptable Evangelical swear words: crap, dangit, freaking, frigging, gosh darn it, shoot, shucks, shucky darn, and son of a gun (Gerencser, 2020). So, let's now turn toward some excellent hell-focused ads in figure 5.20.

We begin our investigation into advertising that embraces the fiery, bottomless pit of everlasting punishment in Ridgeway, Ontario, with Brimstone Brewery in 5.20a. Brimstone's taproom manager, Jamie Gallucci, told us in an e-mail that the brewery got its name and décor theme from its building, which was originally a twentieth-century church but is now called the Sanctuary Centre for the Arts, a premiere venue for weddings, theatrical performances, beer festivals, concerts, and more. Not all of the brewery's craft beverages are named in the same churchy vein, but the one we have focused on is the establishment's flagship I.P.A., "Sinister Minister." These brewers

Figure 5.20 a) An example of the brew called Sinister Minister. b) North American aviation ad from 1944. "Mustangs raise hell in heaven." c) Vancouver Convention Center, "Hell isn't all fire and brimstone. Sometimes, it's carpeted." Conventions *are* hell, but this venue has much better carpeting. d) "Hell no, we're not giving up pizza for Lent." e) Conceptual ad for Big D's Flaming Ghost Hot Sauce. "Hotter'n hell!" f) "For a limited time. A bit like Jesus." *Source: a) Image courtesy of © Brimstone Brewing Co. b) © Rockwell International, public domain image. c) Image courtesy of © Vancouver Convention Centre. d) Image courtesy of © Hell Pizza. e) Image © Larry Zamba 2015, zambaphotography.com. Provided courtesy of Larry Zamba. f) Image courtesy of © Hell Pizza.*

are serious about their product, even though they have some fun with the names of their ales and beers. Says Gallucci, "We stand committed to locally produce unique and drinkable, fresh craft beer of the highest quality. Making beer in small batches has given us creative license to experiment and brew a variety of beer styles."

Other products are called "Midnight Mass Chicory," "Heavenweiss Pear Hefeweizen," and "Beatification English Brown Ale." As expected,

Brimstone is closed on Sundays, but you can always go online to purchase some unorthodox material Christianity. Brimstone sells a broad array of holy hype apparel, among which is a Sinister Minister T-shirt emblazoned with the praying hands that appear on the beer can. Their "Midnight Mass Chicory Oatmeal Stout" clothing items are decorated with a silhouette of a monk kneeling at an altar. Brimstone Brewery even sells beer soap—an amazing combination of two products, beer and soap, that have used holy hype in their advertising campaigns for more than a century!

Figure 5.20b takes us back again to the World War II era, specifically to 1944. North American Aviation informs us that the company's fighter planes, the P-51 Mustangs, "Raise Hell in the Heavens." In *Flying* magazine from 1944, the explanation of the ad is this:

> Here in the arctic cold of the stratosphere a chronicle of victory is sky-written by white vapor trails and by the searing flame of an enemy plane in its last screaming earthbound plunge. The men and women of North American Aviation are proud of the "angels from hell" who pilot these avenging P-51 Mustangs—proud, too, of their own vital part on America's production front. (Cot, 1944, p. 111)

This is what US propaganda looked like during the war. We had the best of all military equipment, weaponry, and personnel, and the public should know this and donate to the cause. The hell-fire from the P-51 made angels of its pilots.

Figure 5.20c is a clever way to speak about hell in its earthly understanding. Some situations are hell . . . for example, conventions. The Vancouver Convention Centre appreciates just how uncomfortable conferences can be. So, the facility ad designers give us this message: "Hell isn't all fire and brimstone; sometimes, it's carpeted." Okay, so if you have to be there and listen to some boring speakers, at least the chair you sit on will be comfier because its foundation will be a cushiony, good-looking carpet. It is definitely an innovative method for promoting the facility as a venue for large groups and meetings.

A pizza business located in New Zealand has connected its success to the name Hell Pizza and promotion using all sorts of allusions to that depraved, lowly place. At times, Hell Pizza, home of the Seven Deadly Sins, uses an icon associated with the Church of Satan, a pentagram-like symbol—an inverted five-pointed star. The "satanic" or "evil" connotation of the right side up version is challenged by a high priestess of the Wiccan tradition, Marsha Shaw (1994, n.p.). She counters:

> It is a beautiful, positive symbol of my spiritual path and that of my ancestors, the Wiccan. In essence, the pentagram means life. It has received an enormous

load of bad press at the hands of "Satanists," who practice a twisted form of anti-Christianity.

Hell Pizza's approach could be either a courageous, gutsy business move or a direct route to failure. It appears to be a huge success. Never too removed from the damnable and infernal theme, the CEO, Ben Cumming, signed his e-mail to us this way: "Evilly yours." The company's website tells us that "the path to Paradise begins in Hell," and visitors to the online location are treated to a virtual tour of New Zealand in the Hell Hearse.

This is the same strategy implemented by some other companies that have dared to stand out among competitors, first in terms of shock and outrageousness, and then by product quality and/or singularity. Some well-known companies that have signed on to this game plan are Sweet Jesus ice cream, Benetton (see figures 5.18a and 8.1a), Federici Italian Cream, and Nike. Not all have found a "shelter from the storm" of censure brought on by their perceived blasphemy (Isaiah 25: 4–5). Figures 5.20d and 5.20f are indications of how far Hell Restaurant is willing to go. As the story goes, "no guts, no glory." The proclamation on the billboard that stands in front of St. Matthew-in-the-City Church is hardly subtle (figure 5.20d). These people are *not* going to give up pizza for Lent. Actually, it is a bit more adamant than that. "Hell no," they will not give up pizza for Lent. They may not have to worry anyway; pizza was the 58th most common thing to be given up for Lent. However, beer was ranked 24th, and cheese was 41st, so they cannot be too sure (*Christianity Today*, 2019). If beer and cheese appear that early in the list, then pizza may be done for. It is better to get the message out that pizza is not something to be surrendered for any period of time. In figure 5.20f, Hell Pizza advertises its special on Hell Cross Buns by alerting customers to the strictly limited time during which this offer is available. The restaurant speaks of this brief duration as being like the length of time the world had Jesus in its midst. This could be viewed by some as blasphemous. Notice that the design imprinted on the bun is an upside-down five-pointed star.

In figure 5.20e, Larry Zamba of Larry Zamba Photography of Salem, Wisconsin, has designed and laboriously photographed possibly the hottest devil imaginable in print. The layout was proposed for the bottle label of a fledgling company that made a hellishly, thus devilishly, hot BBQ sauce in a line of sauces. The company failed to launch commercially, so the design never made it onto bottles, but please recognize the impression this leaves in the potential buyer's mind. This devil looks so hot that it seems like even *he* cannot stand the heat. The owner of the company, Derek Wright, played the devil, and it was photographed underwater. Zamba affirms that Wright was wearing make-up. If you need an image like this, it is possible that Derek still has it available for purchase or lease.

There are plenty of sinful images lurking out there (figure 5.21). Bad behavior can consist of: (1) buying green bathroom fixtures (American-Standard in 5.21a); (2) buying a luxurious automobile during an economic depression (Roadmaster in 5.21b); (3) wearing provocative perfume (My Sin

Figure 5.21 a) American-Standard ad from 1966. "How to turn your friends Surf Green with envy!" b) Buick ad from 1951. "It's almost sinfully luxurious." c) Lanvin ad from 1967. "My Sin . . . a most provocative perfume." d) Tappan ad from 1973. "The estimate, and other air conditioning sins, according to Tappan." e) Ad for Hell Pizza. "Lust." f) Young & Rubicam ad from 1962. "Boredom is the costliest sin in advertising." g) Land O Lakes ad from 1987. "40% sin; 60% forgiveness." *Source: a) © American-Standard, public domain image retrieved from ebay.com listing. b) © Buick, public domain image retrieved from ebay.com listing. c) © Lanvin, public domain image retrieved from ebay .com listing. d) © Tappan, no longer in business. e) Image courtesy of © Hell Pizza. f) © Young & Rubicam, public domain image retrieved from ebay.com listing. g) ©Land O Lakes, public domain image retrieved from ebay.com listing.*

from Lanvin in 5.21c); or (4) charging too much to fix someone's air conditioner (Tappan in 5.21d). Sin is everywhere. Greed and envy are shown in figures 5.21a and b. Figure 5.21c tempts women to wear "My Sin," so someone else may lust after them. Tappan tells us to beware of greedy air conditioner repairmen in figure 5.21d. Hell Restaurant makes another appearance in figure 5.21e. It illustrates a previously mentioned one of the Bible's seven deadly sins—lust. Yes, we do not ordinarily think about passionate longing in terms of lusting after pizza, but it *is* possible. Even advertising agencies get into the act when the conversation turns to sin. Young & Rubicam mentions boredom as the costliest sin in advertising (see figure 5.21f). Okay, it is not one of the seven deadly sins, but a sin just the same. You have designed a pretty bad ad if your cat yawns when viewing it. Land O Lakes Country Morning Blend makes use of a priest eating a dab of the spread on a piece of bread (see figure 5.21g). If we confess to it, he is likely to tell us that it qualifies as 40% sin, but 60% of the behavior is forgiveness. Not such a terrible sin after all, but it *is* "wickedly delicious."

HOLY

Holy is another extremely common word in the religious vernacular that finds its way into frequent use in advertising, but not always in an effective manner. Holy means dedicated or consecrated to God or a religious purpose. It has taken on a life of its own in modern advertising that its synonym, the word "sacred," has not been able to emulate. Like other similar words of this type, the fact that it is at the top of mind is evidenced by its utterance as part of an expletive in colloquial speech. It routinely precedes a word or phrase that combines with it to intensify its emotional power, shock value, and attention-getting effect, but not necessarily its meaning, such as "holy smokes," "holy shit," "holy cow," and "holy moly, holy mother of, and holy Moses." The juxtaposition of a word descriptive of God or a prophet in conjunction with a swear word, one that is taboo, or one that describes something not considered holy serves the purpose of heightening the force of its effect as a profanity instead of mollifying its irreverence.

The ad in figure 5.22a for the Muskegon Luge employs a humorous take on the holy hype approach. The executive director of the sports park, Jim Rudicil, decided to reach out to Team Detroit for its creative design work for an ad campaign. When the ads ran and greatly increased business at the park, Rudicil called the group "angels" for saving his business (Braun, 2020). This is how Greg Braun, professor and original member of the team, summarizes the thinking behind the ad in an e-mail communication to us.

Figure 5.22 a) Muskegon Luge ad. "Many begin their run with a short prayer. 'Holy crap' seems to be quite popular." b) Porsche ad from 1981. "If you listen carefully at 160 mph you can hear the airstream whisper 'Holy mother.'" c) The Jeepster ad from 1967. "Holy Toledo, what a car! Only Toledo could build this rugged rascal." d) Volkswagen ad from 1970. "Is nothing sacred?" e) Coppertail Brewing ad for "Unholy Ale." *Source: a) Image courtesy of © Muskegon Luge. Copywriters: Susan Mersch Parlangeli and John Godsey; Art Director: Beth Hambly Topolewski; Photographers: Brad Stanley and Geoff George; Designers: Beth Hambly Topolewski and Steffan Duerr. b) Image courtesy of © Porsche. c) ©Jeep, public domain image. d) ©Volkswagen, public domain image retrieved from ebay.com listing. e) Image courtesy of ©Coppertail Brewing.*

The Muskegon Luge "Olympian" campaign was a labor of love from the very beginning: 850 feet of 30 mph track crafted by a three-time Olympian. What's not to love? Recreational parks are common in this country, but there's nothing common about this one. In other words, this is not the Tea Cup ride at Disneyland. We talked to people who had actually done it and there were several things common to their experience. They found it thrilling, they found it exhilarating, and they found it scary (in all the best ways). And with a scream on their lips and a smile on their face, they often had conversations known only to themselves, the ice, and their maker. "Short prayer" was the story of one of

> them. And if that's what they said at the top of the run, this is what they said at the bottom of it. "Can I go again?"

The headline reads: "Many begin their run with a short prayer. 'Holy crap' seems to be quite popular." The implication is that "holy" is the worshipful address to God (holy Lord, holy Father, holy God, holy Mother), and that the addition of "crap" is indicating to God that the situation is bad and that God's assistance is desperately needed to get out of or deal with it—a brief religious appeal. In actuality, "holy crap" is a natural, and totally understandable, expletive for the feeling one gets at the top of the luge looking down the winding and treacherous flume that one is just about to traverse. Gerencser has explained that "crap" is one of those words that is not terribly offensive to religious fundamentalists (2020). Using the other word for excrement would not have worked in this ad targeted to anyone looking for a fun and adventurous winter exploit, especially with the family. The object of the headline is to instantly describe the awesomeness of the experience by mildly shocking or amusing the audience into reading further.

The Porsche ad at figure 5.22b is pretty gutsy, considering it was run in 1981 at a time of awakening among politically ultra-right, Republican activists, most of whom were Evangelical Christians, in their launch of the Moral Majority movement. "Holy mother" accurately describes the exclamation from one riding in a Porsche at the speed of 160 mph. Figure 5.22c is a 1967 Jeepster ad featuring Danny Thomas, the venerable comedian and founder of St. Jude Children's Research Hospital, sitting behind the wheel. We see a new use of "holy . . . something" here. The headline in this ad is "Holy Toledo, what a car! Only Toledo could build this rugged rascal."

Figure 5.22d brings us back to the 1970s with a souped-up version of the Volkswagen beetle with the title, "Is nothing sacred?" Here we have the word "sacred" in place of "holy." We will see sacred once again in the next figure. The advertiser is saying that the "bug" in its native state is sacred, and someone is adulterating it with modern fire decals, fancy lights, wide tires, and a strange hood modification, jokingly asking whether anything is sacred.

The Coppertail Brewing Company, whose advertising is overseen by Marketing Director Gary Kost, turns holy on its head by naming one of its brews "Unholy American Trippel Ale" (figure 5.22e). The company advertises this brew as "blasphemy in a glass." The artistic approach of its designer, Evan B. Harris, which is demonstrated in all of the Coppertail beer can labels, ads, and website visuals, is remarkably true to the style of medieval Catholic monks' art in illustrated manuscripts. It brings to mind the religious devotion to the beer-making process that consumes the holy men in monasteries to this day. According to Beer Advocate, an "independent community of enthusiasts and professionals dedicated to supporting and promoting better beer," Belgian tripel or tripel beer refers to the "part of the brewing process, in which brewers use up to three times the amount of malt found in a standard Trappist table beer" (Beeradvocate.com, 2020, n.p.). The ad further accentuates the multiplier of three by delineating its *trinity* of attributes as "Big, bold, and dangerously drinkable." Holy trinity is an expression one will hear frequently on the Food Channel when chefs talk about Cajun cooking and its mixture of chopped onion, celery, and green pepper used in sauces and stews. Coppertail Brewing Company may admit to being generally unholy in its approach, but its faithfulness to good taste is pure.

Another ad we could not display is a fabulously clever ad that stands out among most Absolut vodka ads because it is a double-truck ad, which is an ad that spreads across the gutter of two facing pages. Most of the Absolut vodka ads that were designed to belong to this campaign were single-page ads. The headline is "Absolut Grail." So, what is holy about it? In this advertisement, the word "Absolut" substitutes for the word we normally see with "grail"—"holy." The Holy Grail is a term that comes out of the Middle Ages. As culture relates over the centuries, the Holy Grail is the cup or chalice that Jesus drank from at the Last Supper. Mariel Synan (2018) writes, "Given the importance of Jesus's crucifixion and the eucharist in Christian beliefs, the search for the grail became the holiest of quests as it signified the pursuit of union with God." In the ad, we see the knight's hand covered in chain-mail armor, grasping the Absolut bottle, confirming that the quest has ended successfully.

Another group of "holy" images is offered in figure 5.23. Figure 5.23a is another classic ad for Israel's airline, El Al. This company has effectively taken its location in the Holy Land as its jumping-off point for its decades-old holy hype campaigns. It comes by it honestly, and this is part of what makes it such a successful perspective. It is not put on; it is authentic. Figure 5.23a is from 1965. It implies to the prospective visitor to Israel that there is no need to purchase a book like "Israel on $5 a Day." Yes, that is what you could do about 55 years ago. The ad states: "You already own the best guidebook to Israel" and illustrates the Holy Scriptures as everyone's visitor's guide.

In figure 5.23b, we are reminded of the 1960s, during which time we were introduced to *Batman* on television. Frequently, this character would precede his important points with a "holy" something. In this case, he is exclaiming, "Holy Batmask." It is an ad for General Electric, but the image and headline do not tell us anything about the connection. We must get into the text to discover the meaning, but Batman was and is so popular that we want to see what he is excited about. Lo and behold, this person is excited about a Batmask that can be picked up free at any GE office, just in time for Halloween. Next, we are attracted to figure 5.23c, an ad for a Sacred Foods

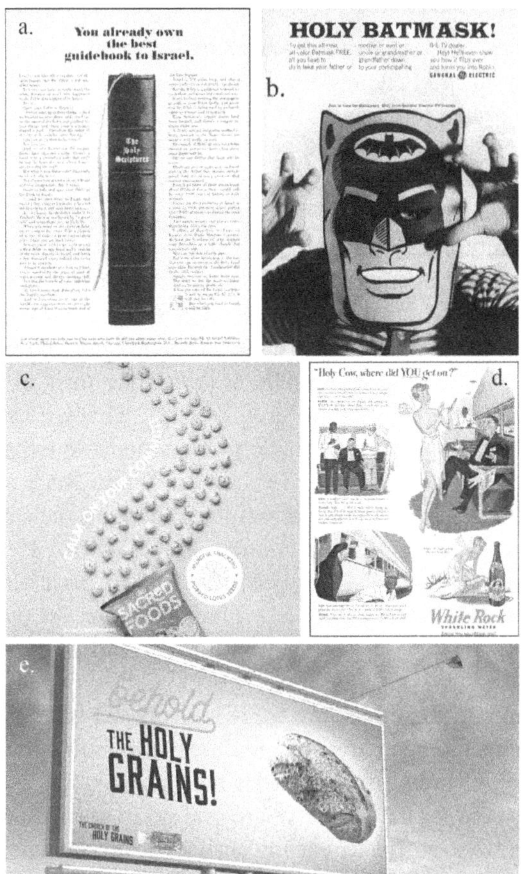

Figure 5.23 a) El Al ad from 1965. "You already own the best guidebook to Israel." b) General Electric ad from 1966. "Holy Batmask!" c) Sacred Foods ad. "Calm on your commute." d) White Rock ad from 1946. "Holy cow, where did YOU get on?" e) Conceptual ad for Food for Life Ezekiel Bread billboard. "Behold, the holy grains!" *Source: a) © El Al, public domain image retrieved from ebay.com listing. b) © General Electric, public domain image retrieved from ebay.com listing. c) Image courtesy of © Sacred Foods. Designed by Kingdom & Sparrow. d) Image courtesy of © White Rock. e) Image courtesy of © Lauren Sitterly and Haley Schrenk.*

snack, popped lotus seeds. The ad does not use the word "holy," but "sacred." Mika, founder of Sacred Foods tells us her story.

> I first discovered popped lotus seeds when I was a little girl in my mother's kitchen in India. She used to roast the seeds and season them with a delicious blend of spices. It was a family recipe passed down for generations and quickly became my favorite snack. When I moved to Canada at 13, I noticed I couldn't

> find it anywhere and that's what inspired me to eventually create Sacred Foods. In my culture, the lotus is very sacred and represents purity, which is one of the core values on which I built this brand. We believe in honoring every ingredient in its most natural form. That's why our snacks are simple, wholesome and minimally processed.

So, as we discover, Mika's use of "sacred" is not an advertising ploy. It is her vision and her culture's vision of the product.

Figure 5.23d is not another sacred or holy product, but rather another use of the word "holy" as part of an interjection slang expression. This is the first time our ads have come across the expression "holy cow." Entering our colloquial language in the early 1900s, it joined the likes of "holy Moses," "holy moly," "holy mackerel," and "holy Toledo," what we refer to as minced oaths. Minced oaths are changes made to objectionable expressions to render them milder and less profane. This ad for White Rock sparkling water is dated from 1943. The men on the train are showing their astonishment at the sight of a topless fairy waiting on them in the bar car. Her partial nudity may be surprising in 1943, but this beautiful, topless pixie was appearing as early as 1905! We do not see holy cow often anymore. As our language has changed, we see greater use now of what then would have been considered coarser language.

The last ad among these is figure 5.23e, a proposed billboard for the Food for Life® Baking Company, which features the "holy grains" that make up its Ezekiel 4:9® brand of sprouted whole grain bread. As the company explains on its website, its products "are crafted in the likeness of the Holy Scripture verse Ezekiel 4:9 to ensure unrivaled honest nutrition and pure, delicious flavors." The verse goes like this: "Take also unto thee wheat, and barley, and beans, and lentils and millet, and spelt and put them in one vessel." Among several of the company's product certifications is even one certifying its bread as kosher. This company's promotional verbiage is not just hype; similar to Sacred Foods, it is the company's actual commitment and "mission" to bring a normally secular product, bread, into a whole new level of sanctity and goodness for the consumer—as they call it, "a most sacred bread."

This billboard ad, though, is not one devised by the company. It is the result of an assignment completed by Lauren Sitterly and Haley Schrenk in 2019 in the creative advertising master's program at VCU Brandcenter in Richmond, VA. As the women explain, students were given a choice of consumer brands for which to design a 360-degree, or integrated, campaign. Noting Food for Life's own use of the biblical verse from Ezekiel, Sitterly and Schrenk set out to "lean into the religious aspect in a fun, over-the-top, humorous way." At the suggestion of their professor, Wayne Gibson, they used the tagline The

Church of the Holy Grains and turned it into a fictitious religion with a web identity, church merch for acquisition, and grain commandments. Regarding the items "for sale," site visitors could "redeem" codes printed on the back sides of stickers inside the bread bags. The image of the loaf on the billboard bestows upon it a heavenly aura against the beautiful, purple background, significant of God's power and authority. This religion requires less of its adherents in that there are only six commandments, two of which are: "Thou shalt not eat any breads before Ezekiel" and "Thou shalt not steal this bread, for it is only $4.99."

VERSE 3

Judaism

It makes perfect sense that most of the secular holy hype we see throughout advertising history is related to Christianity because, as a portion of the world's total population, adherents of Christianity make up about 31.2%, or about 2.3 billion religionists (Pew Research, 2017). Although Jews numbered only about 14.1 million in 2015, secular holy hype from a Jewish perspective is the next most commonly seen version of this advertising approach (figures 5.24, 5.25, and 5.26). The number of Jewish adherents is dwarfed by Muslims, who number about 1.8 billion worldwide, but Islamic contributions to holy hype are scarce (Pew Research, 2017). This paradoxical situation may be best understood by how truly important humor and satire are in Jewish life and culture, and how unimportant or even reviled religious humor has been portrayed among Muslims outside the United States. At least, this is the American perception about humor in Muslim life. Regarding the acceptance of Muslim humor within the United States, Dean Obeidallah, organizer of the 2015 Muslim Funny Fest, sets us straight on the topic: "I think that's something that would shock most Americans—that you can actually do jokes about Muslims and about Islam a little, and Muslims are going to laugh. They're not going to protest and burn the place down" (Muslim Comedian Roundtable, 2015). This is not to say that all or even most of holy hype is humorous. Eisand (2018) reports that about 66% of all award-winning advertising takes a humorous approach. No such analysis of holy hype has been conducted, but it is our educated opinion based on the examination of thousands of exemplars of secular holy hype, the humorous proposition is predominant in Jewish holy hype.

Knox tells us that "Jewish humor is not merely a reaction or response to circumstances and environment but a product of Jewish experience, and is almost as old as the Jewish people itself" (Knox, 1963, p. 327). Knox's piece

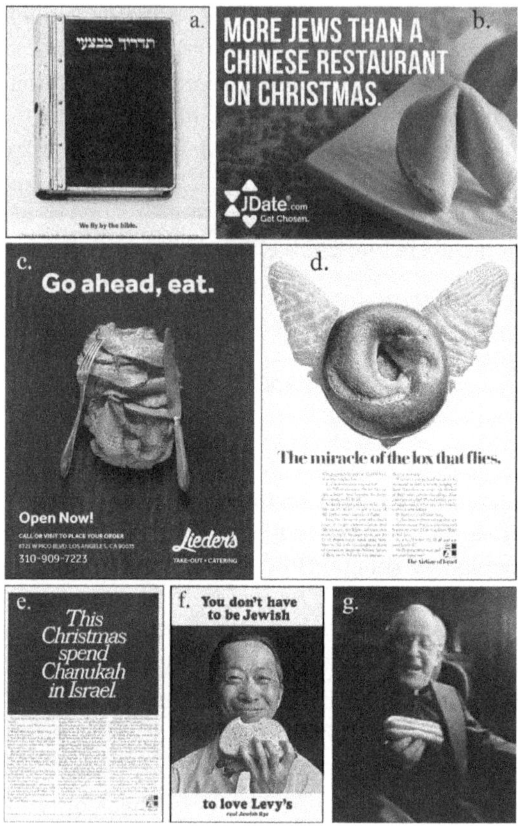

Figure 5.24 a) El Al ad from 1963. "We fly by the Bible." b) JDate ad. "More Jews than a Chinese restaurant on Christmas." c) Lieder's ad. "Go ahead, eat." d) El Al ad from the 1960s. "The miracle of the lox that flies." e) Another El Al ad from the 1960s. "This Christmas, spend Chanukah in Israel." f) Levy's ad from 1961. "You don't have to be Jewish to love Levy's real Jewish rye." g) Hebrew National commercial from 1977. "One taste is enough to convert you." *Source: a) © El Al, public domain image retrieved from ebay.com listing. b) Image courtesy of ©JDate. c) Image courtesy of © Lieder's. Copy written by Justin Oberman. d) © El Al, public domain image retrieved from ebay.com listing. e) © El Al, public domain image retrieved from ebay.com listing. f) ©Levy's, no longer in business. Public domain image. g) Screenshot from 1977 Hebrew National commercial on youtube.com.*

of literature that seriously examines Jewish humor is rare in that it takes us through the humor of the Jewish scriptures, citing the Books of Esther, Deuteronomy, Genesis, I Kings, Psalms, and Isaiah, pointing to the humor of irony—in other words, that which is a surprise or a twist on expectations. Knox refers to this type of humor as "tragic optimism" (p. 331). He explains:

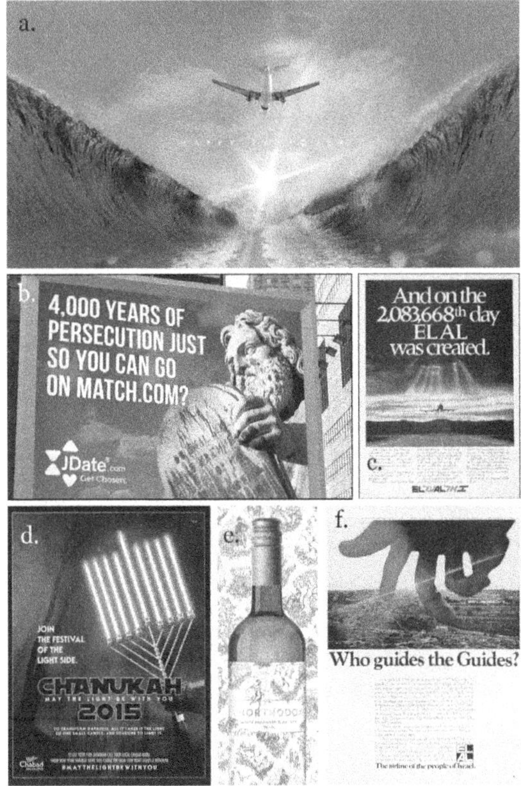

Figure 5.25 a) El Al ad. "Happy Passover." b) JDate ad. "4,000 years of persecution just so you can go on match.com?" c) El Al ad from the 1960s. "And on the 2,083,668th day El Al was created." d) Chabad on Campus ad. "Join the festival of the light side." e) "Unorthodox," Kosher wine. f) El Al ad from 1967. "Who guides the Guides?" It is God's hand that guides. *Source: a) Image courtesy of Izzy Nesselrode from the DA Colony Brand Strategy Creative Design in Tel Aviv-Jaffa, Israel. b) Image courtesy of ©JDate. c) ©El Al, public domain image retrieved from ebay.com listing. d) © Chabad on Campus. Copy written by Justin Oberman, design by Menachim Krinsky. e) Image courtesy of ©Unorthodox. f) ©El Al, public domain image retrieved from ebay.com listing.*

> So long as the actual and the ideal are disparate, so long as the hopes of the heart are not embodied in the contexture of things about us, there is work for man to do, and there is the urgency to stir the conscience to do the work. (pp. 331–332)

For Jews, who do not believe Jesus Christ was the Messiah, God has promised the Messiah is still yet to come, and that is what evokes the optimism. There is something great to look forward to. However, the tragic part is that it seems to take forever for God to get around to it. Knox summarizes it this way: "In this irony, there is a clinging to the Promise, but not without a

Figure 5.26 a) Schick Samson styling dryer ad from 1972. The names of biblical characters are sometimes used for the names of products. b) Daisy rifle ad from 1931. It depicts the David and Goliath story. "One shot from a sling . . . made a shepherd boy king!" c) Nike ad from 1986. "The Rake. Ultimate footwear for the club, the court, or the Colosseum." If you wear the Rake, you will be as strong as Samson. d) Continental Bank ad. "Anticipating the needs of business." e) JDate ad. "She knows JavaScript, Python, and Shirley Finkelstein's grandson. Sign up already." *Source: a) © Schick, public domain image retrieved from ebay.com listing. b) © Daisy, public domain image. c) © Nike, public domain image retrieved from ebay.com listing. d) ©Continental Bank, no longer in business. Public domain image retrieved from adeevee.com. e) Image courtesy of ©JDate.*

smile—a bit skeptical and a bit jovial" (p. 333). This ironic humor is beautifully and adeptly explained in the last verse of the song "If I Were a Rich Man" from *Fiddler on the Roof* by Jerry Bock:

> Lord who made the lion and the lamb; You decreed I should be what I am.Would it spoil some vast eternal plan? If I were a wealthy man.

Jews revere God and his plans, but "would it hurt" if He were to change it up a bit for me? "Would it spoil some vast eternal plan?" The "would it hurt (or 'hoit' per New York accent)" or "it wouldn't hurt (or 'hoit')" phrases are routinely used in Jewish humor as the verbal constructions of the paradox.

In most ethnic and religious groups, food is an essential part of the culture. The Jewish culture does not disappoint in this regard. Hebrew National has created several national advertising campaigns that have brought the brand much attention. One famous Hebrew National tagline was "We answer to a higher authority," and the company's ads were referred to as being "among the longest running and best known ever" (Elliott, 1997, n.p.). One brilliant ad admonishes Jewish consumers to "Be true to your heritage. Eat it from right to left." This is a play on the Hebrew language, which is read from right to left.

Steven B. Silk, president of National Foods in the mid to late 1990s, of which Hebrew National was a subsidiary, offered the rationale for the campaign: "We wanted to take advantage of the brand equity, which is tremendous, but the God in the advertising was very authoritative, a bit to be feared . . . and we wanted to deliver a superior taste message" (Elliott, 1997, n.p.). Kosher food is prepared by the strictest of religious dietary and hygienic standards, which the company maintains results in a product superior to the non-kosher brands. All people involved in the ads expressed their concern about offending anyone because "they recognized the fine line that divides the sacred and the profane when evoking the Lord for commercial purposes" (Elliott, 1997, n.p.). The agency, Grey Advertising, explained that certain tactics were employed to reduce the risk of offense. For example, God's name is never mentioned outright, nor is the Lord ever seen in print or in TV commercials. On TV, the only thing heard is the voice of the actor portraying him, Robert Klein.

Figure 5.24 is a composite of seven examples of Jewish holy hype, five of which are about food. In figure 5.24a, another clever ad by El Al, the airline promotes its adherence to the rules by telling us its pilots "fly by the bible." This advertising approach from 1963 follows its theme of connecting itself with the Holy Land by referring to the scriptures.

Continuing with the array of Jewish holy hype ads, figure 5.24b is an ad for JDate, a Jewish matchmaking service, helping Jewish males and females meet the love of their lives. The ad uses the irony and self-deprecation, which is featured in Jewish holy hype advertising. Jews do not celebrate Christmas, and sometimes the day can feel lonely when all of one's Christian friends are celebrating with family. So, one of the favorite things for Jews to do on Christmas is to take the family out to a movie and then out for dinner at their local Chinese restaurant, which is always open on Christmas day. This time-worn joke was actually used in the movie "A Christmas Story," when the Parker family's hillbilly neighbor's dogs run into the family's kitchen and ravenously consume the unattended Christmas turkey. Without any other way to enjoy a holiday meal, the Parkers head out to the only open place in town, the Chinese restaurant. So, as the ad implies, the site user on JDate.com is more likely to find a Jewish mate there on Christmas day than in a Chinese restaurant.

The ad in figure 5.24c is a daring yet popular one for Lieder's, a greater Los Angeles purveyor and caterer of glatt kosher Jewish food. This ad was copy written by Justin Oberman. The establishment focuses on indulging the Shabbat (Sabbath) dinner choices of Jewish customers who abide by the strictest interpretation of the Torah's dietary laws. Many of these observant Jews are Orthodox. Orthodox Jewish men are forbidden from cutting their sidelocks, the hair that grows from the sideburns. They are much more noticeable on younger men who have not yet begun to grow a beard. In this ad, the roast beef and utensils are arranged so the meat represents a man's round head, and the fork and knife hanging down the sides are positioned to represent the Orthodox Jewish man's sidelocks. This is a representation that could be offensive to some—Jews who may find it offensive on behalf of their more Orthodox Jewish friends or Jews who simply find any ads that seem to mock Jews or Judaism offensive. It certainly would not keep an Orthodox Jew from delighting in Lieder's food. As expected, we found that most non-Jews were at sea regarding the meaning of this ad, but, of course, they are just a small part of the targeted audience. Lieder's knows its clientele.

In some other examples of Jewish holy hype, the Israeli airline, El Al, has consistently placed excellent ads in the mass media, and figure 5.24d is another one. Lox (smoked salmon) and cream cheese on a bagel is a typical treat for people who grew up in Jewish homes. "The Miracle of the Lox that Flies" is the story of the kind of food you can expect on any of El Al's breakfast flights to Tel Aviv. It is El Al's claim that this is a taste of the twentieth-century miracle of flight, so if you have never tried this snack, you will definitely have numerous chances a week during the summer to sample it. The art is perfect in this ad because the lox is positioned on the bagel to make the sandwich look like it has wings. This is a real attention-getter from the 1960s, and one that is unusually sophisticated for the times.

Next, we are treated to yet another El Al ad, this one from the early 1960s, also (figure 5.24e). The beauty of this ad is its copywriting, specifically its headline: "This Christmas, spend Chanukah in Israel." This is a polished and adroit turn of phrase created by a particularly experienced copy writer. It appeals to those celebrating either of the two holidays. Not until the early to mid-sixties do we begin to see the El Al creative work in advertising move into the more modern and cosmopolitan and less parochial approaches that we see in most big company advertising at the time.

The Levy's real Jewish rye bread ad (figure 5.24f) is one in the aforementioned series of ads that is ranked among some of the best ads in history.

In contrast to Lieder's narrow audience, Levy's was attempting to widen its audience with this campaign. The "You don't have to be Jewish" campaign for Levy's debuted in 1961 at a time following a decade or more of social, political, and racial unrest and violence. This era arrived after a brief period of peace and renewal upon the end of World War II. Almost everyone in US advertisements was White, and it would not be a stretch to say that the public perception of Jews was that they were White. At a time of civil rights legislation and Black rights groups coming into their own, there were not many Black people converting to Judaism. If they were converting from Christianity, then it was likely to be a conversion to Islam. One of Levy's ads (figure 2.1c) shows a Black child having taken a large bite out of a sandwich made with the company's Jewish rye bread. Malcolm X, an American Muslim minister and civil rights activist, liked the ad so much that he had his picture taken standing next to a poster of this specific ad in the campaign.

The campaign was a product of the firm Doyle Dane Bernbach. Bill Bernbach conceived the idea, Judy Protas wrote the copy, and William Taubin handled the design (Fox, 2014). These ads were run primarily as posters in the New York City subways. The ads were so striking in not only the headline, but in the photographs of "*conspicuously* non-Jewish New Yorkers" eating Jewish rye (Fox, 2014, n.p.). Back then, according to American stereotypical perceptions of Jews, an Asian person was *definitely* not Jewish. An Irish policeman simply *could not* be Jewish. An Italian mother—there are no Italian Jews, right? Taubin tested the ads on hundreds of people to make sure that they were not found to be offensive (ADC, 1981). The only image that truly represented people who could not possibly be mistaken for being Jewish was the Catholic choirboy in white robe. This campaign was wildly successful, its influence extending to a large national audience. The campaign was ended in the 1970s as more Americans came to learn about Judaism and Jews and as more people from non-White backgrounds began to convert to Judaism. Had this campaign been run in the 1980s, it probably would have fallen on its face. No longer was a non-White person "conspicuously" not Jewish. Today, more than 10% of Jews in America identify as persons of color ("American Jewish Population Estimates," 2015).

And, as Diamond and Bates attest, "Advertising's old-line, Republican WASP [White Anglo-Saxon Protestant] image began to fade, geographically, socially, and ethnically" (1992, p. 111). The creative staff members of an advertising agency must have their ears tuned in to the pulse of society to understand which concepts will fly and which will fail. If the budget allows, extensive interviewing of prospective viewers is always recommended when religious or political contexts appear in an ad. Another point in this regard is that some people not directly affected or targeted by a campaign can be offended on behalf of those who are targeted or embarrassed by an errant representation of themselves.

Figure 5.24g is a still from a 1977 Hebrew National commercial. As Levy's did in the "You don't have to be Jewish" campaign, Hebrew National is going after a much wider audience. There is absolutely no reason for a non-Jew to avoid eating a delicious kosher wiener—well, except for those who are vegetarians or vegans. It is better-tasting and all-beef, so why not? Appealing to a wide audience, the actor in the commercial is dressed as a Roman Catholic priest with an Irish accent. He attests to the deliciousness of the hot dog: "One taste is enough to convert you."

Jews do not think *only* about food and spirits, despite the evidence here. Considering that Jews make up only about 1.5–2% of the US population, there are relatively few businesses that cater only or predominantly to Jewish citizens and very few Jewish-oriented media outlets targeting a Jewish clientele (Pew Research, 2017). Other Jewish-related holy hype involves beer and wine and specifically Jewish-related amusements such as movies, plays, get-togethers, and holidays. Some of these are illustrated in figure 5.25.

In figure 5.25a, our eyes are treated to a beautifully conceived ad, once again for El Al. Many foods are associated with religious holidays or celebrations. The Passover Seder is probably the most well-known meal that is representative of food consumption in the midst of a backstory. It is a ritualistic dinner of symbolic foods explained through a storylike retelling of the Israelites' escape from Egyptian slavery as depicted in Exodus. Matwick and Matwick (2014) assert, "Through storytelling, cooking show hosts [and participants] perform a domestic ritual of cooking transformed from an ordinary practice into extraordinary" (p. 158). The airline's ad in figure 5.25a is wishing ad viewers a "Happy Passover" and, perhaps, implanting the idea that it might be unforgettable to spend this holiday in Israel, where the Passover story concludes. El Al is actually making the biblical story open up to visitors to the Holy Land. Passover, as the Jewish holiday that celebrates and recounts the Exodus narrative, implicates some artful sea-parting by Moses. This biblical miracle is illustrated as a feat accomplished by an El Al plane as it flies over the Atlantic from the United States and was conceived and produced by Israel's own DaColony agency, founded by Izzy Nesselrode. And, just like Moses, the agency attests to its belief that "actions speak louder than words." In this ad, the understated, sophisticated visualization of Moses's dividing of the Red Sea to enable his minions to cross is expertly done. And the bright sun in the distance represents this people as a "light unto the nations" (Isaiah 49:6), representing the goal, the Holy Land. There is so much meaning here with so little complication or fussiness. Only the essentials are necessary, and the essentials are what we see here. A beautiful, clean concept, and an alluring ad—in our estimation, one of the best-conceived and best-executed in this book.

Figure 5.25b, another ad for JDate.com, an online Jewish dating service from which thousands of Jews have found a marriage partner, we see an old theme in Judaism—persecution. And what is the gift for getting through 4,000 years of that—a non-Jewish dating service like Match.com? No, there is one custom-made for Jews searching for Jews. It wasn't until the late 1990s, when the internet became broadly accessible, that Jewish singles could find a resource other than mail-out lists or elderly matchmakers for meeting a large group of eligible Jewish bachelors and bachelorettes. Finally, there were choices. No longer was it necessary to wait for Aunt Sylvia to find a match and set up a blind date. JDate even greets one on the site's home page with "Mazel tov on finding love," that is, *good luck* on finding love. Holy hype advertising was made for a site like JDate. See another of its ads at figure 5.26e.

Looking at figure 5.25c, we are viewing another 1960s vintage El Al advertisement. The headline is "And on the 2,083,668th day, EL AL was created." What a brilliant line, a take-off of the story of creation from Genesis. There is no better place to begin than at the very beginning. God's light is radiating downward to earth from the heavens. When an ad is this good and this thoughtful, very little needs to be said by way of explanation. The designer landed it.

The ad at figure 5.25d is a Hanukkah poster for Chabad on Campus, art directed by Menachim Krinsky and copywritten by Justin Oberman. This Jewish holiday is called the Festival of Lights (Waldman, 2020, n.p.), and this was copywriter Oberman's jump-off point for the ad. Playing off of the *Star Wars* movie's popular phrase, "May the force be with you," Oberman writes, "May the light be with you." And, in acknowledgment of a dark side of life, the ad invites us to join the festival of the "light side." The fully lit Hanukkiah, or Hanukkah candelabrum, appears to be in the extended arms and hands of the good people in a nod to the lasers in *Star Wars*. Figure 5.25e is an illustration that is noticeable more for the name of the product than for any particular copy or art treatment. This is a kosher wine called "Unorthodox," a wine product that would ironically be especially suitable for Orthodox Jews. Imagine the father of an Orthodox family placing a bottle of Unorthodox wine in the center of the dining table. The ad layout is a bit unorthodox as well in that the wallpaper appears to be visible through the bottle.

Finally, figure 5.25f is yet another offering by El Al from 1967. We view what can only be God's fingers and hand doing the walking over the land of Israel. The question posed in the headline is: "Who guides the Guides?" Now, we know. It is God's hand that guides.

An ad that we so dearly wanted to add to the book is an excellent promotional piece for a "traditional Jewish Roman kitchen" located in Rome, Italy, named Nonna Betta. Unfortunately, the pandemic made it impossible for us to contact the owners. What says "Jewish-Italian food" more than an open Torah scroll made of raw pasta dough? Absolutely nothing, and that is exactly why this ad is so effective. For an English-speaking Jewish diner in Rome looking for kosher food, this image is like a sweet aroma that one simply must draw nearer to. This is innovative advertising.

Figure 5.26 offers a few more examples of really good Jewish or "Old-Testament-"inspired holy hype advertising. Figure 5.26a features a 1972 promotion for the Samson styling dryer by Schick. Is that Delilah looking over his shoulder? The connection between the biblical character and the dryer is hair. Samson had long hair that endowed him with almost superhuman strength. The names of biblical characters are sometimes used for the names of products, and their identifying characteristics sometimes inspire the gist of the advertising.

The 1932 ad for Daisy air rifles, figure 5.26b, is not exclusively Jewish, but it does take a story from the Jewish Scriptures, the Old Testament, that provides us with an understanding of this boy's daydream of fending off his enemies with the rifle. It is the story of David and Goliath, and the headline reads: "One shot from a sling . . . made a shepherd boy king!" The Daisy can take this young boy from a 98-pound weakling to a strong young man who will no longer be bullied. And, speaking of biblical strongmen like David, Nike tells its story of Samson in one expertly illustrated full-page ad in figure 5.26c from 1984. Nike would like us to believe that Samson got his superhuman strength not from his long hair, but from his new pair of Nike Airs. The headline, "Fitness for Men," reminds consumers that this ad is for a men's product, despite how many women may be attracted to the handsome, sinewy athlete pushing the pillars down. It is an ad for the Rake shoe, "Ultimate footwear for the court, the club, or the Colosseum."

Figure 5.26d is a return to the David and Goliath theme, which is a common scenario from the Bible used in advertising. Continental Bank is offering its commercial customers a sling shot to use against some of the giants of industry. The competitor, seen as the Philistine's foot wearing the sandal, is closing in on Continental Bank. The customer appears to be flummoxed, wondering how the bank's "tool" can possibly help him against his competition, who is mere steps away. The bank states in the ad, "We try to get to you with solutions before you realize you need them. So, we're always prepared and informed. Because in business, there's always a Goliath." Continental's tagline is: "Anticipating the needs of business." We cannot say how successful this particular ad and the others in the campaign were at the time (date unknown), but after 137 years in the industry, Chicago's Continental Bank went out of business in 1994. Perhaps its business clients were not particularly skilled at shooting rocks with a sling shot.

Figure 5.26e is one ad of a campaign for JDate, the Jewish matchmaking site we saw advertised in figure 5.24b and 5.25b. The narrative that runs through all of the ads is that the company has hired a bunch of older, Jewish ladies, who are coding geniuses, to work the graveyard shift. Each ad features one of the ladies. This lady knows a lot of computer code, but her key qualification is that she personally knows Shirley Finkelstein's grandson, who is obviously quite a catch for a nice Jewish girl.

A special ad we could not publish will provoke an audible chuckle from millions of people, especially those in the home design business. It may be an actual Absolut vodka ad or perhaps just a conceptual one, but it took a lot of creative and production skill to produce. The headline is "Absolut Tchotchkes." The bottle is adorned with little, gauche knickknacks. This ad uses the Yiddish word "tchotchke," pronounced chotch-kee with the accent on the first syllable. The more frequent use of it in national advertising goes to show how this word has eased its way into the English language like many other Yiddish words, such as "maven," "klutz," "chutzpah," "mazel tov," "mensch," "bubbe," and many others. A tchotchke is an inexpensive, ornamental knickknack, sometimes a souvenir and often of questionable taste. My family and I once drove by an interesting home in a moderately priced neighborhood. The front lawn sported about 40 cartoony ceramic creatures of all phyla, mostly vertebrates such as pink flamingos, alligators, and ducks. From that day forward, we referred to that house as "Tchotchkes R Us."

At this point, we leave the Jewish holy hype and go full-on Christian with the Last Supper, an extremely prevalent theme in holy hype.

THE LAST SUPPER

The theme of the Last Supper, based on a painting by Leonardo da Vinci in 1498, is one of the most caricatured artistic compositions of all time. Discovering a unique situation in which to create a parody of it can be an irresistible exercise for an artist with a great sense of humor. A satire of it played out in a US surgery tent in the movie *Mash*. The candlelit table was prepared for 13 doctors in scrubs. Other versions have been created for *The Simpsons*, *Battlestar Galactica*, *The Expendables 2*, *The Sopranos*, and many more examples that were designed as promotional posters for upcoming films and television shows in varying degrees of fidelity to the original (Plumb, 2012). One particularly accurate rendition, unusually true to its Renaissance inspiration, is for an episode of "House." At first count, one might catch the error of arranging only 12 people in the scene, but at closer examination, it is obvious that the anesthetized patient, whose prostrate position functions as the long table in Da Vinci's original, is the 13th figure in the dramatic construction.

Figure 5.27 illustrates four scenarios, all of which were used for advertising purposes.

In figure 5.27a, we see a clever yet elegant adaptation of the Last Supper for the coronavirus age. In Jerusalem on March 15, 2020, gatherings became restricted to no more than 10 people, with required social distancing of 6 feet, 7 inches of space between people. So, Jews could pull together a minyan (10-person minimum) for worshipping, but poor Jesus could not accommodate his 12 apostles. In an effort to flatten the curve of new cases of COVID-19, the Ministry of Culture and Information Policy of Ukraine disseminated this eye-catching and unforgettable poster for its citizens. It is titled "Social Distancing," and it is a prescription for stopping the spread of the virus. Jesus sits alone, dutifully wearing a mask. The apostles must be seated for dinner a safe distance away.

Figure 5.27 a) This is part of Act Responsible, an association to promote socially responsible ads all over the world. "Social distancing. Staying home and keeping social distance is the most effective way to stop the spread of the virus." b) Paddy Power ad. This billboard was taken down due to censorship in Ireland. "There's a place for fun and games." c) Ad for the Folsum Street Fair. d) Photo of side of the building in which Mom's Kitchen restaurant operates in Georgia. *Source: a) © Ministry of Culture and Information Policy of Ukraine, intended for public distribution. Image retrieved from adforum.com. b) © Paddy Power; no longer in business. c) © Folsom Street Fair. Screenshot retrieved from Folsom Street Fair store. d) Image courtesy of © Barbara Aleene Edwards.*

PaddyPower.com (figure 5.27b), an online gaming site, turns the tables on the Old Master. The illustration is correct in the number of people sitting at the table, but they are not eating. They are involved in some heavy-duty gambling. In a 2020 survey of ours about the offensiveness of ads, this was rated as one of the most offensive. Respondents commented on the perceived blasphemy of showing Jesus engaged in such sinful activity.

The ad in figure 5.27c is a fairly well-known artistic take-off on the Last Supper for the Folsom Street Fair. This event in San Francisco, California, is for leather enthusiasts and other fetishists of all sexual and gender identities. Its website explains that its mission is to

> unite the adult alternative lifestyle communities with safe venues for self-expression and exciting entertainment. Our events raise funds to sustain SF Bay Area–based and national charities. We value sexual freedom, diversity, and volunteerism. All of our events are adult-oriented, sex-positive fetish events. (Folsom Street Fair, 2020, n.p.)

The parody in this promotional poster goes to show how versatile the Last Supper theme truly is, and it does not even have to include 13 people to be effective. Versatility aside, there may be opposition to such a holy hype endeavor. There was a swift and vociferous public response against this poster. Eckstrom (2007) of religionnews.com called it "Indigestion over the Last Supper," stating:

> Miller Brewing Co. has apologized for agreeing to sponsor San Francisco's Folsom Street Fair—specifically an ad that parodied the Last Supper with various and sundry sex toys. The annual Folsom Street event is the type of sexuality-on-public-display ("Get a Room!") that makes many roll their eyes at the city by the bay.

In response to vehement pushback and boycott threats against Miller from the Catholic League and others, festival organizer Andy Copper proudly remarked: "Folsom Street Events acknowledges that many of the people in the leather and fetish communities are spiritual and that this poster image is a way of expressing that side of the community's interests and beliefs" (Eckstrom, 2007, n.p.). He further added, "The irony is that da Vinci was widely considered to be homosexual."

Much ink was spilled in the raucous public bickering. Heather Cassell (2007) of the *Bay Area Reporter* wrote about how the Concerned Women for America (CWA) entered the fray:

> "Scripture says that God is not mocked, yet it doesn't stop people from trying," Matt Barber, policy director for cultural issues with CWA, said in the release.

> "As evidenced by this latest stunt, open ridicule of Christianity is unfortunately very common within much of the homosexual community."

Now, some would feel that any publicity is good publicity, but advertisers must weigh the value of the consequences. In the end, Miller Brewing did not take its event endorsement away—just its logo from this particular poster.

Last in this category, figure 5.27d is in this book through the courtesy of photographer Barbara Edwards of Tallahassee, Florida. She teaches traditional film-based and digital photography at Tallahassee Community College. Edwards keeps her camera nearby for great "gets" such as this photo of a rendition of the Last Supper. It is a mural painted on the exterior wall of the restaurant called Mom's Kitchen in Preston, Georgia. When Edwards's photo was taken in 2008, Preston's population was 418. Today, the population has mushroomed to 2,022, and Mom's Kitchen remains in the same building. A person new to the area might wonder what a painting of the Last Supper says about eating at Mom's. Will it be your last supper? It could be a recipe for disaster, but the ratings of the food and staff online are all high, averaging just under 5 out of 5 (TripAdvisor, 2020, n.p.). The hot sun is wreaking havoc on the Last Supper mural, so we are grateful for the photographer's interest in preserving memories of rural Georgia.

An ad for Mortein rat poison, not shown, features 13 rodents dining on cheddar, Roquefort, and brie cheese, the food item most people believe is what rats prefer over any other edible item. It must be their favorite food because it is what scientists have always provided as the reward for those smart rats that can make it through a difficult maze. Deviating from the layout in Da Vinci's original, we are given the view of the neighborhood outside this rodent residence on a cul-de-sac, presumed to be inside the wall of a house like the ones we see out the windows behind the table. Surprisingly, considering that the Jesus figure in this art is a rodent, our survey participants found this variation on the Last Supper theme quite humorous and not at all offensive.

An ad that would have competed for a top spot among the finest of all of the ads in this book would be one for the International Organization for Animal Protection, a nongovernmental organization (NGO) whose mission is animal advocacy and preservation. Translated from the Italian, the headline is: "One of you betrays us 150,000 times every year." The actual poster accommodates 12 dogs and the one human, who is sitting in Judas's place. The dog in the center is the canine Jesus in this arrangement. This means that the traitor, the human being, represents the human race, which is responsible for the deaths of 150,000 canines each year in Italy. In Italy, this version of the Last Supper is especially pertinent to the significance of Da Vinci's painting. This advertisement is the one Last Supper illustration most germane to the intent of the message—betrayal. Da Vinci's original depicts the reaction of Jesus's apostles to his announcement "One of you will betray me" (Suresh, 2019, n.p.). Designing a parody of a well-known image can lay claim to a certain amount of inherent attention-getting power, but the ad that will leave an indelible mark on a viewer will always be one that unmistakably matches its art to its message.

MOSES

The Moses theme is unusually applicable for advertising purposes because Moses is a figure of the Bible well-known for his major role in several different situations. The three most useful in this regard are: (a) Moses who parts the Red Sea; (b) Moses who receives the law directly from God on Mount Sinai; and (c) Moses coming down the mountain with the tablets. We offer 10 ads that have succeeded in the use of holy hype that represent any of these themes. There were so many of these that were excellent examples, it became a difficult task to select only 10. The first half dozen can be seen in figure 5.28.

The ad at figure 5.28a is for Moses Vodka, an alcoholic beverage produced in Finland by Shaman Spirits, Ltd. The company writes on its website:

> Moses Vodka was originally created to be the first super premium vodka certified kosher all-year-round. The brand has since evolved to be something far greater, a symbol of faith, history, tradition, and culture. As Moses did himself, the brand is built to represent similar values and characteristics, such as leadership, innovation, and integrity. (Moses Vodka, 2020)

The label on the vodka bottle shows Moses parting the Red Sea. Recently, the Moses line of products has broadened to include whiskey, gin, and arak. There is a date-flavored vodka that used to be bottled in a container much like the bottle in this ad. It appears that the marketing is in a state of flux because the date-flavored vodka, a product unique in the world, and the other products are now shown in a different type of bottle with all new art in the labeling. The new logo and label art no longer feature an image of Moses. The cleaner, simpler, non-biblical graphics will allow the company to separate itself from the original messages related to Judaism or the Bible if it so desires, but it remains to be seen which approach will be more successful. We find the ad in figure 5.28a to be compelling with its beautiful take on Moses parting the reeds to expose a path through the sea and explaining that Moses accomplished much more than did Van Gogh.

Figure 5.28 a) Ad for Moses Vodka. "Van Gogh may have cut his ear off, but Moses parted a sea." b) Conceptual ad for the American Association of Advertising Agencies. "However powerful a message is, some people may not buy it." c) Hawaiian Tropic ad. Woman wearing the Hawaiian Tropic lotion repels the water. d) Ad for the Newspaper Advertising Bureau of New York. "People who know the power of words put them in print." e) Stock image of Moses revised for use in the American Association of Advertising Agencies ad, figure 5.28b. f) Gracemats placemat. *Source: a) Image courtesy of © Shaman Spirits. b) Image courtesy © American Association for Advertising Agencies. c) Image courtesy of © Hawaiian Tropic. d) © Newspaper Advertising Bureau of New York, no longer in business. e) Stock image retrieved from DepositPhotos.com. f) © Gracemats, image courtesy of Steven Diniaco, owner.*

Figure 5.28b makes use of an illustration of Moses descending Mount Sinai with what the advertisers call "a powerful message." The ad art and copy work together to construct a particularly apt message from the advertising industry as represented by the American.

Association of Advertising Agencies, or 4A's, as it now calls itself. And not only is the organization's message appropriate, but it also suggests the essence of good advertising in one concise headline: "However powerful a message is, some people may not buy it." It brilliantly reduces the practice of advertising to its essence. This ad clarifies for the viewer, the potential purchaser of advertising services, the importance of (a) a powerful message; (b) a deep understanding of the audience; (c) a clear vision of who the ad is targeting or is meant for; (d) realizing that the message must be communicated properly with the right art and the right copy; and (e) testing the art, copy, and composition to evaluate its effectiveness in turning audience members into "believers" willing to "buy" the message. Artists and copywriters cannot convert those who are dead-set against change, but a certain percentage will be open to facts and persuasion and amenable to conversion. This organization makes use of a memorable tagline at the very bottom right of the layout: "Advertising. Another word for freedom of choice."

The next ad we review is the one for Hawaiian Tropic at figure 5.28c. Hawaiian Tropic leads us to believe that the waters will part for us when we simply apply its extremely waterproof sunblock lotion. Drops of H_2O just bounce off of one's repellent-enabled body, allowing a straight shot across a pool or natural body of water. And when you get to the other side, your water resistance is still intact.

Figure 5.28d is the fourth in our assortment of Moses-related, holy hype advertisements, and it is on behalf of the Newspaper Advertising Bureau of New York. The date is not known, but this entity stopped publishing ads in that name in 1992. The art in this ad is an illustration of Moses pointing to the ninth commandment on one of the two tablets he is holding. The commandments are carved in stone and written in Hebrew. That commandment is translated to English in the ad as "Thou shalt not bear false witness against your neighbor," and so those of us who know to which commandment Moses is pointing are immediately alerted to the truthfulness of the ad, or at least to the intention of truthfulness. Not understanding the Hebrew does not detract from the ad's effectiveness. It actually implies authenticity in the message. The headline asserts, "People who know the power of words put them in print." We should allow some creative license here in that the One who put these words in print was not a human. The copy begins, "When you have something to say, no other medium can match the power of the printed word," alluding to the fact that the original Ten Commandments are carved in stone. The ad ends with a statement attesting to its comportment with the ninth commandment: "This series of surprising statements is supported by Roy Morgan Research."

The following ad is not an ad at all. It is a striking stock illustration available on several stock photography sites. After very careful scrutiny, we believe this is the illustration used in figure 5.28b. We cannot be sure, though, because we do not have the date of the advertisement.

We were unable to find the type of evidence that would lead us to believe that it might be the other way around—that is, the illustration from figure 5.28b could be the original, and someone could have come along, made some changes by adding pen strokes and sold it to the stock image sites. AAAAs could not find any verifiable information that would enlighten us to the provenance of this picture or even the date. IStockphotography.com did provide information claiming the engraver to be Gustave Dore (1832–1883). It is "Moses comes down from the mountain with the tablets of law in his hand." It was published in 1875 as an illustration for Exodus 32. The precise Bible or religious publication is not known. At the time of the publication of the ad and the placement on the sites, this was art that was in the public domain.

The sixth "ad" of this series of holy hype based on a Moses theme, figure 5.28f, is another visually compelling ad and probably appeals to just the right audience—kids. Suggesting Moses parting the Red Sea, in this rendition, there is no Moses, but somehow, a different liquid is being parted—the milk in the cereal bowl. We consider this an ingenious way to bring Moses's achievement into the twenty-first century! The placemats, conceived by Steven Diniaco and sold as "Gracemats," deliver on a promise to teach children the stories of the Bible, detailing a separate story on each mat. The cross used as the "t" in Gracemats indicates that this product is a Christian interpretation of the Bible, which encompasses both the Old and New Testaments. The ad ends with the tagline, "The power of the Bible now has a place at the table." The inclusion of religious images and themes is perfectly relevant to the product.

Among the ads not shown is one from the Surfrider Foundation Europe, a subsidiary of the original Surfrider Foundation. The organization is a group of like-minded people who focus on the protection and preservation of the earth's waters against pollution and climate change for the use and enjoyment of all. The art is reminiscent of that in figure 5.28b. The headline reads, "Help us keep the ocean clean." The parting-of-the-Red-Sea Moses theme is employed to show viewers how much garbage has accumulated on our ocean floor—if only someone could divide the water long enough for us to capture the awful sight. The Surfrider Foundation has done just that for us. And thanks to Moses, we discover at the bottom of the sea an old sedan, which tells us that we have brought Moses to the twenty-first century to show us the sins that are usually invisible to us. Though the car may make for a laughable scene, what is not laughable is the amount of detritus we people of the world introduce into the waters of the globe each day. Indeed, it is more than just another plague to endure on Moses's exodus. This ad was produced by Young & Rubicam of Paris. The creative talent were: Herve Riffault, Creative

Director; Sebastien Guinet, Art Director; Josselin Pacreau, Copywriter; and Gerard Trignac, Illustrator.

The next several ads (figure 5.29) in the Moses category are more examples of innovative holy hype in print advertising. One prime example of secular holy hype displayed is a poster for a Jewish film festival. Many large

Figure 5.29 a) 2016 ad for the Toronto Jewish Film Festival. b) Conceptual ad for Levi's Water<less jeans. c) Ad for Moses Vodka. "Savour deliverance." d) Ad for Caparol paint. "Then he raised the roller and the waters were divided." *Source: a) Image courtesy of © Toronto Jewish Film Festival. b) Concept by Jelena Djakovic, jelenadjakovic.com and illustrations by Brandon De Aguero, brandondeaguero.com. Image courtesy of Djakovic and De Aguero. c) Image courtesy of © Shaman Spirits. d) ©Caparol. Image provided courtesy of ABK Communication. Designed by ABK Communication, Tbilisi, Georgia. Creative director: Nikusha Motsonelidze. Art director: David Chabashvili. Copywriters: Mishka Sekhniashvili and Goga Andtidze. Graphic designers: David Tomas and Tekla Baramashvili. CG Artist: Gabo Gatchava.*

cities around the world host one of these Jewish-oriented cinema events, and all promote their festivals with posters. Figure 5.29a shows a poster ad for the 24th annual Jewish Film Festival of Toronto of 2016. Not only does the Moses theme relate to the explicit purpose of the specifically Jewish event, but also, several aspects of the illustration pertain to the deeper meaning of the festival, identification with the Jewish people. There is nothing unwarranted or nitpicking about this metaphorical conceptualization; it is communicated without obsessive attention to every detail in the biblical story. In addition, the image is remarkably compelling and memorable, probably owing to its dramatic use of light and the use of at least two characteristics of the Moses story. Not only do we see the mustachioed and bearded man descending from the doorway down an aisle slanted toward the first rows of seats alluding to Moses's walk *down* Mount Sinai, but in each arm is an extra-large box of popcorn, as essential to the movie-viewing experience as is the code on Moses's tablets to the Jewish living experience. Certainly, this is not to say that eating popcorn is equivalent in importance to receiving the Ten Commandments—just that each activity is essential to its own distinct subject matter and situational set of conditions. The man is bathed in the light radiating from the concession area, implying God's involvement in the action through His aura shining down from the heavens. Finally, the aisle bisects the audience seating into two sections, like Moses's parting of the sea. There is no copy required to explain the photo. The viewer likely "gets it" from the moment it is perceived. An examination of the archive of this organization's promotional posters since 2001 confirms they do not use a story that must be told in words. The art is created to be sufficient to deliver the message.

The second ad in this group of Moses-themed presentations, figure 5.29b, is a conceptual ad designed by Jelena Djakovic and Brandon Deaguero as a university project at Virginia Tech in a course focusing on art direction. The team of two did not have the opportunity to select a brand-name product because the professor assigned them Levi's Water<less jeans. This new product uses up to 96% less water during the jeans' finishing fabrication process. This is how Djakovic describes the creative process for this project:

> During a preliminary check-in with our professor, I was brainstorming ways to portray how little water it costs to fabricate Levi's Water<Less jeans. Thoughts of "repelling," "separating," and "saving" water came to mind. The idea of Moses parting the Red Sea ran through my head and I giggled to myself—the professor then asked me what I was thinking of, and he loved the idea and told us to run with biblical references for our advertisement campaign.

We particularly like the focus on the jeans in that this pair is in color and looks to be more three-dimensional. The simplicity of the lines composing the context add to the way the jeans stand out. This ad would grab our attention, without a doubt. The economy of graphic elements means that no gimmick is needed for drawing in the viewer.

The ad at figure 5.29c is another for Moses Vodka, the bottle for which displays Moses leading the Israelites across the Red Sea in a 40-year trek from Egypt to the Promised Land to find freedom. The headline appropriately invites the viewer to "savor deliverance."

The ad for Caparol waterproof paints, figure 5.29d, reminds us of the Hawaiian Tropic promotion for a water-repellant product (see figure 5.28c) with its horizontal layout and parting of the "seas." In fact, one of the exceptional qualities of this paint is that it can be applied even to a waterway, as the ad explains, "Then he raised the roller and the waters were divided." This is a God-sized paint roller separating the seas to cover the ocean floor. The hand controlling the roller is not seen, but it originates in the heavens. Does the use of biblically styled rhetoric but without any mention of God or Moses manifest as any less provocative than others similar to its approach? This is the kind of judgment an agency must make before going to print.

PRAYER AND WORSHIP

When examining holy hype in any sense, an advertising theme that must be studied is that of prayer and worship. Basically, it is an individual and congregational activity that is expected by most religions. We purposely keep this discussion superficial and generic to avoid a discussion of religion per se. For example, Christianity and Judaism follow the Ten Commandments, the fourth of which states, "Remember the Sabbath day to keep it holy." This implies a rest from work and worshipping in a community of like-minded co-religionists, although it does not command worship. Islamists are taught to pray five times a day. Therefore, prayer is important in any discussion of holy hype.

In figure 5.30, we see seven examples of holy hype featuring prayer. Coming out of World War II and until the mid-1960s, the American social landscape experienced a surge in religious expression, attendance at houses of worship, and public and private prayer. This was America's highest level of religiosity over the past 75 years (Grant, 2014). Ads in figures 5.30a, b, c, d, and e are examples of this immodest display of religious fervor by large companies that realized this type of ad resonated with the newly devout people of the American public. Figure 5.30a was published by Frigidaire in

Figure 5.30 a) 1928 ad for Frigidaire. "Wild turkeys browned and golden and venison and purple grapes for these we offer thanks." b) 1936 ad for Eveready batteries. c) 1955 ad for Massachusetts Mutual Life Insurance Company. "In this season it is well to remember that the hope of our world rests on faith." d) Sunbeam Bakers billboard. "Not by bread alone." e) 1947 US Department of Agriculture Forest Service ad for New Jersey. Smokey Bear kneels in prayer, saying ". . . and please make people careful, amen." The right side of this ad, not shown, employs the new slogan (1947), "Remember—Only you can prevent forest fires." f) Listermint ad. "Bad breath affects those closest to you." g) 2003 ad for Absolut Vanilla. "Absolut Awe." *Source: a) © Frigidaire, public domain image. b) © Eveready, public domain image. c) Image courtesy of © Massachusetts Mutual Life Insurance Company. d) Image courtesy of photographer Susan Sarapin. e) U.S. Department of Agriculture Forest Service. f) Image courtesy of © Listermint. g) ©Absolut, image courtesy of Leon Steele, photographer.*

1928. In a celebration of Thanksgiving, the Puritan family members pray to God in unison to give thanks for the harvest of food and the harvest of industry. All in a hands-folded position with heads bowed except for the father looking upward, they thank the Lord for "Endless research and experiment, a divine curiosity, the open mind . . . these [that] have brought new products and a new and better way of living." The country got through the war, and needed an outlet for thanking the Lord. Advertising became one. In 1936, at the beginning of the trend, the Eveready company advertised its flashlight batteries as an essential part of praying activity at night (figure 5.30b). Using an emotional approach to a scene that most parents can relate to, it shows a little boy in his onesie pajamas with a drop seat, kneeling at bedside with his best friend watching. With his flashlight positioned to allow just enough light and his hands resting on the bed, clasped in prayer position, he bows his head to say his bedtime prayers.

Figure 5.30c is Massachusetts Mutual's famous 1955 ad that owed its broad viewership to the inclusion of a Norman Rockwell illustration, whose photorealistic style added nuances of folksiness, facial expressions, and special lighting to capture the small yet significant moments of everyday life. In this ad, Rockwell represents prayer as that which is done from a church pew. Illustrating a family that could represent any religion, Rockwell artistically tells the story of faith. The daffodils on the pew before them are the only giveaway that this is happening in a Christian church. In Christianity, daffodils represent eternal life and a rebirth. Had the flowers been omitted, any other religious tradition for which its adherents pray in pews could have been included in the message. But remember, this is 1955, and "inclusion" and "diversity" were not yet universal goals. This concept does sneak through a bit in the copy, though. "Through faith, our forefathers—men of varied faiths—built this country." Next, Sunbeam Bakers focuses on Little Miss Sunbeam in prayer on billboards all over the nation (figure 5.30d). It uses a play on words as does much holy hype advertising. Sunbeam is a popular brand of bread, and the headline of the billboard is the biblical "Not by bread alone." This is an abbreviated version of Matthew 4:4 and Luke 4:4, the second of which states: "And Jesus answered him, saying, 'It is written: 'Man shall **not** live **by bread alone**, but by every word of God.'"

A poster in figure 5.30e, attributed to the US Department of Agriculture in 1947, uses the fairly new character, Smokey Bear, created to keep our forests and their creatures safe from forest fires. It is a rare find because it is one of a handful of representations of Smokey praying. He asks God to teach humans to change their careless behavior toward anything that causes a danger to our forests and wildlife. He prays, "and please make people careful, amen." The cut-off right side of the ad states, "Remember—Only you can prevent forest fires." This slogan was introduced the same year.

Figures 5.30f and 5.30g are two more examples of excellent holy hype. At bottom left in figure 5.30f, we see a Listermint mouthwash ad. The people in the far right of the ad are small, so this ad should be run as a half-page or full-page horizontal placement. A priest is standing near the altar, arms extended out to his sides and upward as though beseeching God and his congregants. And yet, not even the passion and transcendent nature of prayer can make us impervious to all earthly odors. The "huddled mass" of worshippers seated at the far end of the sanctuary recoils at the priest's halitosis, which wafts into their pews every time he opens his mouth. They are all covering their noses with handkerchiefs. The tagline positioned near the bottle of mouthwash at lower right is this: "Bad breath affects those closest to you." The bottle of Listermint is radiating a heavenly aura. If the priest had used this product before his sermon, the congregation would find it easier to praise God in the right frame of mind. The final ad of this arrangement of seven is figure 5.30g, an ad for Absolut Vanilia (vanilla) vodka, called Absolut Awe. In this very clever design, photographed by Leon Steele, the bottle of vodka takes a central position around which six vanilla waffle cream cookies bow to the bottle in adoration through prayer. The waffle cookies do not need to say anything because their action says it all. Many religions enjoin the faithful to bow, kneel, or prostrate themselves during prayer, just as these cookies do in the presence of the vodka bottle. Only space constraints prevent us from showing at least a dozen other excellent examples of Absolut holy hype.

CONCLUSION

The three "verses" of Chapter 5 have focused on the most important elements of secular holy hype through brief summaries of the visual and textual advertising approaches in 268 unique visuals, of which about a handful were for nonprofit causes looking for donations. By doing this, we have expounded upon basic principles of effective advertising that jumps off the pages of work accomplished by hundreds of design and copywriting professionals over the past 140 years of modern advertising. We have just begun to tap into the dozens of topics that emerge from biblical and other religious sources and the commercial industries to which they could apply. A cursory run-through of these ads and descriptions of others comes up with more than 65 business types, including some as seemingly ill-suited for religious treatment as pesticides, cosmetic surgery, men's socks, vacuum cleaners, airlines, batteries, and suntan lotions. We hope that this has whet your appetite for using and appreciating this form of advertising in the marketplace. We also hope that these serve as inspiration for ways to reimagine how to incorporate common biblical rhetoric in uncommon ways.

Chapter 6 delves into apparel and other artifacts of mostly Christian culture that people wear to advertise belief in God or their chosen religion. It is truly amazing how many sacred images and words end up in jewelry, wall décor, knickknacks, and bumper stickers—sometimes as personal religious expression or as humorous statements of the recognition of religion as kitsch.

REFERENCES

AdAge. (2003). Absolut Vodka. https://adage.com/article/adage-encyclopedia/absolut-vodka/98299

ADC. (1981). William Taubin. http://adcglobal.org/hall-of-fame/william-taubin/

Ads of the World. (2020). Last Supper. https://www.adsoftheworld.com/media/print/last_supper_1

Akh, M. (2019). When soap companies used God to sell their products. Aworkstation.com. https://aworkstation.com/when-soap-companies-used-god-to-sell-their-products/

"American Jewish Population Estimates." (2015). Steinhardt Social Research Institute. https://ajpp.brandeis.edu/documents/2015/JewishPopulationDataBrief2015.pdf

Athan, L. L. (2020). What is ouzo? *The Spruce Eats*. https://www.thespruceeats.com/greek-ouzo-anyone-1705998

Beeradvocate.com. (2020). Belgian Tripel. https://www.beeradvocate.com/beer/styles/58/

Boorstein, M. (2016). The many meanings of Rio's massive Christ statue. *The Washington Post.* https://www.washingtonpost.com/news/acts-of-faith/wp/2016/08/09/the-many-meanings-of-rios-massive-christ-statue/

Braun, G. (2020). *Personal email communication.*

Brenan, M. (2019). 40% of Americans believe in creationism. *Gallup Politics*. https://news.gallup.com/poll/261680/americans-believe-creationism.aspx

Burns, A., & Schildhause, C. (2018). "Stop crying and fight your father": 'Seinfeld' writers tell us how Festivus came to be. *UPROXX.* https://uproxx.com/tv/seinfeld-festivus-true-story/

Casasanto, D. (2009). Embodiment of abstract concepts: Good and bad in right- and left-handers. *Journal of Experimental Psychology: General, 138*(3), 351–367. doi: 10.1037/a0015854

Cassell, H. (2007). Folsom art draws fire from the right. *The Bay Area Reporter.* https://www.ebar.com/news///238305

CCS. (2020). https://shop.ccs.com/alien-workshop-born-again-skateboard-deck-8-25

Centers for Disease Control. (2020). MERS-CoV Photos. https://www.cdc.gov/coronavirus/mers/photos.html#:~:text=Coronaviruses%20derive%20their%20name%20from,%2C%E2%80%9D%20or%20halo.

Christianity Today Staff. (2019). What to give up for Lent 2019? Consider Twitter's top 100 ideas. https://www.christianitytoday.com/news/2019/march/what-to-give-up-for-lent-2019-consider-twitter-top-ideas.html

Complete Jewish Bible. (1998). https://www.biblegateway.com/passage/?search=Genesis+1%3A26&version=CJB

Cosgrove, B. (2014). The photo that changed the face of AIDS. *Time.* https://time.com/3503000/behind-the-picture-the-photo-that-changed-the-face-of-aids/

Cot, P. (1944). The French air force never fought! *Flying, 34*, 21.

Crean, E. (2004). Of Jacko and Jesus Juice. *CBS News*. https://www.cbsnews.com/news/of-jacko-and-jesus-juice/

Cureton, K. (n.d.). The ten commandments: Foundation of American society. *Family Research Council*. https://www.frc.org/booklet/the-ten-commandments-foundation-of-american-society-

Diamond, E., & Bates, S. (1992). *The spot: The rise of political advertising on television*. MIT Press.

"Do Jews believe in angels?" (2020). My Jewish learning. https://www.myjewishlearning.com/article/angels/

Dolsten, J. (2018). The Super Bowl's best commercial starred a rabbi. *Jewish Telegraph Agency*. https://www.jta.org/2018/02/05/united-states/the-super-bowls-best-commercial-starred-a-rabbi

Eckstrom, K. (2007). Indigestion over the Last Supper. *Religion News Service*. https://religionnews.com/2007/10/30/indigestion-over-the-last-supper/

Eisend, M. (2018). Explaining the use and effects of humour in advertising: an evolutionary perspective. *International Journal of Advertising*, *37*(4), 526–547.

Elliott, S. (1997). Humor and a "higher authority" help spice up a new campaign for Hebrew National franks. *The New York Times*. https://www.nytimes.com/1997/05/23/business/humor-higher-authority-help-spice-up-new-campaign-for-hebrew-national-franks.html

Erizanu, P. (2020). Posters depicting doctors and medical staff as saints deemed "satanist" in Romania. *The Calvert Journal*. https://www.calvertjournal.com/articles/show/11780/posters-doctors-medical-staff-saints-romania

Falls, J., & Deckers, E. (2012). *No bullshit social media: The all-business, no-hype guide to social media marketing*. Pearson Education, Inc.

Feldman, B. (2018). The best meme of the year is T-posing. Intelligencer. *New York Magazine*. https://nymag.com/intelligencer/2018/12/why-the-best-meme-of-the-year-is-t-posing.html

Floros, G. (2020). 10 most controversial United Colors of Benetton ads. *Friendly Stock*. https://friendlystock.com/top-ten-controversial-united-colors-of-benetton-ads/

Folsom Street Fair. (2020). https://www.folsomstreetevents.org/about-folsom-street-events/

Foubert, J. D., Watson, A., Brosi, M., & Fuqua, M. B. D. (2012). Explaining the wind: How self-identified born-again Christians define what *born again* means to them. *Journal of Psychology and Christianity*, *51*(3), 215–226.

Fox, M. (2014). Judy Protas, writer of slogan for Levy's Real Jewish Rye, dies at 91. *The New York Times*. https://www.nytimes.com/2014/01/12/business/judy-protas-writer-of-slogan-for-levys-real-jewish-rye-dies-at-91.html?_r=0

Franklin, N. (2018). *The supernatural, the beautiful, and the halo. Thesis for honors in studio art*. Wellesley.

Fried, Rabbi Y. D. (2017). Angels throughout Torah. *Texas Jewish Post*. https://tjpnews.com/angels-throughout-torah/

Furman, E. (2012). Whiskey business: The many myths of Jack Daniel. https://www.mentalfloss.com/article/31487/whiskey-business-many-myths-jack-daniel

Gerencser, B. (2020). The life and times of Bruce Gerencser. *Evangelical Swear Words*. https://brucegerencser.net/2020/05/christian-swear-words/

Grant, T. (2014). The rise and fall of religiosity in the United States. *Religion News*. https://religionnews.com/2014/12/11/1940s-america-wasnt-religious-think-rise-fall-american-religion/

Grossman, C. L. (2015). Fishy religion-spoof: Do you "sea" fun or blasphemy? *Washington Post*. https://www.washingtonpost.com/national/religion/fishy-religion-spoof-do-you-sea-fun-or-blasphemy/2015/07/28/21edc00c-3562-11e5-b835-61ddaa99c73e_story.html

Hameed, S. (2018). What do Muslims believe about angels. *About Islam*. https://aboutislam.net/reading-islam/understanding-islam/what-do-muslims-believe-about-angels/

Hathaway, J. (2018). How the "T-pose" became a meme. *Daily Dot*. https://www.dailydot.com/unclick/t-pose-meme/

"History." (2020). Communication. https://en.doyouspeakgirbaud.com/communication

Hochman, D. (1993). You don't have to be Jewish to love this business. *The New York Times*. https://www.nytimes.com/1993/04/04/business/you-dont-have-to-be-jewish-to-love-this-business.html#:~:text=Its%20target%3A%20Frank%20Perdue%20and,Not%20surprisingly%2C%20Frank%20Perdue%20Inc

Holyblog. (2020). The halo: Origins and meaning. https://www.holyart.com/blog/religious-items/the-halo-origins-and-meaning/

Hopler, W. (2018). Hindu angels of the Bhagavad Gita. *Learn Religions*. https://www.learnreligions.com/angels-of-the-bhagavad-gita-124013

Jack Daniel's Distillery. (2020). Born to make whiskey. *The Story of Jack Daniel's*. https://www.jackdaniels.com/en-us/our-story

Jones, P. A. (2015). 18 everyday expressions borrowed from the Bible. https://www.mentalfloss.com/article/61964/18-everyday-expressions-borrowed-bible

Kaplan, K. (2014). DNA ties Ashkenazi Jews to group of just 330 people from Middle Ages. *L. A. Times*. https://www.latimes.com/science/sciencenow/la-sci-sn-ashkenazi-jews-dna-diseases-20140909-story.html

Keller, G. F. (2020). The knots of the Franciscan cord. https://stfrancis.clas.asu.edu/article/knots-franciscan-cord

Klee, P. (1961). "Creative credo." In J. Spiller (Ed.) *Paul Klee notebooks, Volume 1: The thinking eye* (pp. 76–80), Percy Lund, Humphries & Co, Ltd.

Knox, I. (1963). The traditional roots of Jewish humor. *Judaism*, *12*(3), 327.

Laird, P. W. (1998). *Advertising progress: American business and the rise of consumer marketing*. Baltimore, MD: The Johns Hopkins University Press.

Levine, D. S. (2004). Angels, devils, and censors in the brain. *ComPlexus*, *2*(1), 35–59.

Lincoln Motor Company Media Center. (2019). https://media.lincoln.com/content/lincolnmedia/lna/us/en.html

Lipka, M. (2019). 10 facts about atheists. *Pew Research Center*. https://www.pewresearch.org/fact-tank/2019/12/06/10-facts-about-atheists/

Louviere, B. (2020). Beer and spirit: A confluence of medieval traditions in brewing and monasticism. Honors thesis at the University of Iowa.

Mallia, K. L. (2009). From the sacred to the profane: A critical analysis of the changing nature of religious imagery in advertising. *Journal of Media and Religion*, *8*(3), 172–190.

Melia, D. (2005). Michael Jackson fuming over "Jesus Juice" wine. *Gigwise*. https://www.gigwise.com/news/10438/

"Moroni, Son of Mormon." (2020). https://www.churchofjesuschrist.org/study/scriptures/gs/moroni-son-of-mormon?lang=eng

Moses Vodka. (2020). https://www.mosesvodka.com/about

Muslim Comedian Roundtable. (2015). *The Takeaway*. https://www.wnycstudios.org/podcasts/takeaway/segments/jokes-and-about-muslims

"Nirvana." (n.d.). https://www.vocabulary.com/dictionary/nirvana

Nsenduluka, B. (2015). Is plastic surgery a sin? Doctor argues "Jesus performed plastic surgery." *Christian Post*. https://www.christianpost.com/news/is-plastic-surgery-a-sin-doctor-argues-jesus-performed-plastic-surgery-140794/?page=2

Palmer, E. (2019). Florida plastic surgeon known as "Boob God" suing ex-patients over negative online reviews. *Newsweek*. https://www.newsweek.com/florida-plastic-surgeon-leonard-hochstein-yelp-reviews-miami-1413772

Pew FactTank. (2018). https://www.pewresearch.org/fact-tank/2018/09/05/u-s-adults-are-more-religious-than-western-europeans/

Pew Research. (2010). https://www.pewforum.org/2010/09/28/us-religious-knowledge-an-overview-of-the-pew-forum-survey-results-and-implications/

Pew Research. (2017). https://www.pewresearch.org/fact-tank/2017/04/05/christians-remain-worlds-largest-religious-group-but-they-are-declining-in-europe/

Plumb, A. (2012). 12 examples of the Last Supper in pop culture. *Empire Online*. https://www.empireonline.com/movies/features/last-supper-pop-culture/

Proctor and Gamble. (2006). A company history: 1837-today. https://www.pg.com/translations/history_pdf/english_history.pdf

Quaker. (2020). Quaker Oats Company. http://www.quakeroats.com/about-quaker-oats/content/quaker-history.aspx

Sampson, H. (1874). *A History of Advertising from the Earliest Times*. Chatto and Windus.

Sarapin, S. H., & Morris, P. L. (2020). Unpublished survey of offensiveness of ads containing religious or sacred images, themes, and/or words.

Shaw, M. (1994). Pentagram is misused as a Satanic symbol. *LA Times*. https://www.latimes.com/archives/la-xpm-1994-03-06-me-30571-story.html

Shurpin, Y. (n.d.). Was the forbidden fruit really an apple? *Chabad*. https://www.chabad.org/parshah/article_cdo/aid/1982723/jewish/Was-the-Forbidden-Fruit-Really-an-Apple.htm

Suresh, H. (2019). An in-depth analysis on The Last Supper. *Medium*. https://medium.com/@shridhay/an-in-depth-analysis-on-the-last-supper-14c46a822baf

Synan, M. (2018). What is the holy grail? *History.com*. https://www.history.com/news/what-is-the-holy-grail

Tennent, T. A. (2014). The Jewish idiom of breaking bread among the early believers. https://themessianicfeast.com/wp-content/uploads/2013/12/MF-PDF-Pages104-105.pdf

The Church of Jesus Christ of Latter-day Saints. (2020).

"The Life and Times of Bruce Gerencser." (2020). Evangelical swear words. https://brucegerencser.net/2020/05/christian-swear-words/

TripAdvisor. (2020). Mom's Kitchen. https://www.tripadvisor.com/Restaurant_Review-g35200-d5025061-Reviews-Mom_s_Kitchen-Preston_Georgia.html

Tyson, J. (2021). How video games systems work. How Stuff Works.com. https://electronics.howstuffworks.com/video-game2.htm#:~:text=Video%20games%20have%20been%20around,man%20who%20developed%20Computer%20Space

"Vital Statistics: Jewish Population of the World." (2020). Jewish Virtual Library. https://www.jewishvirtuallibrary.org/jewish-population-of-the-world

Volokh, E. (2010). Advertisement banned in the UK because of blasphemy. *The Volokh Conspiracy*. http://volokh.com/2010/09/16/advertisement-banned-in-the-uk-because-of-blasphemy/

Waldman, I. (2020). Public displays of Hanukkiyot. *My Jewish Learning*. https://www.myjewishlearning.com/article/public-displays-of-hanukkiyot/

Wulff, A. (2016). A brief history of Cajun cuisine. *Culture Trip*. https://theculturetrip.com/north-america/usa/articles/a-brief-history-of-cajun-cuisine/

Young, J. O. (2020). *Radically rethinking copyright in the arts: A philosophical approach*. Routledge.

Young, W. H., & Young, N. K. (2007). *The great depression in America: A cultural encyclopedia*. Greenwood Press.

Zellman, S. (n.d.). Medium. T posing and its racist origins. *Reddit*. https://www.reddit.com/r/TPoseMemes/comments/8ipdcj/t_posing_and_its_racist_origin

Chapter 6

Apparel

The Fabric of American Faith

"American Christians," opens author Colleen McDannell in *Material Christianity: Religion and Popular Culture in America,* "want to see, hear, and touch God" (1995, p. 1). The Bible even instructs, "Clothe yourself with the Lord Jesus Christ" (New International Version, Romans 13:14). A search on the internet or a visit to a Christian bookstore verifies this, as thousands of items of religious merchandise are available. Holding an item in our hands or wearing it in public identifies us as members of religious groups, and makes faith tangible; "the visual, sensual, and tactile form of the object offers an immediacy that ideas do not always have" (McDannell, 1995, p. 223). In other words, Americans like things that remind us of and communicate our intangible faith. And so, perhaps, it comes as no surprise that in explicating the range of holy hype in society, we devote a chapter of this book to the religiously themed items that adorn homes and bodies.

McDannell posits that "people build religion into the landscape, they make and buy pious images for their homes, and they wear special reminders of their faith next to their bodies" (1995, p. 1). These tokens can include knickknacks, wall hangings, jewelry, clothing, and adornments for our vehicles. Such items compose the material dimensions of Christianity, what McDannell calls the *material culture,* made up of artifacts, landscapes, art, and architecture. In *Brands of Faith,* Mara Einstein offers an important reason for the American obsession with religious stuff; although "religious practice is very much privatized, religious presentation and promotion has become widely acceptable within our culture" (2008, p. 4). At times, material displays of religion were either not allowed or not in fashion, but today it is acceptable to display faith, whether classy or kitsch. The market for such trinkets and tchotchkes is important to larger religious identities: "Having a market and resources that represent your group provides a sense of legitimacy and a form of cultural capital" (Neal, 2017, p. 225).

This chapter explores the *artifacts* of American Christian culture. These items combine or scramble the sacred and profane in a uniquely American way. Like the advertisements presented in Chapter 5, we need to query the content and role of these visible artifacts. When is a T-shirt holy versus irreverent, and when is a velvet painting of Jesus reverent versus kitsch? Opinions are divided on the goodness and usefulness of religious artifacts. McDannell posits that such artifacts on one hand "function like tools: they help Christians to acknowledge common commitments, delineate differences, express affections, or socialize children . . . For these Christians, objects speak to sincere religious needs and sentiments" (1995, p. 57). Wearables and knickknacks may serve to draw the eyes to the religious in a world filled overwhelmingly with the secular. They may teach and remind us of the tenets of our faith. And some feel that symbols of religion are physical reminders of their commitment to their beliefs. Tangible items can also "teach people how to think and act like Christians. They are used to lure, encourage, and shock non-Christians into considering the truth of Christianity" (McDannell, 1995, p. 45). Artifacts speak to others, too, proclaiming that the owner or wearer is a committed member of that faith, and even act as a way to communicate and evangelize for that creed. As discussed in Chapter 3, such "totems" indicate who is in the group and who is not, and can promote solidarity among members. As we travel throughout our days, we may need such projections of identity to locate similar others in the modern world. Einstein asserts that Americans "readily buy products and services that relate to our faith. We do this because . . . traditional religious institutions are not the primary source of spiritual sustenance for most people anymore" (2008, p. 5). As physical church attendance falls, the spiritual still seek ways to connect with their beliefs.

Or, on the other hand, is religious merchandise merely "Jesus junk, holy hardware, Christian kitsch," the much maligned "material culture of contemporary Protestants?" (McDannell, 1995, p. 223). Are Jesus bobbleheads and baby Buddhas merely disposable momentary entertainments, or even a dilution of symbols of faith? Some religious imagery has lost its meaning, and is now reproduced as artsy, exotic, provocative, or campy. "Nostalgia, exaggeration, otherness, artificiality—all of these traits are appreciated" by those who buy, display, and wear them, demonstrating little understanding of the original context and meaning (McDannell, 1995, p. 63). Some may recognize a crown of thorns as belonging to the Christian faith, or the Star of David to the Jews, but they may not know the meaning or proper use of those symbols within the faith. McDannell writes that "critics blithely denounce the whole environment as indicative of how a commercial American mentality has invaded the inner sanctum of religion. They complain about how such products reduce Christianity to the trivial and reflect how profit directs piety" (p. 223). This is a concern we have addressed often in this book as we have explored the intersection of religion and advertising. It is even more relevant when exploring cheap, mass-marketed tees, watches, and figurines imprinted with symbols that trend and sell. In a 2009 research study, Hirdes et al. write:

> Many critics contend that the current assortment of Jesus merchandise is a superficial substitute for genuine faith, a commercial exploitation of spiritual desires for financial profits, and a justification for evangelical consumption . . . and provide oversimplifications of essential biblical truths in other cases . . . such familiarity may also result in flippant or casual attitudes toward God. (Hirdes et al., 2009, p. 142)

Before making a judgment about the value—or not—of religious material goods, we should explore a bit of their history, and look at examples of this merchandise.

RELIGIOUS MERCHANDISE IN HISTORY

Much of Christian religious history features the prohibition of religious items, lest one commit the sin of idolatry. Durkheim, for example, saw the sacred and profane as hostile opposites on either side of a line that should not be crossed. Religious scholars and theologians discouraged images of God. This included John Calvin, the prominent figure of the Protestant Reformation and developer of Calvinism. The Puritan immigrants brought Calvinism to America, and their homes and bodies did not contain Christian kitsch. It is perhaps ironic, then, that modern Americans partake of Christian merchandise with such enthusiasm.

Modern Protestants did not invent the Christian artifact. Items that reminded the spiritual of their religion or religious commitment have been considered a part of many religions (recall the totemism from Chapter 3). Relics, talismans, and symbols have been found in homes and places of worship for centuries. McDannell credits the Victorians, however, with launching the demand for mass-marketed religious goods. Cheaper and faster means of production and a "willingness of Christians to integrate religion into every aspect of their lives" resulted in a rich offering of items to decorate one's home (1995, p. 223). It was fashionable to express one's faith loudly from the walls and mantles. For decades, most of the items were sold door to door or through catalogs. For example, The Gospel Trumpet company of Indiana (now Warner Press) launched a full line of catalog merchandise in the 1930s, including postcards, wall hangings, place mats, pencils, and a lamp featuring the face of Jesus. Such items were clearly branded with common religious images because "they wanted people to feel unequivocally that the object they sold was not just a lamp, it was a Christian lamp" (McDannell, 1995, p. 240). McDannell writes:

> Retailers have developed their own religious marketing niche by emphasizing a generalized Christianity. Christianity becomes, in effect, a type of brand name recognition. Since brand names have to be clear and distinct there must be no confusion as to whether something is or is not Christian. So it is not surprising that suppliers put unambiguous symbols on every item they sell. (1995, p. 260)

Sellers have leveraged religious symbols not only in advertisements, but also on the merchandise they sell. The Christian, Jewish, or Islamic symbols are as much brand as the logos for Izod®, Tommy Hilfiger®, or Chanel®. Instantly recognizable at a glance, they are as much a part of the landscape of the homes and bodies of the faithful as Whirlpool®, GE®, or La-Z-Boy®.

By the 1950s, Christian bookstores were a major source for merchandise. Their sales were boosted in the 1970s by Protestant revivalism, a movement of young evangelicals that "embraced Jesus as a lifestyle" (McDannell, 1995, p. 247), embedding their faith into everyday lives and items. One tenet of evangelicalism is a "commitment to engaging wider culture, while remaining distinct from it" (Neal, 2017, p. 225). Thus, adherents express their faith publicly through T-shirts, bumper stickers, pendants, and other jewelry and often blend popular culture in the form of themes, memes, and logos into those displays. McDannell comments that for evangelicals, "what is important is the promotion of the Bible. Fashion, advertising, popular culture, and style are merely the medium for the message" (1995, p. 261). It is acceptable to let the market create opportunities to embed faith into culture. As this group aged, many became older conservatives with established incomes, and they continue to purchase high-quality merchandise from Christian stores and online sites for themselves and their families; "by buying and displaying Christian art in their homes, giving gifts with biblical sayings, or wearing T-shirts, conservative Protestants translate their beliefs into visible messages" (McDannell, 1995, p. 268).

CHRISTIAN RETAIL

Although online retail sales in the United States are growing (9% of all retail sales in 2017, estimated to grow to 12.4% in 2020) (Statista, 2019), the brick and mortar gift shop industry was valued at $16 billion in 2020

(IBIS World, 2020). Enter the Christian bookstore: "[T]o distribute their alternative versions of secular commodities, evangelicals have created a network of Christian bookstores, and increasingly, these goods are also found in secular bookstores and even movie theaters" (Hendershot, 2004, p. 28). For Christians, the local Christian retailer is the go-to for books, movies, DVDs, and the large variety of paraphernalia available to show one's faith. Figurines, T-shirts, jewelry, signs, and many other items tempt the buyer; "shelves are filled to overflow with a range of religious home décor, toys, music, and clothing designed to appeal to spiritual shoppers. You'll find inspirational figurines, Bible-themed Monopoly-style board games, automobile decals, and even religious breath mints" (Merritt, 2017, n.p.). Whether you love Christian kitsch or feel that "the 'trinketization of Christianity' has plastered a cheap face onto a rich religious movement with a more than 2,000-year history," there is no shortage of religiously branded merchandise to be had (Merritt, 2017, n.p.).

Some have foretold the end of the local Christian store, after closures of several major US chains, Christian Stores (250 stores) in 2017, and Lifeway Christian Stores in 2019 (170 stores). However, the faithful buyer can still find a store selling mostly Christian products among more than 2,000 by checking a map such as www.GetItLocalToday.com/Map (2020). After a number of years of decline, The Parable Group reports that year-to-year sales declines have slowed: "Same-store sales are down 2.5% but the trend is in a positive direction" (2020, p. 33). They collected data from 230 Christian retail sellers and report that gifts made up 26% of the $66 million in sales reported, and was considered the area with the second highest potential, after Bibles (2020). Retailers are banding together; in 2018 the Christian Bookseller's Association (CBA, founded in 1950) reorganized and changed its name to the Christian Retail Association, now boasting 4,000 members. They held their first trade show, the Christian Product Expo, in January 2019 (Weaver, 2019). *Woman's Day* recently featured "36 Christian Gifts that Say 'I Love You': You're going to want everything for yourself, too," showing T-shirts, candles, a mouse pad, rings, necklaces, and a scarf (Free & O'Sullivan, 2020).

What is all this merchandising saying? Hirdes et al. (2009) analyzed merchandise found in the catalogs of several major Christian retailers, from apparel and accessories to decorative art and toys. They found that the most common communication function of merchandise was edification, with evangelism and public relations a distant second and third. They defined evangelism as communication directed outside the church used to persuade people to follow Christ. *Edification* was defined as communication directed at individuals who already have a commitment, to help them make decisions, grow in their faith, and convict wrong behavior. Public relations is used to maintain a positive image of religious organizations among groups outside of its members.

Following Einstein's proposition that messages about religion are persuasive ones, advertisers and marketers promote religion the same way as other products since "religion is a product, no different from any other commodity sold in the consumer marketplace" (Einstein, 2008, p. 4). Hirdes et al. evaluated the types of persuasive appeals of the merchandise. They found that two types dominated: informational and "good times." Informational appeals influence beliefs by explaining what Jesus or Christianity does or how it works. These logical, rational appeals feature Jesus's name and promote positive attitudes toward Christian faith. "Good times" is a tag that associates Christianity with fun, happiness, or warm feelings, and uses emotional appeals featuring Jesus's image. The authors conclude that "frequently, the most direct purpose of a persuasive media message is not to sell a particular product or service as much as it is to promote a positive image or good will in relation to a particular organization (e.g., the Church), individual (e.g., Jesus Christ), or idea (e.g., Christianity)" (Hirdes et al., 2009, p. 143).

A Catalog of Merchandise

Home décor is one popular category of religious merchandise. Religious wall décor was very popular during the Victorian age, and continued into the twentieth century. People proudly displayed high-quality copies of paintings or paper reproductions of religious figures and scenes, and even hand-stitched Bible verses, on their walls. The styles changed with the times as tastes evolved. Fancy, rich-looking materials such as suede and velvet were popular in the 1920s, similar to the velvet Jesus image in figure 6.1a. Companies offered art deco and graphic styles in the 1940s, and modern, less realistic images by the 1970s. Today few people display such images on their walls, but people can still buy a velvet Jesus if they wish. Although the baby Buddha figurines in figure 6.1f probably don't seem religious, and may be found in anyone's home, they mix several religious traditional symbols as well as invoke humor. First, the pictorial maxim "see no evil, hear no evil, speak no evil" is Japanese and traditionally uses "three wise monkeys." Its origin is a carving on a door at Tōshō-gū Shinto Shrine. Second, the maxim has also been found in Chinese Confucian writings. Third, Buddha means "enlightened one," and there are a number of types of statuary with various meanings, the most popular being the laughing Buddha for good luck. Statues and figurines of the historical Siddhartha Gautama, the founder of Buddhism, with various poses and stages of his life, have different meanings. When depicted as a baby or child, the image represents a story in which the infant took seven steps and proclaimed his

Figure 6.1 a) A portrait of Jesus painted on black velvet for sale on eBay. b) Star of David watch for sale on eBay. c) Men's wristwatch with sacred heart of Jesus image for sale on Etsy. d) Jesus tattoo by Scott Wiecek. e) Image of Abdu'l-Bahá of the Bahá'í faith on a necklace being sold on Etsy. f) Baby Buddha version of the three wise monkeys. g) Ring with the Arabic word for Allah (God) for sale at Boutique Ottoman Exclusive Jewelry Shop. h) Neckties with religious symbols and images. i) Religious bumper stickers and auto emblems. *Source*: *a) Screenshot retrieved from ebay.com listing. Hand painted in Mexico, unsigned. b) Image retrieved from ebay.com listing by Collectible Chaos. c) Screenshot retrieved from Etsy listing by TerryTiles2018. d) Image courtesy of tattoo artist, © Scott Wiecek. e) Image retrieved from Etsy listing by Sophie Steinberg. f) Image courtesy of Peggy_Marco on Pixabay. g) Image retrieved from Boutique Ottoman website. h) Images courtesy of photographer Susan Sarapin. i) Images courtesy of photographer Susan Sarapin.*

place in the world, leaving a lotus blossom at each step—his first miracle. Even Jesus is not immune to the kitsch of the bobblehead trend. Christian versions of trends and popular products are not uncommon. Whether on the dash of your car or your kitchen counter, bobblehead Jesus is there to remind you that you are forgiven (figure 6.2d). The keychain or backpack charms in figure 6.2e feature saints and serve as a gift for a child named after a saint or to remind one of the exemplary life and faith of that saint, her feast day, or her patronage. In the middle of figure 6.2e is St. Cecilia,

Figure 6.2 a) A dog wearing celebratory Hanukkah glasses. b) Jewish mezuzah necklace. c) Christian bracelets. d) Bobblehead Jesus for sale at World of Mirth. e) Small trinkets of saints called Tiny Saints, which can be attached to key chains or bracelets. f) The Last Supper tattoo by Scott Wiecek. g) Christian rings. h) Christian wristbands. *Source: a) Image courtesy of Rabbi Emily Losben-Ostrov. b) Image retrieved from Judaica.com. c) Image courtesy of photographer Susan Sarapin. d) Image courtesy of World of Mirth, product designed by Archie McPhee. e) Image courtesy of photographer Susan Sarapin. f) Image courtesy of tattoo artist, ©Scott Wiecek. g) Image courtesy of photographer Susan Sarapin. h) Image courtesy of photographer Susan Sarapin.*

the patron saint of music and musicians, whose feast day is celebrated on November 22.

The Christian fish symbol (ichthys in Greek) sported on many a Christian's car originally was simply an outline of a fish or had "Jesus" in the middle. The fish has been used as a Christian symbol for centuries, and is possibly associated with stories and metaphors linked to Jesus. At several times, Jesus was credited with large catches that fed people both physically and spiritually. In addition, Jesus promised his disciples that he would make them fishers of men (Matthew 4:19). Its popularity as a wearable image began in the 1970s. As shown in figure 6.1i, the car decal or emblem has been co-opted by other faiths, and modified to include stereotypical things about their religions. In addition, parodies have been made that mock the literal interpretation of the Christian creation story, by adding scientific or evolutionary symbolism. Also found on cars are, of course, bumper stickers, which come in all shapes and sizes just like the fish symbol. The faithful may proclaim: "In case of rapture, this car will be unmanned," "Got Jesus?" and "Honk if you love Jesus." In response, parodies and opposing messages appear as well.

Wearing jewelry such as a necklace, ring, or bracelet is another way to take one's faith on the road. Whether cheap and flashy or subtle and pricey, religious symbols have been worn by everyone from nuns to those taking their first communion. Jewelry can be worn as a serious expression of faith, such as the Jewish mezuzah necklace in figure 6.2b, or as a part of a campy, trendy getup a la Madonna. The mezuzah is a piece of parchment containing verses from the Torah placed in a tiny decorative case. It is found on interior and exterior doorways of Jewish homes; on a necklace, it is a sign that the person wearing it lives a Jewish life and a reminder to the wearer of that person's covenant with God. They are often quite beautiful as well. A trendy Christian teen might opt for one of the bracelets in figure 6.2c as a reminder to herself and others of her faith commitment. These are a subtle yet fashionable choice. Unlike the bracelets just described, the colored rubber wristband is unisex and even trendier. Typically, they show support for a cause (one of the original wrist bands [yellow] was from cyclist Lance Armstrong's Live Strong cancer campaign). However, they also now show membership, values, and beliefs of the wearer. Shown in figure 6.2h, the "Left Behind" wrist band is from a popular Christian novel series made into films, and refers to the end times rapture, and this and the "Are You Ready" bracelets refer to that franchise, popular with Christian teens. The others remind the wearer of "God's Big 10" Commandments, and the Christian value of forgiveness. The subtle "InspiRing" rings in figure 6.2g feature Bible verses (and likely can be read only by the wearer) such as John 13:35. ("By this everyone will know you are my disciples if you love one another.") Wearing your religion on your wrist (or sleeve) can remind you of your faith whenever you check the time. The watch in figure 6.1c features a familiar kitschy Catholic image, the sacred heart of Jesus, often found on holy cards and prayer cards. Although a theme long established in Catholic history, the popularity of sacred heart images date from the visions of a seventeenth-century French nun:

> Jesus is said to have appeared to her and, among other things, requested that pictures of His Sacred Heart should be set up and venerated in churches and homes. He also made several promises that people who venerate His Heart would receive special graces for their lives. (Ad Imaginem Dei, 2017, n.p.)

Not all wearables are cheap ones. The 2018 Met Gala theme, "Heavenly Bodies: Fashion and the Catholic Imagination," featured artifacts and objects from the Vatican and famous guests who wore creations full of religious symbolism created by prominent fashion houses. Versace mules with a jeweled cross on the top appeared on that runway, and other styles such as the Sophia Webster Evangeline angel wing sandals were on offer that year. Such fashion bordered on the showy and campy, but also highlighted the rich lexicon of symbolism available to inspire designers and fashionistas. A religious man (or boy) can find many ways to express his faith, but what better way than to proclaim it from his chest when he dresses up? Whether at a religious service, dinner at the country club, or his class reunion, men (and women) of all stripes can choose sacred neckwear. In figure 6.1h, we have a sartorial reminder of the Ten Commandments, an Islamic tie featuring the symbol for Allah and an Arabic calligraphic tie clip, the figure of Jesus walking on water from a stained-glass window, or Samuel the Lamanite, a prophet from the Book of Mormon, indicative of the Church of Jesus Christ of Latter-day Saints.

Other faiths are well-represented in the religious merchandise market, too. Observant Jews are not left out from showcasing their faith through religious merchandise. One can check the correct time and be rewarded with the Star of David (figure 6.1b), a symbol that has existed since antiquity but was adopted in modern times as a general sign of Judaism. Or one can express one's affinity with a traditional Jewish food, matzos, by putting on a pair of socks or a tee (figure 6.3g). Matzos are a key part of the Jewish Passover observance, but also enjoyed at other times and by non-Jews as well.

Figure 6.2a shows that even our pets are not immune from the expressions of our faith. It is not likely that a dog will understand a religious celebration, but its owners can let others know that their dog is a part of their family Hannukah observance. In this photo, George, the canine friend of Rabbi Emily Losben-Ostrov, sports glasses with the nine-candle menorah used to observe Hanukkah. Those following the Islamic faith (Muslims) can purchase the expensive-looking ring in figure 6.1g. The ring contains several important symbols of this faith, the most prominent of which is the Arabic symbol representing Allah (God). The side of this ring features an oil lamp, symbolizing divine light in this faith. Wearers are reminded of the prominence of Allah as well as the tenets of their faith. The ring is large enough to be seen by others, identifying the bearers as members of Islam willing to spend money to display their faith. Figure 6.1e is for adherents to the Baha'i faith. Abdu'l-Bahá (meaning: Servant of Glory) was one of the three central figures of this creed; his writings and speeches are regarded as a source of the faith's sacred literature. In particular, he spoke about peace. Followers of this faith can wear a reproduction of a painting of this important figure to identify and remind themselves of their faith and the teaching of this religious leader.

Tattoos have traditionally been associated with tribal cultures (the word "tattoo" comes from a Tahitian word). Like clothing, they often mark a wearer as a part of a group. They also have been used to mark rites of passage and may have religious meaning. Some Jews or Christians believe that the Bible contains warnings against tattoos (particularly Leviticus 19:28), and, at times, churches have banned them. According to an Ecumenical church council in 787, the church allowed tattoos, but only for truly religious reasons and not superstitious ones; "Tattoos that were worn to honor God and to bear witness to his glory were then said to bring heavenly rewards" (Scheinfeld, 2007, p. 363). Men have traditionally been the primary recipients of tattoo art, and the cross and other religious symbols have been part of their tattoo images. However, it has become more acceptable to sport a tattoo or two, regardless of faith, age or gender, and young people looking for something tasteful may choose religious symbolism whether they call themselves religious or not. Such images counter the negative stereotypes often associated with tattoo wearers. The fish symbol, the cross, crowns of thorns and nails, and words such as "faith" and short Bible verses are common. The tattoo image in figure 6.1d depicts Jesus wearing the crown of thorns, which, according to the Bible, was put on Jesus's head during the crucifixion, both to cause pain and to mock his claims of royalty. The tattoo in figure 6.2f is a real commitment—for both the wearer and the artist. The entire Last Supper (from the painting by da Vinci) is depicted, permanently, on this person's limb. Both of these tattoos were designed by artist Scott Wiecek, who says religious tattoos are a frequent request of his customers.

THE AMERICAN T-SHIRT

Garments communicate to others identity, values, and group membership. Perhaps more than any other wearables, T-shirts can carry a large range of messages, both personal and collective; "the T-shirt is a garment like no other, one in which the language of clothing meets the language of statement, in which textile becomes textuality" (Symes, 1989, p. 88). T-shirts can sport slogans, advertisements, political messages, and sports team logos. And perhaps they are particularly effective at carrying their messages, for as Symes writes, "unlike most clothes which mumble and stammer their messages, the T-shirt 'talks' directly to its audience" (Symes, 1989, p. 98). Lynn Neal examines the history of the garment and finds that the T-shirt garment itself has been used to evoke masculinity, capture the rebelliousness of youth culture, serve as a billboard for slogans, and sell goods. It "has come to be seen as an emblem of individualism, a marker of identity, a space for free expression" (Neal, 2014, p. 187). These are important roles for a mere piece of fabric. And unlike other markers of identity and culture, they are particularly effective because "they do not inhabit a single space but follow the individual into the various spaces they [*sic*] inhabit and engage with" (Ornella, 2019, n.p.).

Identity and individualism are one important role of the T-shirt, but not the only one. Symes explores the tee in "Keeping Abreast with the Times: Towards an Iconography of T-shirts," writing that they "are a convenient medium for self-promotion, a sort of mobile curriculum vitae, offering a summary account of the self for public consumption" (Symes, 1989, p. 93). However, the tee also intersects with advertising. Although not technically advertising because the bearer is not typically *paid* to wear it (rather the other way around), the T-shirt clearly intersects advertising, marketing, and branding. Symes observes:

> The T-shirt combines the art of the advertisement with that of the cartoon, the headline with that of the punchline. Designed to catch the eye, it is the advertisement applied to the self; indeed, in many instances, it is just that: an advertisement using the torso as a billboard, as a peripatetic commercial, on which to exhibit the logos and entreaties of companies. (1989, p. 89)

Perhaps because of their ability to carry a personal statement, no garment is more *American* than the T-shirt. Lynn Neal (2014) writes that "there may be more or less appropriate places to wear them, but the 'Americanness' of the tee remains unquestioned in our culture . . . whether Hanes or haute couture, the T-shirt has come to represent a quintessential American mode of dress and expression" (p. 186–187). The tee has been worn by movie stars and celebrities, on the red carpet and in the movies, as well as on millions of average citizens. The T-shirt is often worn with a suit or tuxedo as a cool, popular fashion statement. The contents of one's T-shirt are emblematic of the American value of free speech. Tees are

> seen by Americans as transparent, as revealing important information about the unique personality of its wearer. Thus, the T-shirt provides people with a culturally acceptable way to be different—to express their ideas, to be provocative, to dissent from politically correct views of Islam or other religions, to literally show something of themselves. (Neal, 2014, p. 200)

In her article "The Ideal Democratic Apparel: T-shirts, Religious Intolerance, and the Clothing of Democracy," Neal further suggests that

> we entertain the notion that the T-shirt functions as *the clothing of democracy*. The T-shirt represents the ideal democratic apparel as it symbolizes cherished American values—individualism and free speech, sameness and difference. Thus, it is *the* clothing of democracy. (p. 203)

The T-shirt is as popular as ever today. Look around at any semi-casual or casual event in warm weather, and you will find a variety of messages. Symes summarizes the power and ubiquity of the tee:

> No other garment is so unambiguous in its communicative power, in offering commentaries about ourselves and about our times. Above all, it contains important messages about contemporary culture, about the contradictions which exist in that culture, about our aspirations and fears. As such, it is a garment whose seriousness and non-seriousness demands to be taken seriously. (1989, p. 98)

RELIGIOUS SHIRTS

As a component of visual culture, the messages on T-shirts often escape the criticism and censorship of other types of messages. Perhaps this is why religious T-shirts continue to be popular, more so than any other type of religious wearable. The tradition of the T-shirt for expressing identity and practicing free speech, posits Neal, allows messages not permissible elsewhere. In Neal's study, this includes attacks on non-Christian religion, but it also creates a space where humor may "foster this sense of 'speaking,' or more precisely 'seeing,' the 'unspeakable' as these tees 'say by laughter what cannot frankly be stated in words' (2014, p. 200). Such provocative Christian slogans as 'Body Piercing Saved My Life" and "Work for God . . . the retirement benefits are great" become acceptable wear.

Christian tees constitute a vital part of commercial evangelical Christianity, "often marketed as 'witness wear'—as a way to evangelize" and announce their Christian identity (Neal, 2014, p. 193; Hendershot, 2004; McDannell,

1995). Any wearable featuring religious imagery or words marks the wearer as a religious believer and communicates religious identity and norms (Neal, 2017). For example, the tee in figure 6.3d, which refers to the evangelical concept of being born again (in Christ), is clever but also clearly labels the wearer (also see figure 5.8). It allows the believer to make his or her outer appearance "correspond with the reborn inner person" (Hirdes, Woods, & Badzinski, 2009, p. 154). Search for Christian apparel retailers online and you will find they push this message, too. Christian Apparel Shop claims:

> Without saying a word, you can share the message of faith in Jesus by simply wearing a Christian T-shirt . . . Christian clothing is a wonderful way for believers in Christ to engage in a conversation with other individuals who otherwise may not have a chance to hear the gospel. (2020, n.p.)

Their message continues, full of hyperlinks to the products mentioned:

> So the next time you decide to go shopping, take in a sporting event or go out to dinner, use that opportunity to evangelize to others wearing your Christian tee shirt, Jesus T-shirt, Christian bracelet, or paying for goods with your Christian wallet. It may just be that next step someone needs to becoming a believer in Christ. (2020, n.p.)

One type of religious T-shirt attracts attention by incorporating popular cultural mottos and logos, but then surprising the viewer with religious content. For example, the familiar Venice Beach Gold's Gym shirt became the Lord's Gym, with an image of Christ struggling to lift the cross. The popular British slogan "Keep Calm and Carry On," along with appropriation of consumer brand logos like Reese's peanut butter cups in figure 6.3b, is popular with Christian tee designers. "With such appropriations of logos and brand names, evangelicals attempt to use humor to bridge the apparent divide between believers and nonbelievers" (Hendershot, 2004, p. 17). They also translate evangelism into the language of popular culture. Parody can be creative; mimicry and imitation may also testify to the commercial success of the original effort (Neal, 2017). The sports jersey-style shirt in figure 6.3h looks a lot like those worn by the football fans and players across the United States. Yet its message is the popular Bible verse John 3:16 ("For God so loved the world, that He gave his only begotten Son, that whosoever believeth in Him should not perish, but have everlasting life"). Christians are not alone in using a clever turn of phrase or image to draw attention to their faith. The Jewish shirt in figure 6.3g refers to a story told at Passover, cleverly spelled out in matzos. The Islamic T-shirt in figure 6.3f reminds the wearer and viewer that the Ramadan fast is happening using

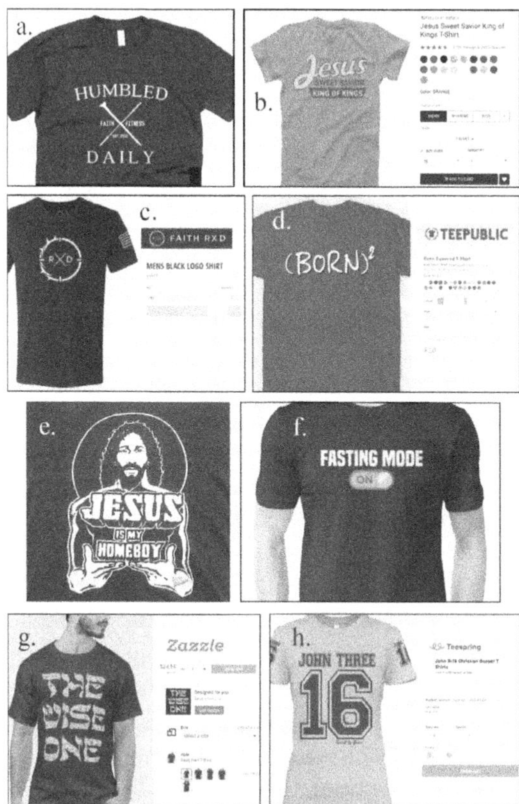

Figure 6.3 a) Christian shirt, "Humbled Daily." b) Christian shirt that parodies popular candy. c) Christian shirt for sale. d) Christian shirt representing the Evangelical concept of being born again. e) Jesus is my homeboy shirt. f) Islamic Ramadan shirt for sale. g) Jewish Passover shirt for sale. h) Jersey style Christian tee with Bible verse John 3:16 for sale. *Source: a) Image courtesy of © Humbled Daily. b) Screenshot retrieved from TeeShirtPalace.com listing. c) Screenshot retrieved from faithrxd.org listing. d) Screenshot retrieved from TeePublic.com listing. e) Image courtesy of © Jesus is My Homeboy Foundation. f) Screenshot retrieved from TeePublic.com listing. g) Screenshot retrieved from zazzle.com listing. h) Screenshot retrieved from Teespring.com listing.*

an icon from a smartphone interface. This would actually work as well for Jews fasting for Yom Kippur.

Neal asks what qualities make a T-shirt (or other Christian merchandise) "evangelical"—as opposed to those creating a parody of these messages. She contends that three characteristics constitute Christian character. First, the companies authenticate their apparel through origin stories which indicate that the company "cares for both their spiritual and sartorial lives" (Neal, 2017, p. 228). An example origin story of the Jesus is My Homeboy Foundation, marketer of a popular T-shirt discussed below (figure 6.3e).

Second, they incorporate symbols and theological ideas into the products, branding them as religious. Finally, they advertise according to Christian conservative principles, offering clothing and models that are modest, products that align with the spiritual and social norms of evangelicalism. Neal notes that slogans with multiple interpretations and double entendre that lack a clearly Christian message would raise questions about the authenticity of the product as evangelical.

Athletics is another area where God, Jesus, and religion cross into the secular. In writing about the CrossFit community, where Christian tees have become popular, Alexander Ornella (2019) states:

> [R]eligiously branded apparel transforms the (clothed) athletic body into a religiously branded body. These branded bodies become powerful communicators . . . a (religiously) branded body, then unfolds this power not only outwardly, for an audience, but also inwardly fostering an intimate sense of connection between the self and the brand (religion). (n.p.)

He continues, "if the faithful perceive of their faith as a brand . . . quite provocatively one could argue that religious athletic garments turn the athlete into 'walking billboards for Jesus'" (n.p.). He concludes by stating that "the religiously inscribed t-shirts do not have an inherent or absolute religious value merely because of their religious inscriptions. Rather, the demand for such T-shirts, and athletes introducing them into secular contexts, bestow them with religious and economic value" (n.p.). In the image, several of the example T-shirts are popular among CrossFitters and other athletes. Humbled Daily ("Lifestyle Apparel and Daily Inspiration") has a vision: "Clothes and content are our avenues. Salvation and sanctification through Christ is our aim" (Humbled Daily, 2020, n.p). The image in figure 6.3a shows a popular T-shirt style favored by active Christians, including those involved in CrossFit. Faith is represented by thorns and fitness by the barbell. Similarly, figure 6.3c is from Faith RXD, an organization of Christian fitness fans similar to the CrossFit movement.

One of the recent notable Christian shirts to hit the mainstream—and the red carpet—is shown in figure 6.3e. The "Jesus is My Homeboy" T-shirt has been worn by Jessica Simpson, Pamela Anderson, Ben Affleck, Ashton Kutcher, Brad Pitt, and others. Says the site selling the shirt, "You've seen the image on T-shirts, hats, and badges. It is the iconic design worn by celebrities too numerous to mention. You might be wearing a 'Jesus is My Homeboy' shirt right now" (Jesus is my Homeboy, n.d.). The design has a story: According to the site, the design, shirt, and movement began in Los Angeles in the 1980s. A man named Van Zan Frater was nearly killed in a gang attack. He claims that shouting the phrase dispersed the gang members, thereby saving his life. Inspired, he designed and sold the shirts for a time in an effort to help end gang violence via the Jesus is My Homeboy Foundation. Sometime later, a fashion designer, Chris Hoy of Teenage Millionaire, came across the lost silkscreen in a secondhand store and began producing the shirts again. The shirt became trendy in the mid-2000s when celebrities were spotted wearing it. Proceeds from sales of the shirts go to the Jesus is My Homeboy Foundation. But the theology behind the image is vague claims blogger Victoria Emily Jones (The Jesus Question), and Frater meant for it to be "a neutral image with which anyone could identify" (2011, n.p.). The blogger interviewed Hoy, who said that the T-shirts "work for everyone, from hipsters to born-again Christians" (2020, n.p).

CONCLUSION

So, is religious merchandise a help or a hindrance to faiths and the faithful? What are the impacts to society, if any, of this form of holy hype? Heather Hendershot argues that "to purchase Christian products is to declare one's *respectability* in a country in which people are most often addressed by mass culture, not as citizens but as consumers. In America, to buy is to be" (2004, p. 30). In other words, the buyers of a religious item may be trying to separate themselves from other consumers. But to some manufacturers and sellers of T-shirts, baby Buddhas, bobbleheads, and ties, it is just another dollar spent. The meaning of the merchandise doesn't matter to them, and maybe not to their customers, either. Neal comments:

> As avenues for distributing evangelical commodities have expanded beyond Christian bookstores, many "evangelical" products have been uncoupled from their origin stories and ministerial frameworks . . . For some in the subculture, this means success—it shows Christianity permeating popular culture and reaching a larger audience with the "good news" of Jesus. Other evangelicals fear that separating the commodity from the "source community" means diluting and confusing the message. (Neal, 2017, p. 240)

In other words, some companies put religious symbolism on artifacts merely to make a buck, not to make an impact. Likewise, some consumers buy and wear signs for their original meaning, while others sport them for other rhetorical purposes, or just for fun.

Authentic merchandisers, on the other hand, claim that their sales are for the greater good, whether for the soul of the wearer, the potential convert who views it, or the uses for the profits. So perhaps it is not the item but the seller who matters to those who see religious merchandise as more than temporary cultural kitsch. For the rest, this type of holy hype becomes just another part of the current zeitgeist.

REFERENCES

Ad Imaginem Dei (2017, June 23). The sacred heart of Jesus-an iconographic introduction. http://imaginemdei.blogspot.com/2017/06/the-sacred-heart-of-jesusan.html

Christian Apparel Shop (2020). Christian T-Shirts Can Change A Life! https://www.christianapparelshop.com/

Einstein, M. (2008). *Brands of faith: Marketing religion in a commercial age.* Routledge.

Free, J. & O'Sullivan, A. (2020, January 22). 36 Christian gifts that say 'I love you': You're going to want everything for yourself, too. *Woman's Day.* https://www.womansday.com/life/g23768575/best-christian-gifts/

Get It Local. Today! (2020). https://www.GetItLocalToday.com/Map

Hendershot, H. (2004). For-profit prophets: Christian cultural products and the selling of Jesus. In *Shaking the world for Jesus: Media and conservative evangelical culture* (pp. 17–51). University of Chicago Press.

Hirdes, W., Woods, R., & Badzinski, D. M. (2009). A content analysis of Jesus merchandise. *Journal of Media and Religion, 8*(3), 141–157. doi: 10.1080/15348420903091030

Humbled Daily. (2020). Vision. https://www.humbleddaily.com/pages/about-us

IBIS World (2020, May). Gift shops & card stores industry in the US: Market research report. https://www.ibisworld.com/united-states/market-research-reports/gift-shops-card-stores-industry/

Jesus is my Homeboy. (n.d.) http://www.jesusismyhomeboy.com/the-story

Jones, V. E. (2011, June 25). Jesus is my homeboy: The story that started it all. *The Jesus Question.* https://thejesusquestion.org/2011/06/25/jesus-is-my-homeboy/

McDannell, C. (1995) *Material Christianity: Religion and popular culture in America.* Yale University Press.

Merritt, J. (2017, August 28). The rise and fall of the Christian bookstore. *The Week.* https://theweek.com/articles/720413/rise-fall-christian-bookstore

Neal, L. S. (2014). The ideal democratic apparel: T-shirts, religious intolerance, and the clothing of democracy. *Material Religion, 10*(2), 182–207. doi: 10.2752/175183414X13990269049400

Neal, L. S. (2017). OMG: Authenticity, parody, and evangelical Christian fashion. *Fashion Theory, 21*(3), 223–244. doi: 10.1080/1362704X.2016.1143574

Ornella, A. D. (2019). 'Jesus Saves' and 'Clothed in Christ': Athletic religious apparel in the Christian CrossFit community. *Sport in Society, 22*(2), 266–280. doi: 10.1080/17430437.2017.1360580

Scheinfeld, N. (2007). Tattoos and religion. *Clinics in dermatology, 25*(4), 362–366. doi: 10.1016/j.clindermatol.2007.05.009

Statista. (2019, July 23). E-commerce share of total retail sales in United States from 2013 to 2021. https://www.statista.com/statistics/379112/e-commerce-share-of-retail-sales-in-us/

Symes, C. (1989). Keeping abreast with the times: Towards an iconography of T-shirts. *Studies in Popular Culture*, *12*(1), 87–100.

The Parable Group. (2020, February 3). 2020 state of Christian retail: Forging ahead with renewed energy. https://www.parablegroup.com/articles/2020-state-of-christian-retailing

Weaver, E. (2019, January 20). Christian product expo attracts former CBA members. *Publishers Weekly*. https://www.publishersweekly.com/pw/by-topic/industry-news/religion/article/79069-christian-products-expo-attracts-former-cba-members.html

Chapter 7

Marketing Religion on the Streets

After reading this far, the pastor of a small church may be scratching his or her head and wondering exactly what marketing, advertising, and branding have to do with getting more people into the church on Sunday morning. The pastor can rest assured that this is not an esoteric topic. In *Selling God* (2008), John Follis writes:

> To the uninitiated, it may seem strange to market a church like a box of Kellogg's Frosted Mini-Wheats. Well, obviously, you don't market a church like a box of Frosted Mini-Wheats. How then? By selling spirituality. More specifically, by selling God. Selling God—what a concept. (n.p.)

But these days, even the smallest congregation's budget usually allows for at least a small weekly advertisement in the local newspaper's religion section promoting special speakers or services. It is a fact of life that many more religious institutions today are dedicating a portion of their financial resources to the public dissemination of their messages through the mainstream media to the American public, quite often through direct-mail promotions. Many more are taking advantage of the attention-getting characteristics of holy hype.

Advertising is not just about selling products; it is also about selling services, organizations, and ideas (American Marketing Association, 2020). The types of holy hype explored in this chapter include proselytistic and self-identifying holy hype and institutional holy hype; both attempt to bring attention to a church or religion, differing in whether they use religious images or secular images to do so. The ads focus on religious ideas, religious experience, or religious practice. However, as Mitchell (in *Media Violence and Christian Ethics,* 2007) commented, among Christian ethicists, "the actual role of visual and other media in moral formation is rarely studied. This is surprising given the long history of media use by local churches and individual Christians to exemplify and express their faith" (p. 5).

Churches and faiths have found themselves in competition both with one another and with the myriad offerings of secular society. Whether in trying to intervene to save souls from the trappings of consumerism or in employing branding and marketing themselves to fill their pews and coffers, churches have employed advertising. Also, perhaps because of its history, the United States has invented and grown some unique forms of institutional holy hype, through church signs and billboards. In this chapter, we describe why churches are involved in holy hype and explore examples of print and out-of-home church marketing.

SELLING FAITH

Churches have historically had an "uneasy" relationship with advertising (Percy, 2000). In 1920, back in the days when advertising was really beginning to take off as a respectable professional enterprise, Ernest Eugene Elliott published a book titled, *How to Advertise a Church*. He explained some of the reasoning behind the eschewing of this modern form of publicity for the church by quoting Dr. Chester C. Marshall, pastor of St. James Methodist Church of New York, as he told the congregation at the First Presbyterian Church:

> Some people . . . say church advertising is undignified. . . . They say it degrades the church to a common level. . . . Finally, they say advertising religion robs it of its sacredness. Is ours a peculiar brand of religion that must be kept sacred by isolation? (1920, pp. 76–77)

Elliott ultimately supported the concepts once advanced by the Rev. E. Robb Sebring of Chicago's Union Methodist Episcopal Church in a sermon delivered to the congregation at the First Presbyterian Church:

> [B]elievers in Christianity must consider their church and religion as a business and themselves as the salesmen . . . no salesman ever had an article or proposition to submit to the public about which he could give a better "selling talk" than he who is talking belief in God. (1920, p. 77)

Elliott even explained how the Bible itself promotes advertising. Speaking about the Rev. Dr. Christian F. Reisner of Chicago, Elliott wrote that the pastor

> justified church advertising from the Bible and the example of Christ. He said that when Christ desired to hold the people longer when they were hungry he sent out for "a few sardines and soda crackers," which was an argument in favor of refreshments at church. (1920, p. 80)

At times, there have been restrictions imposed on church use of advertising by both sacred and secular bodies. Most recently, this has included bans or restrictions on televangelism and fund-raising via broadcast and public television; televangelism did not take off full throttle until the cable era in the 1990s made it affordable and legal. The church itself has also been "conservative in its attitude towards non-print mediums [*sic*]" (Percy, 2000, p. 97).

Seeing a conflict of morals between the tenets of faith and the dogma of advertising, "churches have also been host to a culture of suspicion concerning the general 'alleged' power of advertising," although "these concerns are more to do with the use and abuse of materialism than a critique of the medium of advertising itself" (Percy, 2000, pp. 98–99). In other words, the church, typically preaching the follies of a consumerist lifestyle, clashed with the messages of mainstream advertising and marketing. Faith organizations have even hesitated to employ advertising and marketing to pitch their own brands:

> Churches seem to see themselves more in the role of a "watchdog" rather than as a body that might profit from using a medium that many large organizations take for granted. This tends to result in the churches engaging in tame or lame advertising: under-resourced, unclear about their focus, and over-concerned not to offend their existing constituency. . . . There is little attempt at subtlety or a more arresting form of engagement. (Percy, 2000, p. 104)

Thus, it is rare that church or other faith-based advertising is noted, written about, or awarded (one notable exception includes the Fallon McElligott effort described below).

Perhaps more than anywhere else, the U.S. faith organizations have engaged in their own subdued, yet necessary, sales campaigns. R. Laurence Moore discussed *Selling God* in book-length form in 1994. His popular tome includes a thorough history of religious marketing in the United States. He writes:

> [R]eligion's role "in the marketplace of culture" began in the nineteenth century as an effort to influence and in some cases to ban altogether the commodities being offered for sale. Protestants had special problems with markets that existed to make various forms of leisure and entertainment attractive. (p. 6)

Churches at this time largely engaged media in an effort to counteract the growing capitalist mentality. One effort was to produce its own, approved, forms of entertainment including religious books and nonprofit organizations (usually engaged in some form of service) to lure those who had gone astray into the marketplace of things. However, it wasn't long before religious leaders and moralists realized that they needed to make "their own inventive contributions into the market" in order to succeed (Moore, 1994, p. 6). Eventually overcoming their reluctance to advertise, "religion looked for ways to appeal to all consumers, using techniques of advertising and publicity employed by other merchants" (Moore, 1994, p. 6). Christians "began to embrace advertising as an effective means of communicating . . . in a pluralist age" (Percy, 2000, p. 99). We discuss this more in a few pages.

CHURCH RESPONSE

In modern times, the church is concerned about advertising. For example, communication and media have been addressed in a number of Catholic Church writings, beginning with *Inter Mirifica* (1963), *Communio et Progessio* (1971), and *Aetatis Novae* (1992). In general, these documents are positive about media. *Communio et Progressio* expresses the takeaway from these early documents: "The Church sees these media as 'gifts of God' . . . which unite men in brotherhood and so help them to cooperate with his plan" (Pontifical Council, 1971, n. 2). Media is not seen as inherently good or bad, but rather humankind can make use of it in positive or negative ways. At the time of his writing, Budde (in *The (Magic) Kingdom of God*, 1997) states:

> [O]ne looks in vain for a systematic treatment of global culture industries in the official pronouncements of the Vatican Council, popes, or Curial offices . . . consideration of culture industries as a group is largely absent from the highest levels of church leadership. (p. 97)

Although several new pronouncements have appeared since Budde's writings, this attitude by the Catholic Church still holds true; it has focused on the morality of media content and the usefulness of electronic media for the work of the church and neglected careful analyses of systems and structures. Often quoted are the words of Pope Paul VI, who said the church "would feel guilty before the Lord if it failed to use the media for evangelization" (Pope Paul VI, 1975, n. 45).

In 1997, the Pontifical Council for Social Communications released a report called *Ethics in Advertising*. Echoing earlier statements, it continues to hold that advertising is a morally neutral process, but also argued that advertising techniques have effects on susceptible consumers when they convey values. The council paints a dim view of consumers; the council implies that consumers cannot discern for themselves what constitutes value. Ringold (1998) writes:

> The Council casts consumers as putty in the hands of advertisers. The Council characterizes consumers as base, limited in their ability to take account of information relevant to their own welfare, and unable to exercise their free will in the presence of advertising. (p. 333)

The Catholic Church, in this directive, considers the laity to lack the ability to analyze and evaluate the media they receive (a lack of media literacy and a tenet of the debunked Magic Bullet theory). The council writes that "man's . . . capacity to reflect and decide" (n. 16) is compromised by advertising; the council sees the ability "to move people to act on the basis of irrational motives" (n. 10) and "to cause people to feel and act upon cravings for items and services they do not need" (n. 10) (Pontifical Council, 1997).

The council writes that the "responsibility of media is to contribute to the authentic, integral development of persons and to foster the well-being of society" (n. 1) and concludes by asking advertisers to "eliminate [advertising's] socially harmful aspects and observe high ethical standards" (n. 23) (Pontifical Council, 1997). Thus, the Catholic Church thrusts the responsibility for moral media onto Madison Avenue. Ringold summarizes: "To the council, the morality of advertising practice is based on the degree to which content and technique seeks to inculcate values consonant with the teachings of the church" and objects to the promotion of "harmful or utterly useless goods" (1998, p. 332).

This is hardly an appropriate edict to give to marketers and advertisers, the secular of all that is secular, because "when the council proposes limits on commercial speech, it is seeking, in actuality, to limit choices at odds with the teachings of the church" (Ringold, 1998, p. 335). In the United States, most would scoff at trying to imbue the market with religious values. It is the antithesis of the American desire to separate the secular and profane (however unsuccessful this has been at times).

The council has since released a number of other documents on media. In 2000, they released *Ethics in Communications* and in 2002, both *The Church and Internet* and *Ethics in Internet. The Church and the Internet* states that "the Church has taken a fundamentally positive approach to the media," (n. 1) reaffirming statements in the preceding documents. But the document does at least acknowledge the larger societal effects of media, stating that one concern of the church

> is to encourage their right development and right use for the sake of human development, justice, and peace—for the upbuilding of society at the local, national, and community levels in light of the common good and in a spirit of solidarity. (2002, n. 3)

The council also seems to be more concerned about the socializing influences of modern media. *The Church and the Internet* states:

> One area for research concerns the suggestion that the wide range of choices regarding consumer products and services available on the Internet may have a spillover effect in regard to religion and encourages a "consumer" approach to matters of faith. Data suggest that some visitors to religious web sites may be on a sort of shopping spree, picking and choosing elements of customized religious packages to suit their personal tastes. (n. 9)

Similarly, in 2001, Pope John Paul II said:

> [T]he world of the media can sometimes seem indifferent and even hostile to Christian faith and morality. This is partly because media culture is so deeply imbued with a typically postmodern sense that the only absolute truth is that there are no absolute truths or that, if there were, they would be inaccessible to human reason and therefore irrelevant. (n. 3)

Budde (1997) is particularly critical of the church's lack of substantive response to purveyors of global culture such as media and advertising. He argues that while churches have addressed "matters of media content (sex, violence, and prejudicial stereotyping); matters of media access (the 'fairness doctrine,' public access requirements in cable franchising); and some concerns for a slightly broader media ownership profile," these do not address larger-scale "assumptions or operations of social and political engagement" (1997, p. 53). He likens efforts thus far to the "cultural equivalent of rearranging deck chairs on the Titanic," and writes that failing to look at systemic impacts of media "typify the 'missing the forest for the trees' pattern all too typical of much American Christian social engagement" (pp. 53–54). Yet churches have also been advertisers themselves for millennia (as we saw in Chapter 3) and continue to do so in modern times, as is addressed next. Mitchell counters, writing that Budde, the Vatican, and others assume passive and static audiences, and have "ignored imaginative ways in which Christians might reappraise, resist, and even renew the practice of advertising" (2007, p. 262).

MARKETPLACE OF RELIGION

The United States did not invent religious marketing. Neither did the Christian Protestants. As Moore writes, "religion in Western societies has always had commercial aspects . . . (Martin) Luther was not the first to notice them, nor did he eliminate them" (1994, p. 255). Cathedrals attracted all sorts of sellers and buyers of religion, religious goods, and secular items. The infamous sale of indulgences could be considered selling God and was one of the things that infuriated Luther so much. So, while the intensity of religious marketing may be relatively new, marketing religion is not; it has been going on for centuries. However, in the United States, the condition of freedom of religion produced dozens of denominations. These had to compete for their congregations, and their success depends on their ability to sell their brand of faith to potential members. In America, the need for religious marketing stemmed from the First Amendment right to freedom of religion. Moore writes that "although commercial aspects of religion are traceable in any century . . . clearly the First Amendment was a major factor in accelerating the process of religious commodification" (1994, p. 7). With no state-mandated religion, religions had to compete for parishioners; "the environment of competition among denominations created by the First Amendment's ban on religious establishment simply accelerated the market rationale" (Moore, p. 7).

Originally, one continued to attend the same church, or at least the same denomination, as one's parents and family. It was the place for community. But as the economy changed, so did where people met and where they lived. They moved away from family, and they needed the church less for community as they increasingly worked outside the home. They intermarried into other faith traditions. Various waves of immigrants have brought new and varied faiths, as well as a new population for existing ones, widening the choices available. Nowhere is this more evident than in the landscape of small towns and cities, where the spires and bricks of the many churches dominate the view. In the mid-twentieth century, it became acceptable to rebel against family traditions, including breaking with family religious denominations—or breaking with religion completely. Religion became voluntary, with the elimination of the stigma attached to not attending church (Einstein, 2008). Mass media, too, provided alternatives to physically attending church, and alternatives to church as well. Television, radio, and the internet provided religious programming, and plenty of other options as well. Einstein summarizes:

> Within this environment of being able to select your religion, or religions, combined to unfettered access to information religion must present itself as a valuable commodity, and activity that is worthwhile in an era of over-crowded

> schedules. To do this, religion needs to be packaged and promoted. It needs to be new and relevant. It needs to break through the clutter, and for that to happen, it needs to establish a brand identity. (2008, p. 12)

Especially in the case of Christians, whether in a new hometown or just in the mood for something new, Americans will turn to the brands that they know or trust, and this is as true of faiths as it is of canned green beans. Without some form of getting the word out, congregations cannot attract new members. In fact, not just any message will do. It must compete with the minds and money of major brands that use trained scientists and artists to make themselves heard. Einstein concludes: "In order to be heard above the noise of the rest of society, religion, too, must participate in order to survive" (Einstein, 2008, p. 9). Others agree on this incentive:

> In America a church that seeks to establish and maintain its identity faces serious obstacles. In a land with hundreds of thousands of churches and no end to the multiplicity of denominations, with so many alternatives for worship in a given town or neighborhood, how to attract the interest of potential parishioners? The various denominations and congregations are quite literally scrambling for customers in the religious marketplace. (Zelinsky, 2001, p. 578)

As for Jews, on the other hand, the choice of a house of worship has never been quite so available an option. Small towns often have no Jewish congregation at all, and it is not uncommon for Jews to travel as long as 90 minutes or more to get to a temple or synagogue. Competition is not a factor in this scenario; the issue here is trying to find enough Jewish people to form and support a congregation. For example, a temple in Dothan, Alabama, once advertised housing subsidies for Jewish families to relocate there for a minimum number of years to keep the Jewish community from disappearing and the temple from closing. Pelham Parkway in the Bronx; Springfield, New Jersey; and Meridian, Mississippi, are three other towns that have tried this approach (Hu, 2012). Jewish institutional holy hype cannot hold a candle to similar Christian advertising.

Moreover, religion did not only follow market trends, but began to set them. Churches and "religious leaders played innovative roles during the consolidation of America's market economy in the first half of the nineteenth century"; religious institutions, having put aside their misgivings about advertising, "developed market strategies, ways of advertising itself, and distribution networks" (Moore, 1994, p. 91). For example, the Methodist circuit riders "invented forms of religious proselytizing that could be adapted to the selling of virtually any product" (Moore, 1994, p. 91). From the distribution of pamphlets to the tent revival meeting, the church was now in the marketing game. Publications were written advising churches on how best to reach the masses, and "practical information filled the advertising handbooks for churches. It ranged from suggested slogans to ways to get church news in the papers, to information about how to lay out a church bulletin with maximum eye-catching effect" (Moore, p. 214). As we saw in Chapter 3, there was even overlap between the men of the cloth and the men of early Madison Avenue. Moore adds that "religious entrepreneurs made aggressive use of technological changes in the media that were later copied by businessmen and politicians" (1994, p. 91). The involvement of religious institutions in marketing and advertising in the United States resulted in important changes to the structure of society: "the commercialization of divinity pushed religion into the public arenas of American life and made it central to American mythmaking, to its politics, and to its delineation of social and ethnic divisions" (Moore, 1994, p. 91). The United States may not have a legal national religion, but advertising, in part, has put it square in the view of the people.

On the other hand, Budde was particularly critical of the church's use of media, stating that "a rigorous critique . . . might imply that under given circumstances the Church ought *not* embrace the tools, techniques, and social arrangements" (p. 101). He writes:

> The answer in many quarters seems to involve adopting wholesale the methods and tactics of global culture industries—via corporate public relations campaigns, advertising agencies, market research, motion pictures, radio/TV production, and more. Although such a posture recognizes the utter inability of existing Catholic channels to reach, much less touch the hearts of, the faithful, the push toward greater use of culture industry vehicles is problematic in the extreme. It presumes the neutrality of culture industry tools, ethically and in terms of effects on communicators, messages, and audiences; such is a profoundly naïve and ill-informed view. (p. 84)

He poses questions about the compromises churches may have to make in order to satisfy an audience socialized by mainstream media: "How far are Church leaders willing to go in conforming to the norms of the culture industries? Will the Church train its personnel in manipulative, psychographic-style research, and seductive 'associative advertising' techniques as a part of the media training?" (p. 102)

BRANDING BELIEF

Over time, "by degrees, religion itself took on the shape of a commodity" (Moore, 1994, p. 6), sold with equal fervor as to the names of other major brands. Religious institutions "have become branded in much the same way that consumer products have been branded," writes Einstein, in *Brands of Faith* (2008, p. xi). This is particularly true with the arrival of the megachurch, where brands such as the Church of the Highlands, Crossroads Church, Lakewood Church, Elevation Church, and Willow Creek Community Church boast weekly attendances of the tens of thousands. Many have their own publishing imprint, memorable logos, and are headed by quasi-famous men (yet they are almost exclusively men). Einstein comments that branding of religious institutions is inevitable because of both competition among themselves and with the popular culture. It "makes perfect sense in the current cultural environment . . . branding faith becomes shorthand for reaching the new religious consumer" (2008, p. 13). Einstein, having visited numerous church conventions, seminars, and even a Kabbalah workshop for her research, writes that "religious institutions have taken on names, logos or personalities, and slogans that allow them to be heard in a cluttered, increasingly competitive marketplace" (p. xi). Einstein writes that the fact that religions and religious products have become brands is because most faiths

> offer the same end benefit for the consumer (salvation, peace of mind, etc.). Though packaged differently, fundamentally they are the same product, no different than buying one shampoo versus another. The only way to differentiate one religion from another, or any product for that matter, is through the services provided (the added value) and the symbols that designate it. (2008, p. 13)

Einstein outlines the effects of branding religions and spirituality. She claims that "when you introduce marketing into a category, you change the category and the products that compete in it" (2008, p. xi). First, it introduces the idea that people can shop for it. Indeed, the phrases *church shopping* or *searching for a church home* in American lingo mean visiting multiple houses of worship, evaluating them, and choosing the best fit, not unlike finding a comfortable pair of jeans. Second, in order to be heard among the competition, faiths have to increase the level of marketing and promotion, but also, they become "increasingly prone to creating a product that consumers will buy" (p. xi). The congregant becomes a customer. One critique of churches being in a competitive market is that they may alter teachings and offerings to please the church shoppers or lure away congregants from the competition. The explosion of non-denominational churches of all sizes could be one result. Third, this has led to the church-planting industry with a goal of growth, a bigger yet less personal way to carry out the Great Commission. However, although Americans remain religious, church membership has declined 20% over the past two decades and church attendance is declining, down almost 10% in 10 years (Jones, 2019; Pew Research, 2019). Thus far, then, an increase in or more clever marketing has not made an impact.

INSTITUTIONAL HOLY HYPE EXAMPLES

Percy classifies church or Christian advertising into the following categories (based on a survey of UK ads, 2000): (1) Literalistic: proclamation of biblical texts or doctrinal statements using no illustrations, only pure text; (2) Evangelistic: linked to a place of worship and designed to have an impact on the passersby, although unlikely to be humorous or arresting for non-churchgoers; (3) Modern: appealing to an ethical meta-narrative or universal appeal, and often current, issue-specific; (4) Postmodern: comic and contemporary reflection on well-known stories with the universal story sublimated; and (5) Ironic wry, witty, and (normally) liberal to convey information and a simple message, subtly celebrating communitarian values. Those who are already members of a religious community are targeted by literalistic and evangelistic forms because of their limited appeal. To engage with the marketplace of culture, however, eye-catching modern, ironic, and postmodern forms are used.

In the United States, the groundbreaking work of the Fallon McElligott agency for the Anglican Church (ECUSA) in the 1980s still functions as a benchmark for church advertising. One of the more memorable of its press advertisements includes a picture of Christ with the caption "He died to take away your sins. Not your mind." Another advertisement from the same agency for the same client showed a churchgoer whose mouth was gagged, with the caption stating, "There's only one problem with religions that have all the answers. They don't allow questions" (Percy, 2000, pp. 101–102). The campaign was the product of a brilliant copy writer, Tom McElligott of Fallon McElligott. Dr. George Martin, an Episcopal minister from Minneapolis, contacted McElligott, son of an Episcopal priest, to pitch his desire for a provocative set of ads to get more people to try the church. McElligott executed this campaign pro bono over a six-year period. An example from this campaign is in figure 7.1e. Miguel Ferreira (2020) says of these ads, "They spoke to the reader like God would speak to people in a 1980s way." This was a hugely successful campaign that actually earned money for The Episcopal Church through revenue earned by selling them to other Protestant churches to use in their advertising. Idea man and cleric Martin commented, "Evangelism is believing in your product and putting it out there. It's all about communicating. It has to be compelling, creative, and persuasive" (cited in Ferreira, 2020). Figure 7.1e ends with a tongue-in-cheek remark about being born again. Obviously, every new individual who visits this church will have been born at least once. And according to the criteria for

Figure 7.1 a) Mock church marquee. "Independent Old Timey Hell-Fire Brimstone King James Preaching." b) Mock church marquee. "Savings inside. No coupon needed." c) Mock church marquee. "Adam & Eve, first people to not read Apple's Terms & Conditions." d) 1980s Bible ad by Fallon McElligott agency. "Spoiler alert: The Hero gets killed in the end." e) The Episcopal Church (ECUSA) ad by Fallon McElligott agency. "The Episcopal Church welcomes you. Regardless of race, creed, color or the number of times you've been born." f) Ad for RIAL magazine in conjunction with The Advertising Council encouraging family-focused worship. "Love thy family. Worship together." g) Ashland Avenue Baptist Church ad for Bible study. "Have lunch with the boss." *Source: a) Mockup created by authors. b) Mockup created by authors. c) Mockup created by authors. d) Image courtesy of Father Martin. e) Image courtesy of Father Martin. f) Image courtesy Ad Council Archives, University of Illinois Archives. RIAL is no longer active. g) Image ©Larry Thompson, Eternity Communications.*

joining The Episcopal Church, that one time is fine with them. Figure 7.1d is another ad by McElligot. It proposes the Bible as a dramatic novel, and stories always have a protagonist (Jesus) and an antagonist—a hero (Jesus) and a villain. In his promotion of this "novel," we are provided with the denouement, preceded by a spoiler alert. We discover that the hero dies in the end. With a simple shot of the Bible, the copy does the trick. He had reduced the narrative of the Bible to a mere seven words. Truly admirable. This condensation of such a complicated story as encompassed in the Holy Scriptures is a brilliant, new perspective on the Good Book. This makes the viewer see the Bible in such a new way that the next time your friends ask you whether you have read any good books lately, you can hand them a copy of the Bible. This is one creative way to think about the subject in advertising.

A few more examples of print ads in figure 7.1 show some of the creativity used by church marketers. Figure 7.1f is a magazine page, "A public service of This Magazine & the Advertising Council." Adorable children from diverse backgrounds recite some of the Ten Commandments. The copy asks readers to bring their children to church to worship as a family. This is an appeal to family values and raising children in a faith environment. Figure 7.1g is one of a campaign of ads from the Ashland Avenue Baptist Church, designed by Larry Thompson of Eternity Communications. Using a humorous appeal, one perhaps targeted at the working professional, it asks the reader to come to church to lunch with "the boss," presumably God or Jesus Christ. The smaller copy continues the theme and the humor, asking you to make a date with God Himself at the cleverly named "Mid-Day Manna" Bible study, where busy people can go "straight to the top!" A secondary benefit is a delicious home-style meal for only $3.

SIGNS OF FAITH

As we have discussed in this book, religion is on display in the landscape of American media in a way that is unique. This is also true in the literal landscape. Zelinsky (2001), in a rare treatment of this topic, writes:

> The assemblage of objects that constitute the publicly visible religious landscape of the United States—houses of worship and a variety of church-related enterprises—deviates so markedly from its counterparts in other lands that we can regard its uniqueness as a significant argument for American exceptionalism . . . this includes the widely distributed signage promoting godliness and religiosity. (p. 565)

Zelinsky comments that the frequency of religious billboards and posters along American roadways is a practice that is unlike what foreign countries do. Such signs, including the "catchy and distinctive" naming of the churches themselves, are "flaunted to the passerby" (p. 578). The purpose of the signs, consistent with our definition of institutional holy hype, is to inform and "persuade the unredeemed or to reinforce the faith of believers" (p. 580). And it is one that we include because, as Zelinsky exclaims, "the profusion and nature of religious signs clamoring for the attention of Americans are truly extraordinary" (p. 579).

The names of America's churches may draw attention, but the signs in front of them have gone viral online. At first, humor and religion may seem incompatible. In an analysis of church marquees, Bell et al. write that "the concept of humor was not lexicalized in Hebrew, Greek, or Latin—nor any European language through the Middle Ages—in a form comparable to that expressed by the current English word" (2011, p. 188). Historically, church leaders and members of fundamentalist sects have been skeptical of the congruity between humor and church teachings. Nevertheless, in front of many American churches is a sign on which the letters can be changed, sporting service times and pastors' names but also short phrases to attract the attention of those who pass by. The internet is both a source and recorder of these signs, and Bell et al. write, "If church billboards are any indication of a congregation's sense of humor, put up by the churches themselves, then it seems that, with regard to the form of humor, puns are preferred," partially because they can be conveyed in a limited amount of space (2011, p. 188). Humor is used as a "way for the congregation to succinctly portray themselves as lighthearted, approachable, and 'joinable'" (p. 200). In their analysis of almost 400 "punny" church signs, the researchers found that homonymic puns were popular. They found that the humor was created by and for Christians, drawing on "issues relevant to tenets of faith and Christian morality" (p. 199). Because of that, it may reach those who have a Christian background, but "if, on the other hand, the goal of these messages is, as one website asserted, 'to reach the unsaved,' the message may not reach members of this group who are unfamiliar with the tenets of Christianity" (p. 199). Examples of signs in the analysis include "A lot of kneeling will keep you in good standing"; "Don't give up. Moses was once a basket case"; and "Down in the mouth? It's time for a faith lift." The authors summarize: "[I]ndeed, as a kind of advertisement, the church is perhaps wise to employ punning. Research on the effect of puns in advertisements shows that slogans containing puns are appreciated significantly more than those without" (p. 200).

We created several examples of church marquees based on ones we have seen that tickled our funny bone. In figure 7.1a, a church sign advertises the preaching style: if the King James Bible, hell-fire, and brimstone are to your liking, look no further. You know you can find that here. Figure 7.1b uses punny humor to amuse those who are shopping for savings—of the Baptist kind. You need not bring any special coupons, only come inside. The creation story is featured in figure 7.1c, along with the well-known company Apple. We are almost all guilty of not reading terms and conditions (Sarapin & Morris, 2017) and so were Adam and Eve, apparently. If you are as flawed as they were, you are welcome at this church. Such signs are a popular feature of internet blogs and Pinterest collectors.

BILLBOARDS IN AMERICA

Billboards existed before the advent of the automobile and the US highway system, but it is in this venue that we know it best. Early uses of billboards alerted those traveling by foot, horse, or carriage that a local inn or traveling entertainment awaited them up the road. Early billboards for auto travelers alerted them to the amenities of motels, eateries, and tourist attractions. Soon, "the effectiveness of these advertisements led to creating an entirely new branch of the advertising industry as clients demanded newer and more attractive ads that would catch the eye and entice the traveler to stop and spend money" (Billboard Connection, 2017, n.p.). The organization which today is the Out of Home Advertising Association (OAAA) began as the Associated Bill Posters' Association of the United States and Canada in 1891 (OAAA, 2020). Outdoor signs could be painted on any available space, and eventually merchants and enterprising businesses built (and later standardized the size of, around 1900) signage space for lease; "confident that the same ad would fit billboards from coast to coast, big advertisers like Palmolive, Kellogg, and Coca-Cola began mass-producing billboards as part of a national marketing effort" (OAAA, 2020). Sign painting was also at one time a profession, but one that was later replaced by mass-produced and computer-generated art. Today, billboards advertise all manner of products and services: "[F]rom toothpaste and soaps, to breakfast cereals and sodas, billboards were made to advertise in big, bold pictures and images. . . . [E]fforts to generally improve the way of life" (Billboard Connection, 2017, n.p.). New visual design was created that allowed someone passing by at a high speed to appreciate and remember the ad (OAAA, 2020). Billboards are not always appreciated. In part due to the overabundance of distracting highway signs, the 1965 Highway Beautification Act put restrictions on the number, location, size, and spacing of highway billboards (OAAA, 2020). But such limitations have not stopped the tide of billboard ads; in 2005, the first digital billboard went up, and now a single board can flash several advertisements as we speed by in our cars.

> Whether it's to provide information on gas prices or the arrival of the best burger in town, knowledge is one important element that billboards have imparted. They have become a very popular medium to address current issues and information. Perhaps it's because they reach more people for cheaper prices than any other type of media or maybe it's because people are spending much more time in their vehicles now than ever before. Whatever it is, billboards are here to stay. (Billboard Connection, 2017, n.p.)

Billboards are just one type of "out-of-home advertising." Also included are shelters, transit signs and kiosks, airport advertising, mall displays, airplane banners, and taxis, street furniture, alternative media, cinema, and digital place-based screens. The OAAA of America reported in 2019 that out-of-home (OOH) advertising, of which billboards are a significant part, posted 35 quarters of growth through the end of 2018. In that year, billboards accounted for 65% of OOH advertising, or more than $5 billion. Its report claims that 2019 began with more than 164,000 static billboards and an additional 8,800 digital billboards. A report by Nielsen (Williams, 2016) gives these facts:

- Roadside billboards are the most noticed out-of-home ads.
- 91% of US residents aged 16 or older, who have traveled in a vehicle in the past month, noticed some form of out-of-home advertising, and 79% have noticed OOH in the past week.
- 80% of US residents age 16 or older surveyed have noticed a billboard in the past month and 62% have noted a billboard in the past week.
- 82% of billboard viewers make it a point to look at the advertising message at least some of the time; over one-third look at the billboard ad each time, or almost each time, they notice one.

In his essay, Zelinsky was awed by the prevalence of church signs in the American landscape. Perhaps more than any other type of out-of-home advertising, the billboard promoting faith is an American anomaly:

> [M]uch more remarkable, and suggesting something more deep-seated than the urge to engage in puffery for the local congregation, is the multitude of propagandistic signs along America's highways and byways with little or no reference to specific houses of worship. (Zelinsky, 2001, p. 580)

He continues, describing the signs as promoting "godliness and biblical authority generally without advancing any narrowly defined theology," and that almost all seem to be Protestant (p. 581). But are they effective, and to whom do they actually speak? Percy feels that they were calling to the

> unconverted and the stray lamb, striving to save souls and thwart the Devil, a feverish, never-ending missionary struggle. The signs plead, scold, and nag, and they are meant to shame or frighten into submission those of us who are in spiritual peril. (2000, p. 582)

In contrast, after passing by such highway signs as "Billboards of fiery crosses that say 'REPENT!' Billboards that ask 'Where are you going? Heaven or

Hell?'" a self-proclaimed non-religious blogger asks whether billboards were

> meant as antagonistic messages to nonbelievers, or are somewhat misguided recruiting efforts. It turns out that, according to the people who erect these signs, the billboards' target audience is the already converted. They appear most meaningful to religious people facing tough times, and they are a symbol of community for the rest. (Mayyasi, 2015, n.p.)

Thus, like church marquees, the billboards may be more effective in reeling in those who believe but have fallen away than those who proclaim no religious belief at all.

The blog site *Church Marketing Sucks* claims as its mission "to frustrate, educate and motivate the church to communicate, with uncompromising clarity, the truth of Jesus Christ" and is part of the Center for Church Communication (CFCC), a nonprofit organization. Lively conversation about billboards is a part of the site's offerings. Guest blogger Darren Leach writes in support of church billboard use:

> [O]ne of the greatest strengths of billboard advertising is the ability to reinforce a single message. This characteristic is ideal for church marketing as it can be utilized to reach those looking for answers in their lives by inviting them to look to Jesus and the Bible. Although billboards are not necessarily going to convert anyone, they can be a starting point by influencing people to walk through the doors of the local church. (2013, n.p)

On the other hand, guest blogger Scott McClellan feels church billboards are *not* effective. His post reads:

> White letters against a black background offered these words:
> Read the Bible
> Follow Jesus Christ
> Visible? Yes. Well-intentioned? I'm sure. Theologically unoffensive? Certainly. But that's where the positives end.
> Compelling? No. Substantive? No. Personal (or presented within the context of a relationship)? No. Story? No. Opportunity to dialog? No. (2013, n.p.)

He concludes, "[I]f we're to announce the kingdom of God, we can't settle for a drive-by. Not when there's an amazing story unfolding all around us" (2013, n.p.). McClellan feels the need for a deeper appeal, one that can't be told in six words or less. With questions of audience and effectiveness in mind, let's explore some examples of institutional holy hype that we find compelling.

EXAMPLES

Galiot (2016) reports:

> Thousands of billboards about God and religion have appeared along America's roadways every year since the turn of the 21st century—and the numbers appear to be growing . . . Some of them encourage tolerance of non-Christian religions, and others reassure that a life without religion can still be full. But the overwhelming majority carry an evangelical Christian message. (n.p)

Several prominent campaigns include Christian Aid Ministries, GodSpeaks, the Islamic Circle of North America, and on the other side, American Atheists, the United Coalition of Reason, and the Freedom from Religion Foundation.

An Amish-Mennonite nonprofit organization called Christian Aid Ministries (CAM) displayed more than 500 billboards in 46 states by 2016 (Galiot, 2016). CAM's current 15 billboard designs follow a very specific formula. There's short, attention-grabbing copy—ranging from simple questions such as "Who Is Jesus?" to foreboding declarations like "After you die, you will meet God"—plus an easy-to-remember hotline number. According to the organization, it receives around 200 calls a day on its hotline, or roughly 1 in every 16,000 to 20,000 people who see the billboards. They report that most calls to the hotline "come from people who are struggling and look to religion for help with problems like drug addictions and broken marriages" (Mayyasi, 2015, n.p.).

Several roadside billboards are shown in figure 7.2. The Cedar Creek Church has used a tongue-in-cheek billboard campaign (figure 7.2b) purportedly from Satan himself to promote its institution. Supposedly, the devil has taken a particular dislike to this church, with "Cedar Creek Church Sucks," which must mean that it is a particularly powerful place of worship, and Christians may want to check it out. In figure 7.2c, Catholic Radio is promoting its programming by targeting football fans. The text, "What's football without the Hail Mary Pass?" reminds viewers that their Catholic faith ought to be more important than their football game. In figure 7.2d, a biblical verse and the image of a boat, whose mast forms a cross, invite passersby to attend one of the 6,200 congregations in 18 denominations available and working together in North Carolina. A particular religious event is advertised in figure 7.2g: the celebration of the light of unity of the Baha'i faith. If you want

Figure 7.2 a) Billboard ad for the Islamic Circle of North America. "God does not judge by your face & wealth." b) Billboard ad for CedarCreek Church. "CedarCreek Church Sucks. —Satan." c) Billboard ad for Catholic Radio. "What's football without the Hail Mary pass?" d) Billboard ad for the North Carolina Council of Churches. "Welcome the stranger, for you were once a stranger. —Lev. 19:34." e) Billboard ad for anonymous GodSpeaks campaign. "That 'Love the neighbor' thing. I meant that. —God." f) Billboard ad for the Islamic Circle of North America about Hijab and Islam and women. g) Billboard ad for the Albuquerque Bahá'í Center. *Source: a) Screenshot retrieved from icna .org website. b) Image courtesy of ©CedarCreek Church. c) Image courtesy of photographer M. Viron. d) Image courtesy of North Carolina Council of Churches, photo by Robert C. Reed/Hickory Daily Record. e) GodSpeaks is an anonymous campaign. f) Screenshot retrieved from icna.org website. g) Image courtesy of Albuquerque Bahá'í Center and ClearChannel Outdoors.*

to have a good time at a festival while learning about this religion, you are welcome.

The GodSpeaks campaign (see figure 7.2e) has seen several rounds of billboards. In the late 1990s, an anonymous client gave more than $100,000 to the Smith Agency in Fort Lauderdale, Florida, for a billboard campaign to reach people who had stopped attending church, largely in south Florida (Veenker, 1999). In 2013, the GodSpeaks campaign decided to relaunch its campaign with new copy developed with a less critical, more loving God in mind. "We felt a real sense of hostility towards Christianity, both hostility and apathy towards God and Jesus," said Bradley Burck, chairman of the GodSpeaks board. "We're trying to communicate that there is a God, He loves you, and He wants to have a relationship with you" (Galiot, 2016, n.p.).

The Islamic Circle of North America (ICNA) is a grassroots American Muslim organization that has two outreach programs, "Why Islam?" and "Gain Peace." By the end of 2016, it will have put up 143 billboards in 39 cities (Gaillot, 2015). Waqas Syed, ICNA's deputy secretary general, says that "the target audience mainly is for people who are looking for accurate information about Islam and Muslims" (Gaillot, n.p.). The billboard in figure 7.2a was part of a 2015 nationwide campaign to "encourage dialogue and increase understanding, as well as to dispel the growing disinformation about Islam and its Prophet" (ICNA, 2015). The billboard in figure 7.2f is part of a 2019 campaign in response to misconceptions about Muslim women and discrimination of those wearing the hijab (Chavez, 2019). The campaign associates positive words with the hijab, such as respect, honor, strength, and modesty. The billboard encourages viewers to call to have their questions answered.

While some billboards want to convert people via campaigns, others try to promote understanding and coexistence. Galliot states:

> Though they don't have nearly the exposure, or commitment to billboards, as their evangelical Christian counterparts do, they play an important role in America's landscape. But unlike the Christian organizations, non-theistic organizations report facing much more resistance in getting their messages on billboards. (2016, n.p.)

We see examples in figure 7.3. It may be stunning to discover that atheists, people who lack belief in God, gods, or religion, often use religious symbols or themes to make their anti-God beliefs and associations known. It could seem counterintuitive, but it is a highly visible campaign in a large, competitive market. These ads get attention from some of the people they ordinarily would be unable to reach. The religious images, such as stained glass and the Christmas-related Santa (figures 7.3a, 7.3b, and 7.3c), conceal what many would call an anti-religion message—at least at first. There are a number of groups of non-theists rivaling one another for members (United Coalition of Reason, n.d.; American Atheists, n.d.). Pew Research Center telephone surveys from 2018 and 2019 found that the number of self-identifying atheists in the United States doubled from 2% in 2009 to 4% in 2019 (Lipka, 2019).

Figure 7.3 a) Ad for the Freedom from Religion Foundation (FFRF). "Beware of Dogma." b) Ad for American Atheists. "Go ahead and skip church! Just be good for goodness' sake. Happy Holidays!" c) Ad for FFRF. "Imagine no religion." d) American Atheists bus advertising campaign. "There's probably no God. Now stop worrying and enjoy your life." e) "Beware of the God" sign posted on a fence. f) Ad for FFRF. "The United States government is not in any sense founded on the Christian Religion. —President John Adams." g) Ad for Big Apple Coalition of Reason. "A million New Yorkers are good without God." *Source: a) Image courtesy of © Freedom from Religion Foundation. b) Image courtesy of ©American Atheists. c) Image courtesy of © Freedom from Religion Foundation. d) Image courtesy of © American Atheists. e) Image courtesy of St. Matthew-in-the-City. f) Image courtesy of ©Freedom from Religion Foundation. g) Image courtesy of ©Big Apple Coalition of Reason.*

Add to that 5%, who claim to be agnostics, those unsure about the existence of a higher power. Overall, about 23% of Americans are not affiliated with a religion or a congregation. For short, they are called "nones" (Pew Research, 2020). The Freedom from Religion Foundation (FFRF) is recognizable by its spokesperson, Ron Reagan, the son of the former president Ronald Reagan.

A variety of techniques has been used in these campaigns. Figure 7.3a, FFRF's "Beware of Dogma" is a play on the signs that say, "Beware of Dog." Atheists admonish the viewer to beware of the dogma of religion. Whereas Santa is not usually considered a religious icon per se, he is unequivocally tied to the Christian holiday of Christmas. In figure 7.3b, the American Atheists tell viewers they do not have to be good for Santa's sake or God's sake. Just be good for goodness's sake. Figure 7.3c is also from FFRF, wherein the title of a popular John Lennon song is the headline for this billboard. Lennon was an "unabashed atheist," lending credence to the ad. Its font is a version of Old English, connoting the text in older Bibles. The stained glass and parchment-like background glass are also reminiscent of sacred texts. The photo of a bus driving by in London in figure 7.3d from the Atheist Bus Campaign sports a message for those who like to play the percentages. Because there is probably very little chance of there being a real God, or so the atheists and agnostics believe, why should we spend our time worrying?

The church St. Matthew-in-the-City also uses a play on the "Beware of the Dog" signs seen on the gates of many homes in figure 7.3e. This time, it is "Beware of the God." The FFRF brings us another message in figure 7.3f. This billboard is pushback to those who believe that America was created as a Christian nation. The Big Apple Coalition of Reason brings us its billboard message in figure 7.3g. We could not fit the entire poster into this montage, but in the full image, there is a question at the bottom. After the statement, the question asks, "Are you?"

CONCLUSION

With churches competing for parishioners and their attention, advertising their brand has become acceptable and commonplace, whether in a magazine or along American roads. Despite some lingering doubts about involving themselves in the secular world of advertising, churches should participate. Einstein agrees, writing that "If people are looking for meaning, and marketers readily admit that they are, why not become the prime purveyors of the product and take back from the profane marketplace that which is sacred?" (2008, p. 74) And, such use needs research attention:

> It is surprising that few Christian ethicists have reflected in detail on the related practice of analyzing and imaginatively testing images, let alone the media and industries which produce them, as well as the public which now use and sometimes play with them. Visual representations can be used to form character, to develop virtues and to shape practice, and therefore merits careful attention. Both specific media and media organizations, sometimes described as image-making industries, are regularly overlooked in discussions of Christian ethics. So too is the fact that media have played and do play a central role in Christian worships and communication. (Mitchell, 2007, p. 11)

So, while the secular advertisers continue to sell products, the spiritual should take back the market for meaning through faith, not frivolity. The tools that are so successful in getting us to spend our money can work equally well in persuading us to care for our spiritual needs. The churches have to play on the same field with all of the other products, ideas, and services available to every American. Moore summarizes:

> [A]fter all, if religion is to be culturally central, it must learn to work with other things that are also central. Previously that might have been feudalism, kings, or Platonic philosophy. More recently it has been market capitalism responsive to consumers with spare time and a bit of money to spend. (1994, p. 9)

Rather than seeing religion and marketing as a choice between opposites, Einstein thinks that

> the interaction is more of a mutually beneficial relationship than a contest. It seems that marketers have learned their craft from religion—turning diehard product users into evangelists, for example—and it is simply a situation of religion re-assimilating what is rightfully theirs. (2008, pp. 74–75)

Now, we move into the area of metaphor and how metaphor relates to advertising and particularly how the Bible uses metaphor in a way that can be employed in the creation of memorability in advertising. Chapter 8 highlights the Noah's Ark metaphor used by Greenpeace.

REFERENCES

American Atheists. (n.d.) What is atheism. https://www.atheists.org/activism/resources/about-atheism/

American Marketing Association. (2020). Advertising. https://www.ama.org/topics/advertising/

Bell, N. D., Crossley, S, & Hempelmann, C.F. (2011). Wordplay in church marquees. *Humor, 24*(2), 187–202.

Billboard Connection. (2017). History of Billboards. https://www.billboardconnectionadvertising.com/category/history-of-billboards/

Budde, M. (1997). *The (magic) kingdom of God: Christianity and global culture industries.* Westview Press.

Chaves, S.M. (2019, March 8). Billboard campaign in Dallas in Hijab misconceptions. https://www.icna.org/billboard-campaign-in-dallas-on-hijab-misconceptions/

Einstein, M. (2008). *Brands of faith: Marketing religion in a commercial age.* Routledge.

Elliott, E. (1920). *How to advertise a Church.* George H. Doran Company.

Ferreira, M. (2020). How do you convince people to go to church? In the 1980s you'd hire Fallon McElligott Rice as your ad agency. https://creativesamba.substack.com/p/how-do-you-convince-people-to-go

Follis, John (2001, January 8). Selling God. *Adweek Eastern Edition*, https://www.adweek.com/brand-marketing/selling-god-29981/

Gailot, A. D. (2016, December 15). Signs from God. https://www.thefader.com/2016/12/15/religious-billboards-america

Hu, W. (2012, September 19). To revive communities in U.S., Jewish groups try relocation bonuses. *The New York Times.* https://www.nytimes.com/2012/09/19/nyregion/jewish-groups-across-us-paying-families-to-relocate.html

ICNA. (2015, March 15). ICNA launches historic national billboard campaign. https://www.icna.org/icna-launches-historic-billboard-campaign/

Jones, J.M. (2019, April 18). U.S. church membership down sharply in past two decades. *Gallup.* https://news.gallup.com/poll/248837/church-membership-down-sharply-past-two-decades.aspx

Leach, D. (2013, August 7). How to make billboards work for your church. *Church marketing Sucks.* http://churchmarketingsucks.com/2013/08/how-to-make-billboards-work-for-your-church/

Lipka, M. (2019). 10 facts about atheists. *Pew Research Center.* https://www.pewresearch.org/fact-tank/2019/12/06/10-facts-about-atheists/

Mayyasi, A. (2015, July 12). Why does God have so many billboards? *Priceonomics.* https://priceonomics.com/why-does-god-have-so-many-billboards/

McClellan, S. (2013, February 7). The billboard problem. *Church Marketing Sucks.* http://churchmarketingsucks.com/2013/02/the-billboard-problem/

Mitchell, J. (2007). *Media violence and Christian ethics.* Cambridge Press.

Moore, R. L. (1994) *Selling God: American religion in the marketplace of culture.* Oxford University Press.

Out of Home Advertising Association of America (OAAA). (2019, May 20). OOH Growth Continues Amid Traditional Media Declines. http://oaaa.org/portals/0/Public%20PDFs/Outlook%20Newsletter/OutdoorOutlook_052019.pdf

Out of Home Advertising Association of America (OAAA). (2020). History of OOH. https://oaaa.org/AboutOOH/OOHBasics/HistoryofOOH.aspx

Percy, M. (2000). The church in the market place: Advertising and religion in a secular age. *Journal of Contemporary Religion, 15*(1), 97–119.

Pew Research. (2019, October 17). In U.S., decline of Christianity continues at rapid pace. https://www.pewforum.org/2019/10/17/in-u-s-decline-of-christianity-continues-at-rapid-pace/

Pew Research. (2020). Religious landscape study. https://www.pewforum.org/religious-landscape-study/

Pope John Paul III. (2001). *Message for the 35th world communications day.* Vatican City: Vatican Documents. http://www.vatican.va/content/john-paul-ii/en/messages/communications/documents/hf_jp-ii_mes_20010124_world-communications-day.html

Pope Paul VI. (1975). *Apostolic exhortation Evangelii Nuntiandi.* Vatican City: Vatican Documents. http://www.vatican.va/content/paul-vi/en/apost_exhortations/documents/hf_p-vi_exh_19751208_evangelii-nuntiandi.html

Pontifical Council for Social Communications. (1971). *Communio et progressio.* Vatican City: Vatican Documents. http://www.vatican.va/roman_curia/pontifical_councils/pccs/documents/rc_pc_pccs_doc_23051971_communio_en.html

Pontifical Council for Social Communications. (1997). *Ethics in advertising.* Vatican City: Vatican Documents. http://www.vatican.va/roman_curia/pontifical_councils/pccs/documents/rc_pc_pccs_doc_22021997_ethics-in-ad_en.html

Pontifical Council for Social Communications. (2002). *The Church and the internet.* Vatican City: Vatican Documents. http://www.vatican.va/roman_curia/pontifical_councils/pccs/documents/rc_pc_pccs_doc_20020228_church-internet_en.html

Ringold, D. J. (1998). A comment on the pontifical council for social communications' *Ethics in Advertising. Journal of Public Policy & Marketing 17*(2), 32–335.

Sarapin, S. H. & Morris P. L. (2017). The biggest lie on the web: Coming to terms with the failure to read through the lens of the First Amendment. *First Amendment Studies 51*(2), 86–108. doi: 10.1080/21689725.2017.1388749

United Coalition of Reason. (n.d.) What we do. https://unitedcor.org/what-we-do/

Veenker, Jody (1999, July 12). God speaks to commuters. *Christianity Today, 43*(8). https://www.christianitytoday.com/ct/1999/july12/9t810c.html

Williams, D. (2016). Nielsen out-of-home advertising study. https://theraveagency.com/files/NielsenOAAAOOHAdvertisingStudy2015.pdf

Zelinsky, W. (2001). The uniqueness of the American religious landscape. *Geographical Review, 91*(3), 565–585.

Chapter 8

The Bible Tells Me So

Scriptural Stories of Survival Create Metaphors for the Advertising of Nonprofits

A good story has a moral lesson: For example, you may recognize the end of this story: "Every living thing on the face of the earth was wiped out; men and animals and the creatures that move along the ground and the birds of the air were wiped from the earth. Only Noah was left, and those with him in the ark" (New International Version, Genesis 7:23). What has been missing in the research into secular holy hype is an exploration of advertising that employs a religious theme in terms of the moral lesson of the original scriptural tale. In particular, long-standing social causes, such as ending world hunger, developing solutions for natural and man-made environmental disasters and ruination, and driving efforts for biodiversity, require billions of dollars over decades in capital investment and manpower. For these nonprofit organizations to survive, they need to implement cause-related marketing (CRM) campaigns that are instantly noticed, perceived, appreciated, and favorably recalled when it is time to donate manpower, time, or money.

In today's marketing environment of advertising clutter and homogeneity, two of the few ways to break through for attention is through metaphor (Ang & Lim, 2006) and by crossing the line from religious satire to the provocative, blasphemous, and scatological (Pope et al., 2004). In this chapter we: (a) explain the study of metaphor; (b) describe the most easily identifiable and most frequently appropriated attributes from three popular scriptural narratives; and (c) delineate the singular advertising needs of nonprofit organizations (NPOs). In particular, we focus attention on one ad run for the Green Building Council, Brazil, and two of Greenpeace's ads as exemplars of the kind of wordplay and neoiconistic design that incorporate the Noah's-Ark lesson and images into a multimodal metaphor for the communication for survival of environmental protection interests. It should be noted that not all illustrations of the biblical themes are for nonprofits. They are included for a review of the motifs overall, especially in terms of their use of metaphor.

METAPHOR

The way secular holy hype works on its mass of viewers can be explained by a compilation of several metaphor theories. Researchers have struggled to develop a unified theory of metaphor since Aristotle's *Poetics* from 335 BCE. Richards (1936) resurrected the study of metaphor. Today, there are numerous theories of metaphor, most of which are verbally or linguistically oriented (e.g., Black's interactive metaphor theory, 1962; Lakoff and Johnson's conceptual or cognitive metaphor theory, 1980; Martin and Harré's comparison metaphor theory, 1982). More recent research has added the visual metaphor and the multimodal construction of metaphor, the two theoretical frameworks we focus on as they apply to advertising. Despite such a wide array of theories of metaphor, many share similar assumptions. For example, Krippendorff (1993) explains several assumptions of a theory of communication metaphors "that goes beyond mere rhetorical formulations and links language with the creation of perceived realities" (p. 1):

- "All metaphors carry explanatory structures *from a familiar domain* of experiences *into another domain* in need of understanding or restructuring."
- "Metaphors require seeing some *structural similarities between these two domains*, however far-fetched these may be."
- "Metaphors *organize their users' perceptions and*, when acted upon, *can create the realities* experienced." (p. 2–3)

Forceville (2008) expounds on Lakoff and Johnson's (1980) construction of metaphor as not being limited to linguistic usage, harking back to Black's (1962) interaction theory of creative metaphors. In fact, Forceville insists, language is not necessary in order to create a metaphor. He calls for the extension of conceptual metaphor theory (CMT) to progress beyond language to include visuals, sounds, and the representations of our other senses. In research predating Forceville's studies and citing neurobiologist Arturo Damasio, Zaltman and Coulter (1995) concur that the mind must satisfy the essential criterion of having "the ability to display images internally and to order those images in a process called thought. The images are not solely visual; there are also sound images, olfactory images, and so on" (p. 37).

Further, still, is the discussion of multimodal metaphors, which Forceville defines as "metaphors in which target, source, and/or mappable features are represented or suggested by at least two different sign systems (one of which may be language) or modes of perception" (Forceville, 2008, p. 463). The target, or the new image, represents the semantic domain, which is newly structured in terms of another domain, that is, the source, or original image. The source is the antecedent, the object or event to which a symbol alludes.

Figure 8.1a is a particularly powerful example of a visual metaphor that requires almost no text. From the apples and our beautiful, nubile female handing the fruit over to a handsome, young man for him to take a bite of a juicy one, we are instantly struck by the biblical metaphor for temptation.

Figure 8.1 a) 1987 Benetton ad depicting Adam and Eve as teenagers. The serpent is wrapped around Eve's neck as she is offering the apple to Adam. b) 1939 ad for Fruit of the Loom men's shirts. Back then, shirts were selling for $1.65 each. c) DKNY also employs the sexual attraction and temptation theme with its seductive Eve. Eve is holding an apple and the headline is "Be delicious," from the 2013 campaign of the same name. Another line states, "Take a bite out of life." d) 1947 ad for American Wheelabrator & Equipment Corp. uses David and Goliath with the headline: "Strength is no longer a matter of size." e) Lattice Engines ad using the David and Goliath theme. "You can really be David to the big companies' Goliath by leveraging data effectively." *Source: a) © Benetton. Public domain image. b) © Fruit of the Loom, public domain image retrieved from ebay.com listing. c) © DKNY. Image retrieved from adforum.com. d) © American Wheelabrator & Equipment Corp, no longer in business. e) © Lattice Engines, no longer in business.*

This woman is our Eve. In this 1987 Benetton ad, as unconventional as ever, she is seducing us with her open denim top, exposing her breasts. Not too easy to miss is the black snake wrapped around her neck, its tail end draping down over her left breast. Is this an ad for jeans? Did Benetton ever make jeans? Just what is going on here? If they are selling jeans, I can understand the take on Adam and Eve.

THREE UNIVERSALLY RECOGNIZED BIBLICAL SURVIVAL NARRATIVES

There are several prominent stories of survival from the Hebrew Bible: the creation story involving Adam and Eve; the tale of David and Goliath; and the story of Noah's ark and the deluge. These three are so well known by the worldwide public that one need not be especially biblically literate to understand their significance. To be sure, all of these narratives communicate survival. The creation story of Genesis is so salient that a poll conducted for the Biologos Foundation in 2014 found that more than 50% of Americans believe that "Adam and Eve were real people" (Burton, 2017) despite the fact that only 24% of Americans believe the Bible is the literal word of God (Saad, 2017).

Adam and Eve

When we examine advertising over the last century that uses the Adam and Eve theme, we are usually treated to a humorous advertisement that plays on one or more of the following motifs: (a) embarrassment from one's nudity; (b) the precious value of apples; or (c) the irresistibility of sexual temptation leading to the violation of God's laws and a subsequent fall from grace—irreverence and blasphemy for their own sake or for amusement and shock. At the outset of designing appeals for a social cause, this theme would seem to be inappropriate because, as Pope et al. (2004) report, "In advertisements with nudity, the associated company is deemed to be less reputable and the producer of a lower-quality product" (p. 71). What we do *not* see in ads using the creation story is the implication of the moral, the goodness of the Lord in allowing humankind to survive despite Adam and Eve's exile from Eden for disobeying. Therefore, we would expect to see this theme used in more humorous, daring, or whimsical product advertising, such as what we view in the 1939 Fruit of the Loom ad for men's shirts in figure 8.1b. We imagine that women giving advice to me on their clothing began in the Garden of Eden. As the ad states, "even before men wore shirts, women gave lots of good advice on men's attire." In figure

8.1c, DKNY, or Donna Karan New York, gives the sensuous Eve a chance, too. This Eve seduces us with her pouty, partially open mouth. DKNY is a famous brand for feminine products, so we are led to believe that we may also possess this sensuality and sexuality if we use whatever this product is. Looking closer, we see that the words "Be Delicious" are actually the name of a new fragrance from this company. Aware of the Adam and Eve story from the Bible, we know what this is supposed to do to our ability to tempt and attract our "Adam." In very small type, this woman taunts us to "take a bite out of life." Our first instinct, which is to believe that this is temptation and, perhaps, sin, is confirmed in the scant text. We have been drawn in by the visual metaphor.

Some advertising images might lead us to believe that the Adam and Eve story from the Bible could not be employed for the marketing of a social cause (e.g., figure 8.1b), but there is one NPO known for its commonly over-the-top, sometimes shocking, advertisements—PETA (Bhasin, 2011). Figure 5.2b illustrates PETA's perspective on the Adam and Eve narrative, another reference to religion. A vine of vegetation wraps around the nude body of Angela Simmons, substituting for the serpent of the creation story. The metaphor plays off of the story's lesson about original sin and temptation, clearly stating that eating meat is a sin as well. In fact, the ad tempts us to eat the apple the model is holding instead, contrary to God's admonition.

David and Goliath

The story of David and Goliath, portrayed in the Hebrew scriptures, is often an ad theme in a lighter approach, but can also figure prominently in a serious ad (see figures 8.1c and 8.1d, and in figures 8.5a through 8.5h). In a 1947 ad, figure 8.1c published by American Wheelabrator & Equipment Corp. uses David and Goliath with the headline: "Strength is no longer a matter of size." Figure 8.1d shows an ad for a company that is no longer in business, Lattice Engines. The headline is: "You can really be David to the big companies' Goliath by leveraging data effectively." David and Goliath is a biblical story of survival of the Israelites, and is most often used in modern advertising to illustrate the difference between the advertiser's product and the competitor's product in terms of strength and effectiveness and not size—David, representing the advertiser, is small but mighty, resourceful, and good, and the rival, portrayed as Goliath is, of course, large but unintelligent, bad, and awkwardly inadequate (Gatchet & Cloud, 2012). It would be nothing short of sacrilege to compare the advertiser to Goliath, the Philistine. David and Goliath make frequent appearances, and we can see more of them later in figure 8.5.

Noah's Ark and the Flood

The third well-known biblical story to examine is that of Noah and the flood from Genesis 6–9. It is, perhaps, the most frequently used visually rhetorical device among the three discussed herein. The metaphorical "low-hanging fruit," probably a more appropriate term when analyzing the Adam and Eve story, would be accessible through these characteristics of the ark itself: (a) has a huge capacity as a container; (b) was laboriously constructed of wood that survived a 40-day rain; (c) is loaded with male-female pairs of every species on earth; (d) is dark and dreary inside; and (e) is resistant to water. These are the qualities of the ark that advertisers have played upon in numerous advertisements since the turn of the twentieth century, tying these few memorable characteristics to that of the advertised product or service. This theme has consistently appeared in advertising for more than a century and lives on into the 21st. It appears that there is no end to the inspired applications of the ark story's metaphorical attributes (figures 8.2, 8.3, and 8.4).

A British company established in 1865, Liebig's Extract of Beef Company, published the earliest advertisement we have found using the Noah's Ark theme in 1898. In figure 8.2a, Liebig claims that its extract of beef has been eaten by laborers since Noah's time and that it is recognized as the "greatest source of vigor and refreshment." The company was sold in 1968. Figure 8.2b shows animals boarding the Ark, two by two. Even the Reddi Wip spray whipped cream is entering the Ark in pairs. The 1966 headline: "What would one gnu be without another gnu? Extinct! Pair it with pies, cakes." This is an ad which begs the question: What does Noah's Ark really have to do with whipped cream? One of the older ads is figure 8.2c from 1953 for REO Motors, which advertised its "more-pay-load" design. Noah adds, "Biggest truck news since the Flood." This comes from the Ark's ability to carry a large amount. Figure 8.2d, which touts Continental Can Co. from 1949 and its solutions to "Problems in Packaging" is another go at the Noah's Ark metaphor. Figure 8.2e, a 1969 ad for GATX, a company that leases railcars, uses the rare 40-days-40-nights theme, the length of time Noah captained the Ark. The last line of the text reads, "You can call General American Transportation Corporation, even on a rainy day." AIG Companies insurance spent large on this 2-page, black-and-white ad layout in figure 8.2f comfortingly stating, "AIG would not have cancelled Noah's flood insurance!"

Figure 8.3 is a display of eight more advertisements dating back to 1914, that make use of the Noah's Ark metaphor.

In figure 8.3a, Pirelli finds use for a Noah's Ark in the desert. A long semi fitted with hundreds of Pirelli tires can tow a filled ark with no problem. Figure 8.3e takes a more humorous approach than did Pirelli, both in art and in concept. Pirelli's art is realistic and dramatic, while Eureka Tents from 1989 is cartoonish. Pirelli emphasizes the heavy payload its tires can support

Figure 8.2 a) 1898 Liebig ad claims its extract of beef has been eaten by laborers since Noah's time. b) 1966 ad for ConAgra and Beatrice Foods. "What would one gnu be without another gnu? Extinct! Pair it with pies, cakes . . ." c) In 1953, REO motors advertised its "more-pay-load" design. Noah adds, "Biggest truck news since the Flood." d) 1949 ad for Continental Can Co. offers its solutions to "Problems in Packaging." e) 1969 GATX (a company that leases railcars) ad uses a 40-days-40-nights theme. "You can call General American Transportation Corporation, even on a rainy day." f) AIG ad. "AIG wouldn't have canceled his flood insurance!" *Source: a) © Liebig. Public domain image retrieved from ebay.com listing. b) © ConAgra and Beatrice Foods. Public domain image retrieved from ebay.com listing. c) © REO, no longer in business. d) © Continental Can Co. Public domain image retrieved from ebay.com listing. e) ©GATX. Public domain image retrieved from ebay.com listing. f) Image courtesy of ©AIG Companies.*

Figure 8.3 a) Ad for Pirelli tyres [*sic*]. The Ark is being transported on a truck with new Pirelli tyres for safety. b) 1934 ad for Taylor Instruments. "Friend Noah, what does your Stormguide say?" "Looks like we're in for a bit of rain." c) 1950 ad for American Airlines Airfreight. "Noah didn't pick 'em by size, shape or weight!" d) 1965 ad for London Fog. "When it looks like rain, believe in London Fog." e) 1989 ad for Eureka! Tent, which provides a dry place for all of the animals left out in the "wet and windy" weather. f) In 1914, Black Flag insect killer printed an 8-page brochure advertising the product Noah could have used to rid himself of the insect-control problem he had with so many animals on the ark. g) 1928 Marlboro ad. Captain Noah on his ark. "When it's dark and rainy outside, smoke a Marlboro." h) 1973 RCA ad. "Satellites have taken up where Noah left off." *Source*: *a) © Pirelli. Screenshot retrieved from adeevee.com. b) © Taylor Instruments. Public domain image. c) © American Airlines. Public domain image. d) Image courtesy of London Fog. Creative directors: Ana López & Marina Cuesta. Illustrator/designer: Jorge López. e) © Eureka Tents. Public domain image retrieved from ebay.com listing. f) ©Black Flag. Public domain image. g) ©Marlboro. Public domain image. h) ©RCA. Public domain image.*

as they safely transport the cargo, and Eureka focuses on its ability to provide safety and protection against the elements.

In figure 8.3b, Taylor Instruments gives us this humorous ad from 1934. Someone, perhaps one of Noah's neighbors who helped him build the ark,

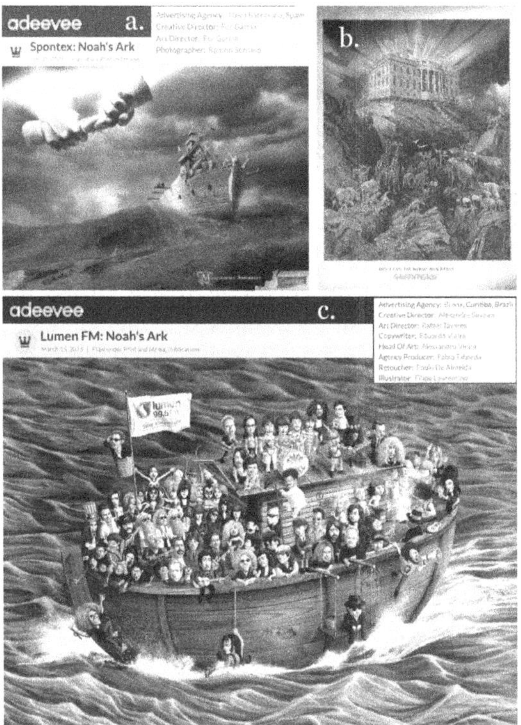

Figure 8.4 a) 2009 ad for Spontex. Even God uses Spontex wipes because, in a storm, they are "miraculously absorbent!" b) 1997 Greenpeace ad, a plea to the White House. "Don't fail the world. Sign Kyoto." c) 2016 ad for Lumen 99.5FM, a plea to save the station. Many famous musicians are being saved by an ark. *Source*: *a) ©Spontex. Screenshot retrieved from adeevee.com. b) Image courtesy of ©Greenpeace. c) ©LumenFM. Screenshot retrieved from adeevee.com.*

asks Noah, "Friend Noah, what does your Stormguide say?" Noah, checking his Taylor nautical instrument answers, "Looks like we're in for a bit of rain." Moving right to figure 8.3c, another black-and-white ad, American Airlines Airfreight runs its ad in 1950. This shipping company demonstrates the utility of the Noah's Ark perspective on capacity as its justification for the biblical theme. It addresses its ad "to every management seeking better methods of distribution." The headline is: "Noah didn't pick /em by size, shape, or weight!" Later, "Airfreight, too, invites every kind of cargo—the ponderous as well as the perishable." This is the most commonly used perspective of this Bible story.

The popular British rainwear company, London Fog, shows how well its raincoats hold up in a deluge in figure 8.3d from 1965. The headline is "When it looks like rain, *believe* in London Fog." This is the original double-truck, or 2-page, layout, but it was sometimes published as a one-page display. This ad sports a double entendre, not in a risqué way, but in a subtler way. It rains quite a bit in London. If you have ever seen an old movie set in that wonderful city, you know that the actors spend a lot of time in precipitation and fog. The other meaning here is that anyone boarding an ark, especially the original one, must expect nothing less than a deluge. In England, they may tell you that it is bucketing down or that you are experiencing a Scotch mist. What a perfect opportunity for rainwear by London Fog.

In one of the most imaginative appropriations of the ark theme from 1914, Black Flag (figure 8.3f) thought about the less attractive repercussions of caring for so many animals on board. The varmint-killing company printed an 8-page brochure advertising the product Noah could have used to rid himself of the insect-control problem he must have had. It is difficult to imagine the design meeting that preceded the Marlboro cigarettes ad in figure 8.3g. One brave creative soul piped up: "I've got it! Let's use a Noah's Ark theme for this ad!" Where did that come from? It's hard to say, but it is an ad that was really published in 1928. Who's to say that this interesting scenario did not work well as an attention getter? The headline, "When it's dark and rainy outside, smoke a Marlboro," certainly encapsulates Noah's predicament. The copy continues on its optimistic outlook: "Rain or shine—Marlboro cigarettes will see you through." RCA published in 1973 an ad (figure 8.3h) with a Noah's-Ark motif, stating, "Satellites have taken up where Noah left off." The connection appears tenuous, but the ad's first sentence helps us understand how this approach came about: "The Ark may be obsolete, but there's a new way to help preserve the species against flood—and a host of other perils."

Figure 8.4 expands upon the Noah's Ark presence in advertising with three more examples. In a visually metaphorical advertisement, Spontex (figure 8.4a) gives credit to God, whose hands have wrung the rain from its "miraculously absorbent" wipes, while serving as the source of the rain keeping Noah and his family and animals holed up inside the ark. The illustration uses dramatic lighting and colors to render Noah's predicament in the most serious of depictions. God has used these maximally absorbent wipes to collect the moisture from the clouds and wring it out as rain. The Spontex brand is so absorbent that its wipes can hold enough moisture for 40 days and 40 nights! Figure 8.4b is explained later in this chapter and figure 8.4c is described in the caption.

UNIQUE NEEDS OF NPO ADVERTISING

While all corporations do or should consider how their marketing influences public perceptions of their business or industry, that is, their corporate image, cause-related organizations may need to be more sensitive to this in today's business environment. Their campaigns must spur and improve the health of not only the organization but also of the cause itself.

Branding has long been studied as it pertains to tangible goods and, after that, to services. It has been only over the last two decades that the branding of nonprofits has been seriously considered and empirically investigated (Mort et al., 2007). Charity NPOs that survive on individual donations or that form associations with for-profit businesses must be sensitive to the effect their advertising has on the public's propensity to contribute to the cause or to buy the associated or partnered businesses' products and services. Branding has been shown to be as important to an NPO as to a for-profit company because it is the "primary point of differentiation between competitors and, as such, they are [*sic*] increasingly acknowledged as critical to a nonprofit organization's success in both cross sector and intra-sector competition" (Mort et al., 2007, pp. 108–109). Additionally, a nonprofit must be aware of the images of its partners due to the effect of cross-branding. They all affect each other's public images. For example, a for-profit's spokesperson may have negative qualities in the estimation of some segment of the public, which could then spill over into the image of the nonprofit partner. Branding factors, such as logo, name, and slogan are the stalwart identifiers that must be considered, but, today, there is a new characteristic being examined in the relationship between the for-profit or NPO and their audience of consumers and potential consumers—brand personality. The brand personality can result in "stronger emotional ties and greater trust and loyalty" (Mort et al., 2007, p. 109).

Sargeant et al. (2007) find that an NPO's personality trait of emotional engagement can be responsible for increased donor financial support through enhancement of the memorability of the donor's contact with the organization. Emotional engagement can be due to the level of excitement generated in addition to other personality characteristics. Sargeant et al. (2007) report: "Traits such as strong, bold, exciting, fun, heroic, and inspiring were commonly linked to the level of arousal brands were able to generate and appeared linked to giving behavior" (p. 8). Whereas some shocking approaches undoubtedly can raise awareness of an issue or differentiate an NPO among others in the same "good-cause" sector, it is not necessarily the case that high arousal levels and memorability from boldness will lead to greater financial contributions to the specific organization. It could foster awareness, but also revulsion. However, despite heavy use of shocking visuals in its marketing literature, Barnardos, the United Kingdom's largest children's charity, claims its violent graphics, which have elicited some of the largest numbers of complaints, have converted viewers into donors (Isaac, 2016).

We do not often encounter cause-related advertising that takes advantage of the moral of the story, that man can survive and defeat the enemy

Figure 8.5 a) In 1931, David can even slay the scourge of tuberculosis, represented by Goliath. b) 1904 ad for Postum, an instant coffee product, tells a David-and-Goliath tale about the product. c) 1956 ad for Republic Airlines promoting its fighter planes for the US Air Force. d) to g) Greenpeace ad features David and his slingshot against dirty industry. h) 1966 ad for Calvert. "Calvert Gin vs. The British Gin Empire." *Source: a) Public domain image retrieved from U.S. National Library of Medicine digital collections. b) ©Postum. Public domain image retrieved from ebay.com listing. c) Public domain image retrieved from ebid.net. d) to g) Images courtesy of ©Greenpeace and FCB/Lower Group. Illustrator: Anatolij Pickmann. h) ©Calvert. Public domain image retrieved from ebay.com listing.*

despite his shortcomings and the clearly apparent futility of the situation of the moment. Using the David-and-Goliath theme, we have found only one ad for a tuberculosis charity (figure 8.5a) and one campaign for the NPO Greenpeace. In figures 8.5d–g, the four different ad panels for Greenpeace pit David and his slingshot against the monstrous, looming, heavily capitalized corporate interests that are ruining our land and water, their tentacles reaching into every industry with the potential to spoil our natural resources. This implies a vicious fight between a largely defenseless good cause (right), which could even need divine intervention, against an enemy (might) that will not go down easily.

NEOICONISTIC MODEL FOR THE BIBLICAL SURVIVAL STORY OF NOAH'S ARK AND THE FLOOD: CASE STUDIES: GREEN BUILDING COUNCIL, BRAZIL, AND GREENPEACE

Social movements carry an inherent moral foundation and they have long "channeled their moral energy into causes in the name of the dispossessed" (Mika, 2006, pp. 916–917). Mika explores activism on behalf of the world's non-human animals, specifically the animal rights group PETA, and asserts that causes such as this have particular salience for activists, "who do not typically engage in traditional forms of religious practice" (p. 917) and yet hold a fervent, near-religious devotion to the cause. PETA's members, for example, are more than 65% atheistic or agnostic (Mika, 2006). Mika attests to the importance of the ardent dedication to PETA as a substitute for orthodox religion in that "commitment to the principles . . . is part of an individual, even communal, spiritual ethic" (p. 918). We must then ask: If this is what a cause-centered group means to a member-adherent or supporter, then how can that nonprofit, social organization entice potential constituents to join its ranks? Jasper and Poulsen (1995) affirm, "They are recruited to a group or movement, not converted to a belief system" (p. 497). The organizers must find a way to "frame," or fabricate an attractive or malleable vision of, the movement "to achieve a common definition of a social problem and a common prescription for solving it" (p. 495), aligning the moral mission and methods of the organization to those of the prospective recruit. This is accomplished through the use of strategic rhetorical appeals, both linguistic and visual, and the use of a device that Jasper and Poulsen attribute to Sapir (1935), who calls it a "condensing symbol" or "condensation symbol," which "strikes deeper and deeper roots in the unconscious and diffuses its emotional quality to types of behavior or situations apparently far removed from the original meaning of the symbol" (1995, pp. 493–494). Jasper and Poulsen (1995) expound:

> Organizers use such symbols to recruit members, especially strangers. A powerful symbol lends credibility to an explicit argument by connoting the implicit

> assumptions embedded in worldviews and common sense. The best evoke what Burke called a "god term:" a moral absolute that appears to be unquestionable. Like all culture, symbols are both connotative, evoking associations in an audience, and constitutive, helping to create the audience's world. (p. 498)

Acknowledging that not all condensation symbols or god terms will resonate with everyone in the audience with the same valence or even with the same meaning, it is logical that an appeal should employ the most widely comprehended symbol in the most commonly intended connotation. However, another, less explicit, approach is finding resonance with potential members and contributors around the world. Just as we see pervasive use of neologisms in advertising, an innovative perspective, what we call a "neoiconism," is making its appearance in CRM marketing. We now look at two NPOs and some of their neoiconisms.

Green Building Council, Brazil

Neologisms are new words coined by, most relevantly, copywriters and art directors to particularize a meaning. Organizations, few at this time, are experimenting with new meanings for old icons, or neoiconisms. One Brazilian NPO, the Green Building Council, has accomplished this in an ethereal, otherworldly advertisement. With industrial smokestacks choking the air out of what used to be a clean, livable environment, a modern spaceship parked on a Mt.Ararat–like hill offers hope of a green environment, a fresh start, on another planet. In the biblical story of Noah's Ark in Genesis, after 40 days and 40 nights, the ark lands on Ararat. In figure 8.6a, we are launching from where we once landed. Once again, the Noah's Ark metaphor evokes a message of survival for humankind. Whereas the organization advances green principles of building here on earth, we understand that this resolution of finding another place to live will be our species' last chance if we continue to abuse and spoil God's gifts for us.

The space[ship] is the focus of a bright, white, divine light, which shines down from heaven, and, as such, is the neoiconism. Despite the new certainty of a "God-given" way out of the terrible circumstance, we would prefer to avert what would certainly be a disaster in the end. As we know from the first ark experience, humanity will perish except for a righteous few persons and all of the animal kingdom. Can we be sure we will be the righteous ones on board that ship? On Ararat, Noah's family enters into a covenant with God. If we were to change our ways, become good instead of evil, the planet and the planet's people would never again be destroyed in a flood. Now we are receiving a communication, which forces us to acknowledge we have not been good stewards of our environment. We have not upheld our end of the

Figure 8.6 a) 2011 ad for the Green Building Council of Brazil (GBCB). The animals walk in pairs up the mountain to the spaceship for the GBCB. The ad asks, "Where to now?" b) 2006 Greenpeace ad. Inset at lower left: close-up of Greenpeace ship called the Arctic Sunrise, painted with a rainbow and a dove with a fig leaf in its beak. *Source: a) Image courtesy of ©Green Building Council of Brazil. b) Image courtesy of ©Greenpeace.*

bargain. The minimal text, "Where to now?" makes this a multimodal metaphor, one in which two domains, textual and visual, are used in conjunction with each other. Those three words are the simplest way to communicate the exigent nature of our situation. We must decide whether we act now or wait until there is no other choice than to leave this planet while the mass of humanity dies out. Do we inform others, donate money to this cause, volunteer our time? Has something in this ad resonated with us in such a profound, emotional, and immediate way as to compel us to act? Has the ad successfully communicated the existential threat? Unfortunately, what occurs to us is this: There is no other place to go. If we are concerned, we must act now.

In a response to Garrett Hardin (1974), an American ecologist and philosopher, Verghese (1976) summarizes the author's argument, declaring, "Hardin contends that the widespread use of the spaceship metaphor to describe the plight of our planet [i.e., overpopulation] is inappropriate, except perhaps as *a justification for certain pollution control measures*" (p. 244; emphasis added). Hardin's claim seems to give credence to the metaphor used in the ad by the Green Building Council, Brazil. The toxicity of the belching smoke-stacks speaks to a need to rid the planet of air pollution. This would comport with the "mission" of the Council, which is:

> Transforming the civil construction industry and the culture of society towards sustainability, using market forces to build and operate buildings and communities in an integrated way. And, ensure the balance between economic development, socio-environmental impacts and use of natural resources, contributing to the improvement of the quality of life and well-being of present and future generations. (Green Building Council, 2014)

This unusual, creative, and thought-provoking ad uses metaphor in the three main ways described by Krippendorff (1993). It employs explanatory structures, such as the animals walking two by two into the spaceship atop a small mountain, from the familiar domain of the biblical story experience, into another domain, the spaceship, an icon in need of reorientation. This ad meets the second of Krippendorff's assumptions, too. The absence of the ark does not detract from the meaning or the salience of the connotation. It lives in our consciousness and is replaced almost seamlessly by the spaceship because we know of no other experience that calls for so many animals to be collected in male-female pairs and ushered into a large vehicle to hold them all together. There is no other signification so broadly comprehended for the image of animals walking two by two into a house-like structure. Even the experience of viewing zoo or circus animals being coaxed into a container for rest or transport is nothing like the animal parade of Noah's Ark tale. We have seen some movies and at least one "Twilight Zone" episode that dramatically enact this frightening scenario. Quite literally, the source, or ark, is absent from the advertisement in figure 8.6a, and the qualities of the ark are mapped onto the new vehicle, the spaceship. The animals walking two abreast into the "ship" represent the structural similarity between the two domains, that element, which connects one to the other. Its "condensing symbol," per Sapir (1935), is the imminent destruction of our world and the extinction of all people on the earth until or unless we change our ways and become the stewards we have committed to be.

With regard to the third assumption, the Noah's Ark metaphor organizes the viewers' perceptions such that they can imagine the real effects, that is, the realities, of the threat of extinction if survival tactics are not employed. The lesson of this story is salient for Brazilians, who make up the majority of the audience for the Green Building Council. The country is highly religious, with 90% of its people reporting adherence to a Christian denomination. Only 7% report no religious affiliation (World Population Review, 2019). They would be expected to know Noah's story well. And, they are particularly vulnerable to the emotional and cognitive pull of this ad because they live among fellow citizens afflicted daily by the plagues of water and air pollution. Henley et al. (2009) suggest that "academics and practitioners should garner better results by including relevant Christian symbol product linkages while avoiding irrelevant Christian symbol product linkages when targeting religious consumers" (p. 100).

Greenpeace

Greenpeace has been using the Noah's Ark metaphor for more than 20 years. This group, also an NPO, makes a promise to work for survival on its website's home page: "Greenpeace will never stop fighting for a greener, healthier world for our oceans, forests, food, climate, and democracy—no matter what forces stand in our way." This is most assuredly stewardship. The first example we have been able to find is shown in figure 8.4b. It dates to 1997, when more than 150 nations adopted the Kyoto Protocol, the first international treaty for environmental protection around the world (United Nations Framework Convention on Climate Change, 2019). The caption reads, "Don't fail the world. Sign Kyoto." Once again, there is no ark. The ark's attributes have been mapped onto the man-made White House, our new target image, signaling that the US government must become a part of this pact by signing onto the agreement's policies protecting the environment. The White House is our new ark. The continuity of life as we know it depends on our nation's enthusiastic participation, including government regulation. The target audience is all Americans interested in or curious about environmental protection. The animal pairs, walking with singular purpose into the protective surroundings of the building on the mount, are the remnant from the source whose presence in the ad stands in for the Noah narrative and connects us with it, but we must understand that the new "vehicle" for survival is no longer a means of physical transport—now, a metaphysical or transcendental one. It is a neoiconism, a new interpretation of the original ark, not as an object that carries the few righteous people away from the certain jeopardy of extinction, but as an instrument or mechanism for changing the way the world deals with the evil God finds on earth. The allusion to extinction is not as strong as in the council ad with the spaceship, which is a perceived vehicle for survival. Extinction is secondary to political action necessary to avert it. The situation can be perceived in both a pessimistic and an optimistic way. The glass-half-empty view is that our situation is dire because there is no real transport to take us to a safe place. If the administration's agenda does not achieve policies of environmental protection, life is in danger of becoming extinct. On the other hand, the glass-half-full perspective shows us that the policies are communication for survival, a way we can stave off the worst-case scenario.

The onus is on us, as stewards of our country's resources, to put appropriate political pressure on those in the White House and in other institutions of government to create the laws necessary to regulate those committing environmental crimes against life on earth. In this advertisement, though, we are emboldened by the implicit message that we *do* have power over the vectors of evil, even in this dire situation. God has obligated us to the conservancy of the world he has created for us. Are we able to fulfill this duty? Through stewardship, we exert our power. Cryer explains:

> The link between stewardship and environmentalism is a contentious one. What does it mean for humans "to take care of the world"? Environmental stewardship is typically thought of as entailing reducing human impacts into the natural world. However, philosopher Neil Paul Cummins claims that humans have a special stewardship role on the planet because, through their technology, humans are able to save life from otherwise certain elimination. This is a modern-day interpretation of Noah's Ark, the cornerstone of human stewardship being technological protection and regulation. (Cryer, 2018, n.p.)

We now come to a more recent Greenpeace advertisement reminiscent of the Bible's Noah-and-the-flood narrative. On the basis of the population estimate of 6.6 billion, we can date the ad, figure 8.6b, to about 2006 (Worldometers, 2019).

Unlike anything we have seen so far, this ad (figure 8.6b with close-up of ship) features no ark and no parade of animals. It does, though, feature an ocean-going ship moving through treacherous waters, which is singularly connotative of Noah's ark through the image painted on the side, a close-up of which is seen, also in figure 8.6b. The end of the biblical ark narrative begins with Noah, the captain, releasing a dove from the ship. Eventually, the dove returns with a twig and leaf in its mouth, an indication that land and flora are near. Soon thereafter, Noah sets the ark down on Mt. Ararat. It is then that God makes the covenant with Noah, of which the rainbow will be a sign to remind humankind of this divine agreement that as long as man takes care of the earth as dutiful stewards, the Lord will never again destroy it in a deluge. Consequently, the rainbow and dove on the ship evoke this story almost immediately, especially if this is what the viewer looks at first.

The awareness of the biblical referent is reinforced by the text in this multimodal ad. The message is that this is a life raft—a means of survival for 6.6 billion people . . . at the time, the population of the entire world. We are next invited to "come on board." Is humankind in danger of mass death . . . extinction? The ship is likely navigating through waters full of shards of one of the polar caps. After all, the name of the ship is the Arctic Sunrise. If the polar icecaps melt, is the earth in danger of complete environmental and human annihilation? Will our world and its people be covered with water as in the biblical flood? It seems almost impossible that viewers would not imagine these potentialities, but we cannot know this with certainty without surveying public opinion. The rhetorical invitation to come aboard alludes to an invitation to join the movement. The public is being recruited to work alongside like-minded people to use whatever legal means available to inhibit the human-directed behavior that is one of the agents of climate change. If we cannot give the time to volunteer for the group, then perhaps we can donate financial resources to the social cause. Just as Noah built an ark to actualize the survival of the human species and all animal species, Greenpeace built a "life raft for 6.6 billion people."

As for the alignment with Krippendorff's (1993) criteria for effective metaphor, the Greenpeace "life raft" ad borrows some explanatory structures from the Noah story's domain, such as the boat, the rainbow, and the dove, and carries them into the new domain of the boat in an ocean of ice fragments, where they work with the textual element to account for the boat's new position and new purpose. The structural similarities between the two domains are the boat and the water. In biblical days, the flood destroyed all life on earth except for the few righteous and all animal species on board. Today, with polar ice caps melting, much of our land and the structures and life on it will flood and be destroyed as a result of rising water. The entire metaphor, if even remotely understood, organizes the viewers' perceptions of the urgency of the coming disaster, and, in this way, the reality of the destruction can be experienced as the looming crisis it is. We can almost perceive the imminent ruination as humankind's failure to heed the divine warnings, and, therefore, realize our personal part in it. Consequently, it is now the call we are hearing that compels us to act.

Verghese (1976) informs us that Hardin recommended the lifeboat metaphor as a substitute for the spaceship metaphor. Offering his opinion of that alternative, Verghese argues, "If there is one conclusion that is growing upon most informed persons in our time, it is the idea that we are all 'in the same boat'" (p. 244).

CONCLUSION

Its persistent use of Noah-inspired advertising would seem to indicate that Greenpeace and all others who have taken this approach have had success with this formula. Our e-mails and phone calls sent to the appropriate people at the NPOs and the advertising agencies to inquire about the effectiveness of these ads in terms of monetary donations have gone unanswered. Greenpeace is a huge organization that works with numerous advertising agencies in many countries, including its own in-house creative agency. Their communicative efforts are addressed to a multitude of publics around the world. Their website displays many of their ads, but these are not accompanied by any descriptive text. We believe that their continued use of this theme and the graphics on their boat attest to the success of this advertising approach until verification is obtained. This is the most consequential limitation of this study and any study of advertising. Even if we could communicate with the right people involved, we might not be able to gather that kind of information, which is usually proprietary.

Additional methods for determining the success of campaigns and individual ads using biblical themes of survival would be experimental surveys, providing an array of creative approaches for the same narrative, from outrageous to respectful, from humorous to serious, and more, and testing participants' appraisals of the advertisements in a variety of ways.

NPOs that concentrate on environmental and animal protection would probably do well using the Noah's-Ark metaphor. Although a large portion of those on the Christian political right in their audiences of potential recruits have adopted an anti-climate-change position, they may find comfort with a biblical message that perhaps only they perceive or that does not appropriate cherished religious symbols for the base purpose of selling things (Mallia, 2009). The message could break down barriers between their political and religious beliefs. It is unlikely these fundamental Christians would be particularly deterred from recruitment or making donations simply on the basis of being exposed to a biblically inspired message that does *not* mock religion (Edwards-Levy, 2015). It is also expected that less religiously conservative or nonreligious viewers of the ad would not be put off or deterred from donating upon seeing this ad because it is not religiously offensive, which is something they might find distasteful.

Of course, not every NPO can be successful using the Noah's-Ark theme. However, we have reviewed several adaptations of the theme that employ the underlying moral message in lieu of playing off of the physical attributes of the ark. Noah's Ark and the flood as a theme just happens to be uniquely modifiable to organizations whose mission is the preservation of our earth's resources. We believe there are other biblical or universal nonreligious tales with morals that can be used in this way to fit the needs of NPOs whose beneficent objectives are different from those of Greenpeace and the Green Building Council of Brazil.

In a study about communicating the "incommunicable green" to Americans and the Chinese, Li agrees, stating, "The Judeo-Christian Bible is rife with apocalyptic references and they become the rich repertoire of environmental rhetoric," (p. 95). Especially in the early twenty-first century, "Psychologically and institutionally, environmentalism has taken the place of religion in the secular world" (Li, 2010, p. 201).

Those engaged in advertising for NPOs that are focused on protecting our natural resources can use universal moral tales from other sources to sell good instead of goods—promoting, through survival metaphors, the appreciation, maintenance, and non-destructive use of what we already have while subconsciously eschewing consumerism.

REFERENCES

Ang, S. H., & Lim, E. A. C. (2006). The influence of metaphors and product type on brand personality perceptions and attitudes. *Journal of Advertising*, *35*(2), 39–53. doi: 10.1080/00913367.2006.10639226

Awad, M. (n.d.). Greenpeace Noah's Ark illustration. http://mikeawad.tumblr.com/post/130109608258/greenpeace-noahs-ark-without-trees-to-build

Ayman. (2013). Viral tech ads. https://www.trendhunter.com/trends/sony-store-impossible-ii

Bhasin, K. (2011). 13 most offensive PETA advertisements. *Business Insider*. https://www.businessinsider.com/peta-shocking-controversial-ads-2011-10

Burton, N. (2017, March 18). The meaning of Adam and Eve: Was the fall from Eden a price worth paying? *Psychology Today*. https://www.psychologytoday.com/us/blog/hide-and-seek/201703/the-meaning-adam-and-eve

Cryer, A. B. (2018). Stewardship (theology) explained. https://everything.explained.today/Stewardship_(theology)/

Edwards-Levy, A. (2015, January 12). Even Americans who don't favor mocking religion support the right to do it. *Huffington Post*. https://www.huffingtonpost.com/2015/01/12/charlie-hebdo-poll_n_6457212.html

Forceville, C. (2008). Metaphor in pictures and multimodal representations. In R. W. Gibbs, Jr. (Ed.) *The Cambridge handbook of metaphor and thought* (pp. 462–482). Cambridge University Press.

Gatchet, A. D., & Cloud, D. L. (2013). David, Goliath, and the Black Panthers: The paradox of the oppressed militant in the rhetoric of self-defense. *Journal of Communication Inquiry*, *37*(1), 5–25. doi: 10.1177/0196859912466411

Green Building Council. (2019). http://www.gbcbrasil.org.br/sobre-gbc.php

Hardin, G. (1974). Lifeboat ethics: The case against helping the poor. *Psychology Today*. http://schoolforethics.org/wp-content/uploads/2017/06/Hardin.pdf

Henley Jr, W. H., Philhours, M., Ranganathan, S. K., & Bush, A. J. (2009). The effects of symbol product relevance and religiosity on consumer perceptions of Christian symbols in advertising. *Journal of Current Issues & Research in Advertising, 31*(1), 89–103. doi: 10.1080/10641734.2009.10505259

Isaac, A. (2016, April 20). Have charity shock ads lost their power to disturb? *The Guardian.* https://www.theguardian.com/voluntary-sector-network/2016/apr/20/charity-ads-shock-barnados

Jasper, J. M., & Poulsen, J. D. (1995). Recruiting strangers and friends: Moral shocks and social networks in animal rights and anti-nuclear protests. *Social Problems, 42*(4), 493–512. doi: 10.2307/3097043

Krippendorff, K. (1993). Major metaphors of communication and some constructivist reflections on their use. *Cybernetics & Human Knowing*, *2*(1), 3–25.

Le Gaston. (2013). The IliAD. Sony & Store the Impossible. 21w2https://legaston.wordpress.com/2013/11/05/the-iliad-second-act-sony-store-the-impossible/

Li, X. (2010). Communicating the "incommunicable green": A comparative study of the structures of desire in environmental advertising in the United States and China. https://ir.uiowa.edu/cgi/viewcontent.cgi?article=1884&context=etd

Mallia, K. L. (2009). From the sacred to the profane: A critical analysis of the changing nature of religious imagery in advertising. *Journal of Media and Religion*, *8*(3), 172–190. doi: 10.1080/15348420903091162

Mika, M. (2006). Framing the issue: Religion, secular ethics, and the case of animal rights mobilization. *Social Forces, 85*(2), 915–941. doi: 10.1353/sof.2007.0017

Mort, G. S., Weerawardena, J., & Williamson, B. (2007). Branding in the non-profit context: the case of Surf Life Saving Australia. *Australasian Marketing Journal (AMJ), 15*(2), 108–119. doi: 10.1016/S1441-3582(07)70047-2

Pope, N. K. L., Voges, K. E., & Brown, M. R. (2004). The effect of provocation in the form of mild erotica on attitude to the ad and corporate image: Differences between cause-related and product-based advertising. *Journal of Advertising*, *33*(1), 69–82. doi: 10.1080/00913367.2004.10639154

Richards, I. A. (1936). *The philosophy of rhetoric.* Oxford University Press.

Saad, L. (2017, May 15). Record few Americans believe Bible is literal word of God. *Gallup Social & Policy Issues.* https://news.gallup.com/poll/210704/record-few-americans-believe-bible-literal-word-god.aspx

Sapir, E. (1935). Symbolism. *Encyclopaedia of the Social Sciences*, *14*, 492–495.

Sargeant, A., Ford, J. B., & Hudson, J. (2008). Charity brand personality: The relationship with giving behavior. *Nonprofit and Voluntary Sector Quarterly*, *37*(3), 468–491. doi: 10.1177/0899764007310732

United Nations Framework Convention on Climate Change. (2019). http://enb.iisd.org/climate/cop23/enb/11nov.html

Verghese, P. (1976). Muddled metaphors: An Asian response to Garrett Hardin. *Soundings: An Interdisciplinary Journal, 59*(2), 244–249.

Worldometers. (2019). World Population by Year. http://www.worldometers.info/world-population/world-population-by-year/

World Population Review. (2019). http://worldpopulationreview.com/countries/brazil-population/

Zaltman, G., & Coulter, R. H. (1995). Seeing the voice of the customer: Metaphor-based advertising research. *Journal of Advertising Research*, *35*(4), 35–52.

Chapter 9

Revelations of the Future of Holy Hype

At first glance, the combination of the sacred world of religion and the profane world of marketing and advertising may seem incongruous. However, as we describe in this book, the two have developed together throughout time. Whether in purpose or content, they overlap. We have written this book because despite modern manufacturers and retailers in America having used religious themes consistently in their marketing communications since the Second Industrial Revolution of the late nineteenth and early twentieth centuries (Niller, 2019), there has been a noticeable increase in it for consumer products over the past 50 to 60 years. An even bigger surge over the past 20 years has occurred (Mallia, 2009). We have sought to explore, categorize, and begin a conversation about the intersection of the two dimensions which on the surface seems to be quite different.

OVERVIEW OF THE BOOK

At the outset, we define four categories of holy hype, so as to help organize the ways in which religion and advertising meet. As you look around at the media messages as a consumer or student, we hope you can identify these categories. *Secular holy hype*, the use of religious imagery or rhetoric to sell nonreligious goods, is highly conspicuous in advertising, as presented through numerous examples in Chapter 5. *Proselytistic and self-identifying holy hype* is the use of religious imagery and rhetoric to promote one's personal religion, and we provide examples in Chapter 6, focusing primarily on wearables—from T-shirts to jewelry—that proclaim the wearer's faith. *Institutional holy hype* is the use of secular imagery to promote the various houses of worship, denominations, and religious causes. We showed examples in Chapter 7, with a concentration on church billboards. Finally, *religious holy hype* is the use of religious images and rhetoric to promote and sell religious consumer products. These products include holy texts, items needed for religious rites and rituals, and products for the church, churchgoers, and clergy themselves. This category is relatively rare and limited in audience scope because there is a limited demand for these products. A few examples are included in Chapter 2.

We describe the overlap of the ideologies of religion and advertising, exploring briefly the research that attempts to match ideas and purposes of both in Chapter 3. Some experts declare that the overlap is large enough to see advertising *as* a religion, albeit a primitive one (e.g., Sut Jhally). Others, notably Mara Einstein and Tricia Sheffield, point out significant commonalities, but do not go so far as to equate the two. Advertising miraculously presents finished goods, which it tells us we need to possess in order to be fulfilled, to be redeemed, and to be member of the culture. Its messages include showing the power of individual items, which become sacred, as well as showing the way to a better life. Advertising purports to know better than we what we need.

The heart of this book is an overview of some of the many thousands of advertising images that use secular holy hype—almost 300 ad examples throughout. From angels to prayer, from ancient times to the present, we offer a wide variety of symbols and rhetoric that marketers have borrowed from religion. Our aim has been to raise the reader's awareness of the symbols and words that pervade the ads we see—and perhaps amuse and shock along the way. So many of these ads persuade us without our being conscious of it. We hope the reader has gained curiosity that in turn will provoke a heightened awareness of how religion is used to enhance product sales. Those familiar with biblical stories will note that many marketers use images and words from these stories as a shortcut for telling stories about the products, services, and ideas in the advertisements.

THE CULTURE OF HOLY HYPE

The prevalence of holy hype mirrors the scrambling of the sacred and profane in culture. For decades, the more religiously rigid Christian element of the U.S. population has lamented the secularization of our society (Sullivan, 1992), perhaps not recognizing the parallel decline of religion's prominence in everyday life.

Crossman (2019) defines it this way: "Secularization is a cultural transition in which religious values are gradually replaced with nonreligious values. In the process, religious figureheads such as church leaders lose their authority and influence over society" (n.p.). Societal changes and conditions have contributed to holy hype's acceptance and popularity, and perhaps nowhere is secularization more evident than in the use of religious rhetoric and images to sell consumer goods.

We have conducted several studies that look at the possible offensiveness of ads featuring holy hype, and discovered that there is overall acceptance of most of these images. Still, using religion in marketing requires a keen understanding of societal norms, especially those of the targeted audience. Holy hype should not be used without caution; whether to be clever or to shock, the use of the religious realm in advertising is still seen as taboo by some demographic segments of the audience, and its use may offend and invite negative responses. We believe there is a paucity of current research in this specific area that would guide acceptable use, in terms of both the audience response and the type of message in which holy hype is a natural fit for the message.

Uncertainty about meaning can contribute to the interest an ad can generate (Mitchell, 2007). Those who design ads must first get the viewer's attention, and the use of holy hype is a part of that. To break through the "noise" of millions of advertisements in all media and in all places (even on the backs of bathroom stall doors), the approach to the audience in visual terms can be as important and persuasive as the message itself. Sometimes, messages and images can be taken into areas of indecency, tastelessness, and insensitivity—areas that elicit negative associations with the product. We discuss this as to certain advertisements in this book. If an advertiser, meaning the company or institution that actually oversees and approves the design and pays for the dissemination of the ad, knows his audience well, then perhaps criticism of the ad or the business is a risk the company is willing to take in exchange for the segment of the audience that will love it. The United States has its First Amendment regarding the relationship between individuals and companies and government suppression of expression, while the United Kingdom has its Advertising Standards Commission. Romania has an organization similar to the United Kingdom's it calls the PR office for the Romanian Patriarchy. It has censoring power (see figure 5.17a).

Some in society, like Vance Packard (*The Hidden Persuaders*, 1957), one of the earliest scholars of advertising persuasion, and Christopher Lasch (*The Culture of Narcissism*, 1979), are fearful of advertising's power to manipulate people to buy things simply because they are too psychologically weak to resist the persuasive effects of a well-designed ad. Lasch writes:

> In a simpler time, advertising merely called attention to the product and extolled its advantages. Now it manufactures a product of its own: the consumer,

> perpetually unsatisfied, restless, anxious, and bored. Advertising serves not so much to advertise products as to promote consumption as a way of life. It "educates" the masses into an unappeasable appetite not only for goods but for new experiences and personal fulfillment. (1979, p. 72)

With holy hype, this is an especially paradoxical notion in that consumerism seems to exist in opposition to a religious, or at least Christian, lifestyle. Mitchell was, in her conclusion, indecisive, wondering whether further critical questioning would find that

> the borrowing by advertisers of particular religious images and icons is doing violence to these symbols and by extension love for God and neighbor, or actually providing impetus onto further reflection of how to trust in God and not goods, to care for and not do violence to God's good creation and reject rather than embrace the violent idolatry so often lurking at the heart of a modern advertisement. (p. 266)

THE FUTURE OF HOLY HYPE

Holy hype continues to be a popular means for attracting audiences. Since we began writing this book, we have continued to discover new uses across many media. Holy hype is found in: (a) politics (e.g., photographs of elected leaders in front of a golden orb, making the subjects look like angels or illustrated with halos over them); (b) product ads; and (c) public service announcements. From a TV commercial for heavenly chicken to one displaying God's consumption and spilling of flavored water (as in Hint trademark fruit-infused water commercials), advertisers of popular products continue to use religion to sell. Even serious messages, such as those dealing with insomnia and domestic violence, invoke sacred rhetoric. Are these inappropriate and offensive, or funny and clever? Culture, norms, and audiences all play a role in deciding. In the meantime, marketers seem willing to continue to test the boundaries of holy hype.

The adoption—or appropriation—of religious symbols, images, and rhetoric by advertisers can be seen either as a brilliant tactic or a predatory move. In 1997, Budde, a scholar in Catholic Studies and Political Science, lamented:

> In recent decades, global culture industries like television and advertising have begun to exploit religious imagery in ever more overt, crass, and trivial ways. They have come to operate as "symbolic predators," cultural parasites seeking to profit from repositories of meaning and socialization they did not create and which they weaken by their encroachment. (p. 84)

His harsh words are no surprise, as his writing criticizes postmodern culture in general, and the media specifically, for drowning out the spaces where religion has traditionally formulated the devout, that "the process is impeded when outside forces threaten to overwhelm, undermine, or drown out the communicative functions of religious symbols and images" (p. 84). In other words, the sanctity of religious communicative language is irreparably tainted by its use in advertisements. Budde, however, also lays blame at the feet of religious organizations as well. Their failure to teach proper responses to and protect the inviolability of "sacred symbols of the faith" has made "their corporate hijacking simultaneously easier and non-controversial (because those symbols, stories, and images are both vaguely familiar and not especially vital to most people) . . . Indeed, all too often, they seem not to recognize the pillaging in process" (p. 84).

Despite his overall pessimism about religious symbols in advertising, Budde stated that not all uses of religion in advertising are "overt or crass." As of 1997, he writes:

> Religious symbols are still too "hot" to manipulate with abandon—we won't see Jesus on the cross used to pitch deodorant anytime soon—but when appropriately subdued, buried, and nonobvious, many of the classic narratives of Judaism and Christianity (e.g. Exodus, miracles, resurrection) act effectively as deep structures in commercial messages. (p. 92)

As Chapter 5 in this book indicates, in the 20-plus years since he wrote the above comment, ads *have* come very close to Budde's deodorant-selling Jesus, and indeed it seems that just about all religious communicative symbolism is fair game for marketers today. The flip side of the crossroads of advertising and religion is ingenious use of well-known symbols and language that captures attention but stops short of offending the audience.

If we keep our eyes and ears open to seeing new holy hype, we will find it. Biblical themes continue to offer the salience necessary to send a message of meaning to prospective buyers of things. This is how we discovered the conceptual advertising output of a group of college students who posted online their campaign for a Toronto "classic cheeseburger joint" called The Burger's Priest. The eatery promotes itself as "redeeming the burger one at a time." Its commandments are quality, purity, and simplicity. One of its real ads announced the chain's sinful new burger, garnished with gratitude. A Twitter ad boasting its London site read, "You're about to be blessed." The names of the burger choices make use of holy hype as well and are presented on a repurposed hymn board. Some of the sandwiches are: High Priest; The Vatican City; Holy Smokes; The Religious Hypocrite; The Tower of Babel; and the Four Horsemen of the Apocalypse. The eatery came about when a

Californian, Shant Mardirosian, took up religion. He moved to Canada to attend seminary to become a priest. The website tells us: "Shant prayed every day with all his heart to find his calling. His nose and stomach delivered, and Burger Redemption was born." This establishment served as inspiration for college students art director Kaitlyn Stegmaier, Strategist/Account Manager Anastasiia Liahusha, Art Director Valentina Fortun, and Art Director Alexandra Richards in 2019.

After brainstorming several "Big Ideas," the group decided to focus the executions of their ads around a semi-religious rhetoric. In their own words:

> At this stage in the project, we spent a lot of time researching religious-related terms, religious stories from the Bible, and religious sayings that would be easily understood and recognized by the average consumer. From that research, we found a perfect balance between rhetoric and religious terminology/sayings in order to write the headlines for the campaign. We knew that we wanted the copy to be the hero of the executions, so we intentionally kept the art direction very minimalistic by using a black background and simple images of the burgers so as to not distract consumers from the headlines. Once we finalized the copy and the art direction for the campaign, we brainstormed where the ads would be placed in the real world in order to reach our target market effectively. For this campaign, we were targeting individuals aged 18–35 years old who worked and lived downtown, so we knew that the ads would be most effective placed on billboards, transit shelters, subway platforms, and on Instagram. Based on these locations, the layout and dimensions of each ad was determined in order to be contextualized appropriately in each location. (Kaitlyn Stegmaier, 2021, e-mail communication)

In figure 9.1, we see the result of the students' campaign proposal. It is nice to be able to say that these ads are self-explanatory. Each ad or subway poster is designed to comport with the restaurant's established color scheme and take on biblical rhetoric. This is a perfect situation for the use of holy hype; however, there will continue to be numerous opportunities to employ this approach as a one-off advertisement or a one-time campaign.

Advertising creatives do not profess to be seers. Their messages are created for the here and now—although in years to come, they will represent a window into today's culture. Today, with the increasing speed and breadth at which messages are circulated, creators of advertising find that the "sell-by" freshness date is much closer than ever before to the launch date. Perhaps we cannot even foresee social conditions three to four months ahead. Just as the service industry is having to change its methods of meeting consumer needs in this age of the novel coronavirus, its advertising must adapt as well. It remains as true today as when Budde wrote in 1997:

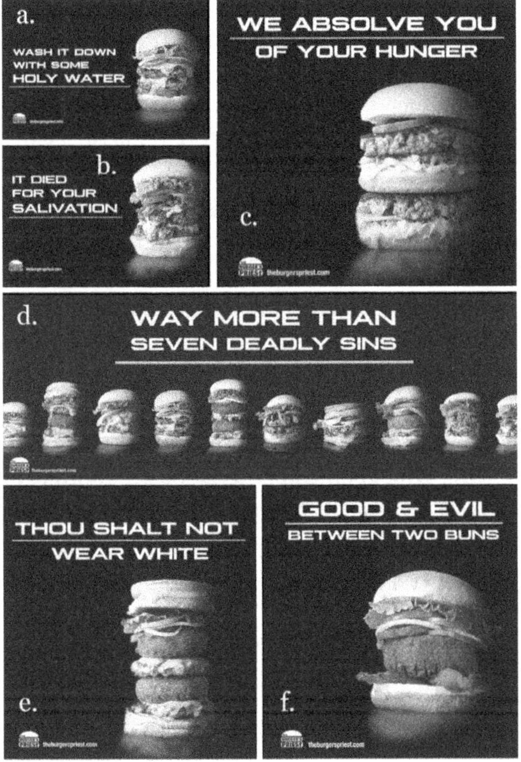

Figures 9.1 a) to f) 2019 Conceptual Campaign for The Burger's Priest Cheeseburger Joint. "Wash it down with some holy water." "It died for your salivation." "We absolve you of your hunger." "Way more than seven deadly sins." "Thou shalt not wear white." "Good and evil between two buns." *Source: a) to f) Images courtesy of ©Kaitlyn Stegmaier. Art directors: Kaitlyn Stegmaier, Valentina Fortun, and Alexandra Richards. Strategist/Account manager: Anastasiia Lia.*

> Various programs of psychographic research continue searching for emotional, precognitive, and value-based "triggers" that can be grasped in efforts to generate consumption-oriented behaviors. Those words, concepts, pictures, sounds, and other components that "resonate" favorably among various segments of mass markets (determined by extensive advance testing and research) become the stuff of modern ad appeals. (p. 41)

Before the pandemic hit decisively in March 2020, nobody could have anticipated its devastation or the changes all of us would have to make to accommodate the requisites of a new normal. For example, Taco Bell has announced that due to the pandemic, certain items that are consumer favorites must be removed from the menu (Walansky, 2020). These menu items take more time to prepare, use ingredients not easily obtained, or require more hands to put together and deliver. Removing these offerings from the lineup helps the company streamline service and conduct business more hygienically with fewer hands touching the product and fewer employees overall. Many of Taco Bell's most faithful customers have registered their outrage on Twitter. For instance, blog commenter Sarah Malone laments, "Taco Bell's announcement that they're 'removing all potato items' should just be read as 'removing all the heart from my body and soul'" (Walansky, 2020, n.p.). Perhaps the most holy hype-ish of the comments came from a social media user, who paraphrased an oft-cited quote by the well-known, anti-Nazi, Lutheran pastor from Germany, Martin Niemöller: "First they came for the power burrito and I said nothing, for I did not order the power burrito. Now they've come for the quesarito, and there is no one left to speak for me" (Fox6Now, 2020). If the consumers are complaining about Taco Bell's news in spiritual terms, how will Taco Bell handle this in its ads? Might some holy hype be appropriate and effective?

As of 2018, 66% of Americans expressed "at least some curiosity to know more about what the Bible says, including one in three (29%) who express a strong desire" ("State of the Bible," 2018, n.p.). Almost half of Americans (48%) consider themselves Bible users in that they "engage with the Bible on their own by using, listening to, watching, praying or using Bible text or content in any format (not including use at a church service) at least three to four times a year" ("State of the Bible," 2018, n.p.). The effectiveness of holy hype depends on a certain minimum level of consumer knowledge of biblical stories and rhetoric. How low must these numbers go for sociologists to feel that most Americans no longer have a basic familiarity with the Bible? If current trends toward secularization continue, it is possible that, within a century or two, holy hype will become an advertising approach that most people simply won't grasp due to a lack of knowledge about the Bible. Until then, we predict a healthy use of biblical themes, rhetoric, and images in promotions for secular consumer goods targeted to biblically conscious or knowledgeable audiences.

REFERENCES

Crossman, A. (2019). What is secularization? *ThoughtCo.* https://www.thoughtco.com/secularization-definition-3026575

Fox6Now. (2020). Taco Bell rumored to be removing popular menu item, social media erupts. https://fox6now.com/2020/07/18/taco-bell-rumored-to-be-removing-popular-menu-item-social-media-erupts/

Lasch, C. (1979). *The culture of narcissism: American life in an age of diminishing expectations.* W.W. Norton and Company.

Mallia, K. L. (2009). From the sacred to the profane: A critical analysis of the changing nature of religious imagery in advertising. *Journal of Media and Religion, 8*(3), 172–190. doi: 10.1080/15348420903091162

Mitchell, J. (2007). *Media violence and Christian ethics*. Cambridge Press.

Niller, E. (2019, January 25). How the second industrial revolution changed Americans' lives. *History.com.* https://www.history.com/news/second-industrial-revolution-advances

Packard, V. (1957). *The hidden persuaders*. New York: McKay.

"State of the Bible 2018: Seven Top Findings." (2018). *Barna.* https://www.barna.com/research/state-of-the-bible-2018-seven-top-findings/

Sullivan, K. M. (1992). Religion and liberal democracy. *The University of Chicago Law Review, 59*, 195–223.

Walansky, A. (2020). Taco Bell confirms it's removing several popular menu items. *NBC Los Angeles.* https://www.nbclosangeles.com/the-scene/taco-bell-confirms-its-removing-several-popular-menu-items/2398593/

Index

Note: Page numbers in *italics* refer to figures.

Abbey beers, 60
Abbot Ale, *59*, 60
Absolut Vodka, *108*, 109, 126, 139, *150*, 152
act-of-God theory, 19–20
Act Responsible association, *140*
Adam and Eve theme, 68–74, *69*, *71*, *73*, *207*, 208–9. *See also* creation stories
advertising, 1–2, 24–26. *See also* holy hype; marketing
Advertising the American Dream (Marchand), 31
afterlife images, 103–6, *105*. *See also* angel images; devil and evil images; heaven; hell and sin
AIDS pandemic, *112*, 112–13
AIG Companies, 210, *211*
Alberta College and Association of Chiropractors, 77–78, *78*
Albuquerque Bahá'í Center, *197*
Aldine Press, *51*
Aldus Manutius (publisher), 58
Allen, Peter, *71*
Altoids, 68, *69*, 70
American Airlines Airfreight, *212*, 213
American Association of Advertising Agencies, *144*, 144–45
American Marketing Association, 24
American Standard, 122, *122*
American Wheelabrator & Equipment Corp., *207*, 209
ANCAP, 104
ancient Babylonians, 10
Andtidze, Goga, *147*
angel images, 74–81, *76*, *78*, *80*, 88
Ansco Films & Cameras, 104, *105*
Apostle Spoons, *51*, 56–57
apparel: differing views on, 160–61; Gingiss formalwear, 90–92, *91*; Jesus belt buckles, 15, *15*; Jesus Jeans, *112*, 113; "Left Behind" theme, *166*, 167; Levi's jeans, 87, *147*, 148–49; neckties, *165*, 168; shirts, 169–75, *173*, *207*, 208
Apple ads, 98–99
Armour & Company, *88*, 89
ARP guitars, *108*, 111
Ashland Avenue Baptist Church, *190*, 191
Atheist Bus Campaign, *199*, 200
atheists, 198–200, *199*

audiences, 3–4
Ayer, Francis Wayland, 38, 40

Bahá'í faith, *165*, 169, 196–97, *197*
Banana Boat, 79–80, *80*
Banlon socks, 75, *76*
Baramashvili, Tekla, *147*
Barnardos charity, 215
Barr, B. A., 53
Barton, Bruce Fairchild, 38, 39–41, *40*, 47, 110
Barton, Durstine & Osborn (BDO), 39
Bates, S., 135
Batman image, 126, *127*
Batten, Barton, Durstine & Osborn (BBDO), 39, 41, 47
Batten, George, 38, *40*, 41
BDO (Barton, Durstine & Osborn), 39
Beazer, Ed, 75
beer breweries: Brimstone Brewery, 26, 118–20, *119*; commercial production replacing monasteries, 55–56, 60; Coppertail Brewing, *124*, 125–26; Green King Brewery, *59*; guilds, 55–56; medieval illustrations, *51*; Miller Brewing Company, 141–42; monk images, 87; origin of secular holy hype and, 59–60; Resurrection brand, *85*, 86; signs during Middle Ages, 55–56; Unholy Ale, *13*, 14
Bell, N. D., 23, 192
Bellah, Robert Neely, 1, 35
Bell & Howell, *91*, 92
Benetton, 102, 111–13, *112*, 121, *207*
Bernbach, Bill, 135
Betta, Nonna, 138
Betty Crocker, *76*, 77
Bibles, online, 73, *73*
Bible stories: Adam and Eve, 68–74, *69*, *71*, *73*, *207*, 208–9; David and Goliath, 138, *207*, 209; Last Supper, 139–43, *140*, *166*, 169; Moses, 136, 143–49, *144*, *147*; Noah's Ark, 210–14, 217–23, *219*; parables, 41; Samson and Delilah theme, 138; Ten Commandments, 83–84, *84*, 148, *165*, 168. *See also* creation stories; Jesus theme
biblical sayings and words, 10, 81–84, *82*, *84*
Big Apple Coalition of Reason, *199*, 200
Big D's Flaming Ghost Hot Sauce, *119*, 121
billboards: church marquees, 11, 189–92, *190*; examples, 196–200, *197*, *199*; on roadside, 193–96, *197*
Bird's Custard, *69*, 70
Black, Max, 206–7
Black Death, 52–53
Black Flag insect killer, *212*, 214
Black Lives Matter, 102
Blair, J. A., 47–48
blasphemous expressions, 5
bobbleheads, 166, *166*
Bock, Jerry, 132
body art, 66, *166*, 169
The Book of Mormon (musical), 23–24
BooneOakley agency, 111
"born again" phrase, 81–83, *82*
Boxing Clever agency, 77
brands and branding, 25–26, 66, 187–89, 215–17, *216*. *See also specific brands*
Brands of Faith (Einstein), 30, 159–60, 188
Braun, Greg, 123–25, *124*
Brimstone Brewery, 26, 118–20, *119*
Budde, R. N., 2, 21, 182, 184, 187, 231–33
Buddha figurines, 164–66, *165*
Buddhism, 115–16
Buick cars, 122, *122*
Burck, Bradley, 198
Burger's Priest, 231–32, *233*
Burton, Laurel, 29
Bush, George W., 37
buzzwords, 72–73

Cadillac Superline Victoria, 103–4, *105*
Calvert Gin, *216*
Calvinism, 161

CAM (Christian Aid Ministries), 196
Candler, Asa, 38, 42
Cannon towels, *82*, 82–83
Caparol paint, *147*, 149
capitalism, 2, 34–35, 54–55, 61n2. *See also* consumer culture
Carvana logo, 116
Casasanto, D., 99
Cassell, Heather, 141
catalog merchandise, 161–62
Cathedral Church of Saint John the Divine, 83, *83*
Catholic Church: images used in, 49; popes, 102, 182, 184; responses to church advertising, 182–84. *See also* clergypersons in ads
Catholic Radio, 196, *197*
cause-related marketing, 205. *See also* nonprofit organizations (NPOs); religions
Cecilia, Saint, *166*, 166–67
Cedar Creek Church, 196, *197*
censorship, 106–7, *108*, 229
Center for Church Communication (CFCC), 195
certitude rhetoric, 36, 44n4
CFCC (Center for Church Communication), 195
Chabad on Campus, *131*, 137
Chabashvili, David, *147*
Chapel Bar & Bistro, 114
Chartreuse liqueur, *88*, 89
Chegleev, Stanislav, *73*
Cherry Blossom presentation cases, 87, *91*, 92
Chevrolet, *76*, 76–77
Chicago Cubs, *117*, 118
Christian Aid Ministries (CAM), 196
Christian apparel shops, 171–72
Christian bookstores, 162–64
Christian ethics, 200–201
Christianity: catalogs of merchandise, 164–67, *165*; ethics and, 200–201; institutional holy hype and, 186; population statistics, 129; retail sales of artifacts, 162–64; symbols as logos, 162. *See also* Catholic Church; Church of Jesus Christ of Latter-Day Saints; Episcopal Church; Evangelical Christians; Methodists; Protestant Christianity
Christmas ads, 5
A Christmas Story (movie), 133–34
The Church and the Internet (Pontifical Council), 183–84
church attendance, 188–89
church fans, 7, *7*
Church Marketing Sucks blog, 195
church marquees, 11, 189–92, *190*
Church of Jesus Christ of Latter-Day Saints, 23–24, *24*, *165*, 168
civil religion, 35–38
Clanchy, M. T., 56
Clegg, N. W., 54
clergypersons in ads, 87–92, *88*, *91*, 102–3
CMT (conceptual metaphor theory), 206
Coca Cola, 26
The Codes of Advertising (Jhally), 30–33
colonial-era flyers, 10
colophons, 57–58
conceptual metaphor theory (CMT), 206
Concerned Women for America (CWA), 141–42
condensation symbol, 217–18
Connell, Bard, 77–78
consumer culture: advertising as persuasion, 1; institutional holy hype and, 182–84; mixing of sacred and profane, 227–30; persuasion and, 229–30; reconciliation and, 34; religious terms describing, 30–33. *See also* capitalism
consumer research results, 24–25
Continental Bank, *132*, 138
Continental Can Co., 210, *211*
Copper, Andy, 141
Coppertail Brewing, *13*, 14, *124*, 125–26
Cosgrove, Ben, 112–13
Coty Musk and Wild Musk, *69*, 70

Coulter, R. H., 206
"Court of the Ladies of Queen Anne of Brittany," *51*, 52
COVID-19 pandemic, *73*, 73–74, 140, *140*, 233–34
CPH Vision, 93, *94*
Cranach, Lucas the Elder, *51*
creation stories: Adam's creation, 70–74, *71*, *73*; in El Al ad, 137; Garden of Eden, 75. *See also* Adam and Eve theme
CrossFit community, 174
Crossman, A., 228–29
Crown Royal Canadian whiskey, 87
crucifixes and T-poses, 92–98, *94*, *96*
Cryer, A. B., 222
Cuesta, Marina, *212*
The Culture of Narcissism (Lasch), 31–32
Cumming, Ben, 121
Cummins, Neil Paul, 222

DaColony agency, 136
Daisy air rifle, *132*, 138
Damascus Road Church, *17*, 18, *112*, 113–14
Damasio, Arturo, 206
Daniel, Jasper Newton, 86–87
Das Kapital (Marx), 31
David and Goliath theme, 138, *207*, 209
Da Vinci, Leonardo. *See* Last Supper images
Deaguero, Brandon, *147*, 148–49
Decoding Advertisements (Williamson), 1, 32
demographics, 24–25. *See also* statistics
devil and evil images, 98–103, *101*
Diamond, E., 135
Diniaco, Steven, *144*, 146
Dirt Devil, 102–3
divine, words evoking, 84–87, *85*
divine mediator figure, 34
Djakovic, Jelena, *147*, 148–49
DKNY, *207*
dolphin symbol, 58
Dore, Gustave, 146
Doyle Dane Bernbach agency, 12, 135
Duct Tape Marketing, 20
Duerr, Steffan, *124*
Dukes Bread, 111
Durkheim, Émile, 33–34, 161
Duval Guillaume agency, 93–95, *94*

Ecclesiastes, Book of, 10, 81
Eckstrom, K., 141
Edwards, Barbara Aleene, *140*, 142
EF Hutton, *13*, 14
Einstein, Mara, 29, 33–35, 43, 159–60, 164, 186, 188, 200–201, 228
Eisand, M., 129
El Al airline, 126, *127*, *130*, *131*, 133, 134, 136, 137
Elliott, Ernest Eugene, 16, 180–81
Ellison, Keith, 37
Emery, Timothy, 23
emotional associations, 25–26
environmentalism as religion, 225
Epic Burger, 72
Episcopal Church, 17, *17*, *108*, 110, 189–91, *190*
ESPN Classic, *96*, 97
Ethics in Advertising report, 182–83
Ethics in Communications (Pontifical Council), 183
Ethics in Internet (Pontifical Council), 183
Eureka Tents, 210–12, *212*
Evangelical Christians: as institutional marketing category, 189; merchandise for, 162, 163, 171–75, *173*; swear words and, 118; televangelism, 181
Eveready batteries, *150*, 151
Exakta camera, *88*, 90

Fables of Abundance (Lears), 38
Faith RXD, 174
Fallon McElligott agency, 17, *17*, 181, 189–91, *190*
family values, *190*, 191

Federici ice cream, 121
Ferreira, Miguel, 189
Festivus holiday, 86
fetishism, 32
FFRF (Freedom from Religion Foundation), *199*, 199–200
Fiddler on the Roof (musical), 132–33
Fine, Carole Ann, 109
Finlandia Vodka, 77, *78*
First Amendment, 185, 229
fish symbol, *165*, 167
Flexor parts, 70–71, *71*
Floros, George, 102
Follis, John, 179
Following Christ in a Consumer Society (Kavanaugh), 33
Folsom Street Fair, *140*, 141
Food for Life Baking Company, *127*, 128–29
Forceville, C., 206–7
Fortun, Valentina, 232, *233*
Foubert, J. D., 81
fragmentation in current culture, 21
Frangelico liqueur, 87–89, *88*
Franklin, N., 107
Franzikaner brewery, *59*, 60
Frare, Therese, *112*, 112–13
Frater, Van Zan, 174–75
Freedom from Religion Foundation (FFRF), *199*, 199–200
Free My Lungs, 93–95, *94*
Fresh Awards competition, 83, *83*
Fried, Rabbi, 74
Frigidaire, *150*
Fruit of the Loom, *207*
functional overlaps, 33–35
funeral images, 103–6, *105*
Fust, Johann, 57–58

Galiot, A. D., 196, 198
Gallucci, Jamie, 118–19
Garden of Eden, 75
Garden of Eden (Plat), 58–59, *59*
Gatchava, Gabo, *147*
GATX company, 210, *211*
Gautama, Siddhartha, 164–66, *165*
Gauthier, Shawn, 79, *80*
Gemmy Industries, *15*
General Electric, 126, *127*
George, Geoff, *124*
George Batten Newspaper Advertising Agency, 41
Gerencser, Bruce, 118
Gibson, Wayne, 128–29
Gilchrist, D. B., 57–58
gingerbread man image, 77, *78*
Gingiss formalwear, 90–92, *91*
God, 20–21, 106–7, *108*, 110–11, 217–18
God's Capitalist (Kemp), 42
Godsey, John, *124*
GodSpeaks campaign, 20, *197*, 197–98
"God's works is the world's wonder" campaign, 58, *59*
"God talk," 36, 43n3
God the Economist (Meeks), 34
godvertising, 11
Goodall, Troy, 114
Goode, Virgil, 37
"good times" appeals, 164–65
Goodyear blimp, 90, *91*
Gospel Trumpet Company of Indiana, 161–62
Gracemats, 146
Green, Nathan "Nearest," 86
Green Building Council (Brazil), 218–21, *219*
Green King Brewery, *59*
Greenpeace, *213*, *216*, 216–17, *219*, 221–24
Grey Advertising, 133
Grilled Cheesus, 15, *15*
Gubanov, N. I., 22
Gubanov, N. N., 22
guild system, 54–55
Guinet, Sebastien, 147

halo images, 107, *108*, 109
Hansen, Steve, 114
Hanukkah poster, 137

Hardin, Garrett, 219–20, 223
Harley-Davidson, 75, 82, *82*
Harris, Evan B., 125
Havas London agency, 111
Hawaiian Tropic, *144*, 145, 149
Hayes, Geoff, 109
heaven, 115–18, *117*
Hebrew National, *130*, 136
hell and sin, 98–103, *101*, 118–23, *119*, *124*
Hell Pizza, 26, *119*, 120–21, *122*, 123
Hendershot, Heather, 175
Henley, W. H., Jr., 221
Hennah, Angus, 114
He Upset the World (Barton), 41
Hiltzik, M., 14
Hinduism, 115–16
Hirdes, W., 161, 163
historical perspective: artifacts, 161–62; church fans, 7, *7*; early tribes, 48–49; Middle Ages, 49–52; post-World War II culture, 149–51, *150*; print ads, 4–5, 10; printing press, 50, 53–54, 57–59; religious institutions, 185–87
Hochstein, Leonard, 72
holy hype: about, 2–5, 9–10; act-of-God theory, 19–20; awareness of God and, 20–21; differing views of, 49, 228–30; future of, 230–34; "holy" terminology, 123–29, *124*, *127*; "hype" terminology, 11; institutional holy hype, 16–18, *17*, 189–90, *190*, 227; proselytistic (witnessing) holy hype, 14–16, *15*, 227; religious holy hype, 18–19, *19*, 52–55, 228; self-identifying, 227; usage of sacred themes, 4. *See also* secular holy hype; secular holy images; *specific themes*
home décor, 164, *165*
Hopkins, Claude C., 38, 42
Hotten, J. C., 56
How to Advertise a Church (Elliott), 16, 180–81
How to Fill the Pews (Elliott), 16
Hoy, Chris, 174–75
Huizinga, J., 52
humor, 22–24, 129–33, *130*, *131*, *132*, 192. *See also specific products*
Hutira, Wanda, 106–7, *108*
"hype" terminology, 11
Hypo stain remover, 116–17, *117*

Iams, 78–79
ICNA (Islamic Circle of North America), *197*, 198
iconoclast debate, 49
iconology stage of advertising, 31
"The Ideal Democratic Apparel" (Neal), 170–71
identity, 170–71. *See also* apparel; religious artifacts
idolatry, sin of, 161, 230
idolatry stage of advertising, 31
IGFM (International Society for Human Rights), 98, 114
images, 21–22, 47–48. *See also specific images*
immortality, images of, 103–6, *105*
inflatable nativity scenes, 15, *15*
informational appeals, 164
institutional holy hype, 16–18, *17*, 189–90, *190*, 227. *See also* billboards; *specific religions*
International Organization for Animal Protection, 142–43
International Society for Human Rights (IGFM), 98, 114
interviews with prospective viewers, 135–36
ironic category of institutional marketing, 189
Islam: humor and, 129; institutional marketing, *197*, 198; Islamic Circle of North America (ICNA), *197*, 198; Qur'an, 37; religious merchandise, *165*, 168–69, 172–73, *173*; symbols as logos, 162
IStockphotography.com, 146

i3Lab, *71*
Ivory soap, 66–67, *67*

Jack Daniel's whiskey, *85*, 86–87
Jacobellis v. Ohio, 25
Jantsch, John, 20
Jasper, J. M., 217–18
JDate, *130*, *131*, *132*, 133–34, 137, 139
Jeepster, *124*, 125
"Jesus Is My Homeboy" T-shirts, 174–75
Jesus theme: about, 39–41, 111–15, *112*; in Christian merchandise, 164–66, *165*, *166*, 174–76; crucifixes and T-poses, 92–98, *94*, *96*; images of, 111–15, *112*; Jesus belt buckles, 15, *15*; Jesus Jeans, *112*, 113; Last Supper images, 139–43, *140*, *166*, 169
jewelry as religious merchandise, *165*, 167, 168–69
Jewish Film Festival of Toronto, *147*, 147–48
Jewish-Italian food, 137–38
Jhally, Sut, 29–33, 228
John Paul II, Pope, 184
Jolly Green Giant, 79
Jones, Victoria Emily, 175
Joplin, Janis, 110
Joyce Aviation, 116, *117*
Judaism: food as part of culture, *130*, *131*, 133–38; Hebrew Scriptures, 49–50, 74; humor and, 129–33, *130*, *131*, *132*; institutional holy hype and, 186; Israel's civil religious rhetoric, 36–37; Levy's Rye Bread, 12, *13*, 14, *130*, 134–35; not using proselytizing hype, 15; population statistics, 129; prosecution theme, 137; rabbis, 90–92, *91*; religious merchandise, *165*, 167, 168, 172–73, *173*; symbols as logos, 162; Torah, 19. *See also* Adam and Eve theme; Bible stories; creation stories
J. Walter Thompson Group, 100, *101*

Kavanaugh, John, 29, 33
"Keep Calm and Carry On" slogan, 172
"Keeping Abreast with the Times" (Symes), 170
Key, Martin, 89–90
Kids Cancer Project, 72, *73*
Kim, Dr., 71–72
Kim, Paul, 114
The (Magic) Kingdom of God (Budde), 182
Kirby, Bill, 113
Klee, Paul, 65
Klein, Robert, 133
knickknacks, 160
Knox, I., 129–30
Kodak, *101*, 102
kosher food, 133
Kost, Gary, 125
Kramer, Jack, *84*
Krinsky, Menachim, *131*, 137
Krippendorff, K., 206, 220, 223
Kudirka, Žygimantas, *112*
Kyoto Protocol, 221–22

Land O' Lakes, *122*, 123
Landor (branding business), 25
language in ads: biblical phrases, 10, 81–84, *82*, *84*; blasphemous expressions, 5; "born again" phrase, 81–83, *82*; scripturally laced speech, 36. *See also* metaphors
Lanvin, *122*, 122–23
Larry Zamba Photography, *119*, 121
Larwood, J., 56
Lasch, Christopher, 31–32, 229–30
Last Supper images, 139–43, *140*, *166*, 169
La Trappe products, *59*, 60
Lattice Engines, *207*, 209
Leach, Darren, 195
Lears, Jackson, 38
Leffe brewery, *59*, 60
"Left Behind" apparel, *166*, 167
Leilani Hawaiian Rum, *108*, 109–10
Lennon, John, *108*, 109, *199*, 200

Levine, D. S., 99
Levi's jeans, 87, *147*, 148–49
Levy's Rye Bread, 12, *13*, 14, *130*, 134–35
Lexical ad, *108*, 109
Li, X., 225
Liahusha, Anastasiia, 232, *233*
Liebig's Extract of Beef Company, 210, *211*
Lieder's kosher food, *130*, 134
lifeboat image, *219*, 222–23
Lifeway Christian stores, 163
Lincoln Aviator, 84–85, *85*
liquor ads: Absolut Vodka, *108*, 109, 126, 139, *150*, 152; Frangelico, *88*, 88–90; Leilani Hawaiian Rum, *108*, 109–10; Moses Vodka, 143, *144*; Olmeca Tequila, 104–5, *105*; Smirnoff, 100–102, *101*. *See also* beer breweries
Listermint, *150*, 151–52
literalistic category of institutional marketing, 189
LOGIN ad, *112*, 113
logos, symbols as, 55–56. *See also specific products*
Lombardi, Vince, 116, *117*
London Fair, 58, *59*
London Fog, *212*, 213–14
López, Ana, *212*
López, Jorge, *212*
Lord's Gym, 172
Lumen 99.5FM, *213*
Luther, Martin, 185

magic, 32
Maguire, G., 4
Mainz Psalter colophon, 57–58
Making Good in the Local Church (Elliott), 16
Malone, Sarah, 234
Manchester United Red Devil, 72, *73*
Manning, Paul, 114
The Man Nobody Knows (Barton), 39, 110
Marchand, Roland, 31
Marco, Peggy, *165*
marketing: advertising *versus*, 24–26; branding, 25–26, 66, 187–89, 215–17, *216*; Christian ethics and, 200–201; competition in, 179–80; institutional marketing, 185–87, 189; responses to, 182–84; societal context, 102. *See also* historical perspective; holy hype
Marlboro cigarettes, *212*, 214
Marshall, Chester CV., 180
Martin, Father George, *17*, *108*, 189, *190*
Marx, Karl, 31
Massachusetts Mutual Life Insurance Company, *150*, 151
mass media programming, 185–86. *See also* televangelism
Material Christianity (McDannell), 159–60
material culture, 159–60
Matthew-in-the-City Church, *119*, 121
Matwick, K., 136
McCann Erickson agency, 114–15
McClellan, Scott, 195
McDannell, Colleen, 159–62
McElligott, Tom, *17*, *108*, 110, 189–91, *190*
McLuhan, Marshall, 26
meaning making, 30
Media Violence and Christian Ethics (Mitchell), 179–80
Meeks, M. Douglas, 34
megachurches, 188
Memorex, 110
memory and symbolic images, 56
merchandise. *See* religious artifacts; *specific type of merchandise*
Merton, Thomas, 9
Messaris, Paul, 21, 48
metaphors, 205, 206–7, *207*. *See also* Bible stories; nonprofit organizations (NPOs)
Met Gala themes, 168
Methodists, 186–87

mezuzahs, 49–50, *166*, 167
Michelangelo's Sistine Chapel, 70–74, *71*, *73*
Middle Ages, 49–52, 125
Mika, M., 217
Miller, L. J., 53
Miller Brewing Company, 141–42
mindfulness, 72
Mini cars, 79
Mirk, John, 53
Mitchell, J., 179–80, 184, 230
Mlenny (photographer), *15*
modern category of institutional marketing, 189
Mom's Kitchen restaurant, *140*, 142
monks, 125. *See also* clergypersons
Monks Meadery, *88*, 89–90
Moore, R. Laurence, 181–82, 185, 187, 201
Moroni, Angel, 75
Mortein rat poison, 142
Moses theme, 136, 143–49, *144*, *147*. *See also* Ten Commandments theme
Moses Vodka, 143, *144*, *147*, 149
Mt. Ararat image, 218–21, *219*, 222–23
Murray, Bruce, 35–36
Muskegon Luge, 123–25, *124*
Mustang fighter planes, *119*, 120
My Homeboy Foundation, 173–75
My Sin perfume, *122*, 122–23
"The Mystic Marriage of St. Catherine," *51*

narcissism stage of advertising, 31
Neal, Lynn, 170–74, 175
Needham, Harper & Steers agency, 12–14, *13*
neoiconistic model, 217–23, *219*
Nesselrode, Izzy, *131*, 136
Newspaper Advertising Bureau of New York, *144*, 145
Nielsen report, 194
Niemöller, Martin, 234
Nike, 26, *96*, 97, *105*, 106, 116, *117*, 121, *132*
nirvana, 115–16
Nissan, *94*, 95
Noah's Ark agency, 116–17, *117*
Noah's Ark theme, 210–14, 217–23, *219*
nonprofit organizations (NPOs): about, 205–6; Green Building Council (Brazil), 218–21, *219*; PETA, 68–69, *69*, 75–76, *76*, 209, 217; unique needs of, 214–17
North American Aviation, *119*, 120
North Carolina Council of Churches, *197*
Norval United Church, *17*, 17–18

OAAA (Out of Home Advertising Association), 193–94
Obeidallah, Dean, 129
Oberman, Justin, *130*, *131*, 134, 137
obscenity definition, 25
offensiveness to viewers, 22, 229–30
Ogilvy, David, 20
Ogilvy agency, 114
O'Keefe, Daniel, 86
Old Spice, 79, *80*
Olmeca Tequila, 104–5, *105*
On the Social Contract (Rousseau), 35
Ornella, Alexander, 174
O'Shaughnessy, J., 9, 22
O'Shaughnessy, N. J., 9, 22
Outdoor Advertising Association of America, 20
Out of Home Advertising Association (OAAA), 193–94

Packard, Vance, 229
Pacreau, Josselin, 147
Paddy Power, *140*, 141
Parable Group, 163
parables. *See* Bible stories
Parlangeli, Susan Mersch, *124*
Parscale, Brad, 38
Passion of the Christ (movie), 18
Paulose, K. O., 72
Paul VI, Pope, 182

Peirce, Charles Sanders, 21
Percy, M., 189, 194
persuasion, 26–27, 47–48, 164, 229–30
PETA, 68–69, *69*, 75–76, *76*, 209, 217
pet merchandise, *166*, 168
Philadelphia Grocer, 41
Pickmann, Anatolij, *216*
Pirelli tires, 210–12, *212*
pizza ads: Hell Pizza, 26, *119*, 120–21, *122*, 123; Pizza Hut, 71, *71*; Pizza Time, 70, *71*
plastic surgeons, 71–72
Plat, Sir Hugh, 58–59, *59*
Playbill ads, 23, *24*
Pledge of Allegiance, 43n2
Polaroid, *91*, 92
politics and religious rhetoric, 36–37
Pontifical Council for Social Communications, 182–84
Pope, N. K. L., 208
Porsche, *124*, 125
postmodern category of institutional marketing, 189
Postum, *216*
Poulsen, J. D., 217–18
Prager, Dennis, 37
Presbrey, F., 10, 48–49
printing press, 50, 53–54, 57–59
Procter, Harley, 66–67
professional photographers, 19, *19*
proselytistic (witnessing) holy hype, 14–16, *15*, 227. *See also* religious artifacts
Protas, Judy, 135
Protestant Christianity: Americans' belief in, 37–38; capitalism and, 61n2; pioneering ad agencies and, 38–43; Reformation, 49; religiously themed advertisements and, 22; revivalism movement, 162; soap manufacturers and, 66–67
Prothero, Stephen, 83
public service, ads as, 20
puns in advertisements, 192

Quaker Oats, 42, *67*, 67–68
quality of merchandise, 54–55
Qur'an, 37

rabbis in ads, 90
RCA, *212*, 214
reader boards on churches, 11, 189–92, *190*
Reagan, Ron, 199
"Reason-Why" method, 42
reconciliation and consumerism, 34
Reddi Wip spray, 210, *211*
Reed, C. G., 54
Reed, Robert C., *197*
Reisner, Christian F., 180–81
religions: civil religion, 35–38; clergypersons in ads, 87–92, *88*, *91*, 102–3; consumer culture as new religion, 30–33; functional overlapping, 33–35; holy hype compared to religious rhetoric, 36–37; increased mixing of, 227; religious knowledge *versus* practice, 83; stages of, 31; study of, 29–30; symbols and images for, 21–22; universality of angel images, 74–75. *See also* Bahá'í faith; Buddhism; Christianity; Hinduism; Islam; Judaism
religious artifacts: catalogs of merchandise, 164–70, *165*, *166*, *173*; historical perspective, 161–62; interest in, 159–61; jewelry, *165*, 167; judgments about, 160–61, 175–76; tattoos, *166*, 169. *See also* apparel
The Religious Dimensions and Advertising (Sheffield), 33–34
religious holy hype, 18–19, *19*, 52–55, 228
religious manuscripts, 19, 53. *See also* Bible stories
REO Motors, 210, *211*
Republic Airlines, *216*
resurrection, images evoking, *85*, 86
RIAL magazine, *190*
Rice, Nancy, *17*

Richards, Alexandra, 232, *233*
Richards, I. A., 206
Riffault, Herve, 146–47
Ringold, D. J., 183
Rionda, Diego, *96*, 97
roadside billboards. *See* billboards
Robb, Charlie, 20
Rockwell, Norman, 151
Rokotyanskaya, L., 22
Rousseau, Jean-Jacques, 35
Routen, Joseph, *40*
Rudicil, Jim, 123

sacramentality, 34
Sacred Foods, 126–28, *127*
saints, merchandise depicting, *166*, 166–67
salvation, focus on, 52
Samson and Delilah theme, 138
Santa, *199*, 199–200
Sapir, E., 217
Sapolio Soap, *40*, 41, 100, *101*
Sarapin, Susan, 57, *150*, *165*
Sargeant, A., 215
Schick Samson dryer, *132*, 138
Schoeffer, Peter, 57–58
Schoendorf, Justin, *88*, 89–90
Scholz & Friends Group, 102–3
Schrenk, Haley, *127*, 128–29
Schuchardt, Read, 11
Scrabble game, 110–11
Sealtest logo, 99–100, *101*
Sebring, E. Robb, 180
secular holy hype: about, 12–14, *13*, 65–68, 227; emergence of, 55–56; factors in, 50; movement from religious holy hype to, 52–55; origin of, 59–60; printing press and, 57–59. *See also* historical perspective
secular holy images: Adam and Eve, 68–74, *69*, *71*, *73*; afterlife, 103–6, *105*; angels, 74–81, *76*, *78*, *80*, 88; biblical phrases, 10, 81–84, *82*, *84*; clergypersons, 87–92, *88*, *91*; crucifixes and T-poses, 92–98, *94*, *96*; devil and evil, 98–103, *101*; of the divine, 84–87, *85*; God, 106–7, *108*, 110–11; heaven, 115–18, *117*; hell and sin, 98–103, *101*, 118–23, *119*, *124*; "holy" terminology, 123–29, *124*, *127*; Jesus, 111–15, *112*; Last Supper, 139–43, *140*; Moses, 143–49, *144*, *147*; prayer and worship, 149–52, *150*. *See also* Judaism
secularization, 228–29
Sekhniashvili, Mishka, *147*
self-identifying holy hype, 227. *See also* religious artifacts
Selling God (Follis), 179
Selling God (Moore), 181–82
semantics, 21–24
"Seven Capital Sins" ad, *13*
Shaw, Marsha, 120–21
Sheffield, Tricia, 29, 33–34, 38, 228
Sherrill, Rowland, 35–36
shirts, 169–75, *173*, *207*, 208
Short, Jessica, 114
Showler, James, 114
Shurpin, Y., 69–70
Silk, Steven B., 133
Sills, Phil, 87–88
Simmons, Angela, 209
Simpson, Gavin, 71, *71*
Sinclair Oil Corporation, 100, *101*
Sinister Minister, 118–19, *119*
Sitterly, Lauren, *127*, 128–29
Smiedt, Jennie, *73*
Smirnoff, 100–102, *101*
Smokey Bear, *150*, 151
Snider's catsup, 100, *101*
snow angels, 77–81, *78*, *80*
soaps, 66–67, *67*, 100, *101*
societal context, 102
sociological analysis, 4
Sorels by Kaufman, *108*, 109
spaceship metaphor, 218–21, *219*
Spitzer, Leo, 30
Spontex wipes, *213*, 214
Stanley, Brad, *124*
Star of David, *165*, 168

statistics: Americans with Bible knowledge, 234; Brazilians as religious, 221; church attendance, 188–89; PETA members, 217; religions by population, 90, 129
Steele, Leon, *150*, 152
Stegmaier, Kaitlyn, 232, *233*
Steinberg, Sophie, *165*
Stelzle, Charles, 38–39
Stewart, Potter, 25
Stewart, Volker, *85*, 86
St. Matthew-in-the-City church, *13*, 14, 16, *199*, 200
stock photos, 5, 19, *19*
Stonkus, Dovydas, *112*
Stoops, Herbert Morton, *40*
Strate, Lance, 25
subcultures, 22
success of campaigns, 224
Sunbeam Bakers, *150*, 151
Surfrider Foundation Europe, 146–47
Sweet Jesus ice cream, 121
Syed, Waqas, 198
Symes, C., 170–71
Synan, Mariel, 126

Taco Bell, 116, 233–34
Tappan, *122*, 123
Target store, 75
tattoos, 66, *166*, 169
Taubin, William, 135
Taylor Instruments, *212*, 212–13
Teenage Millionaire, 175
televangelism, 181
Ten Commandments theme, 83–84, *84*, 148, *165*, 168. *See also* Moses theme
Tenser, Josh, 104–5, *105*
Thomas, Chris, 23
Thompson, J. Walter, 65
Thompson, Larry, *190*, 191
Tiles, Terry, *165*
Toastmasters International, 104
Tomas, David, *147*
Topolewski, Beth Hambly, *124*
Torah, 19
Toronto Jewish film festival, *147*, 147–48
Toscano, Oliviero, 102
totemic stage of advertising, 31
totemism, 33–34, 160, 161
Toyota, *80*, 80–81, *82*, 83
T-poses in ads, 95–98, *96*, 111
Trachtenberg, J., 49–52
tragic optimism, 130–32
Trignac, Gerard, 147
Tropical Tobacco, 116, *117*
Trump, Donald J., 37–38
T-shirts, 169–75, *173*
tuberculosis, *216*
Turner, Graham, 109

ultimate concern dimension, 34–35
Underwood Deviled Ham, 100, *101*
Unger, R. W., *59*
Unholy Ale, *13*, 14
Unorthodox wine, *131*, 137
US Department of Agriculture Forest Service, *150*, 151

Valančiauskas, Džiugas, *112*
Vancouver Convention Center, *119*, 120
Van Raalte lingerie, 85–86
Verghese, P., 219–20, 223
Vespa, *88*, 90
Viron, M., *197*
VO5, 111
Volkswagen, 79, *124*, 125

Wanamaker, John, 20, 38, 42–43
Ward, Artemas, 38, *40*
Warhol, Andy, 109
Warren's Standard Printing Papers, *40*
wearables. *See* apparel
Weatherby, G. A., 4
Webster Cigars, 116
Wesley, John, 66
White, J. F., 49
White Rock, *127*, 128
Wiecek, Scott, *165*
Williams, Raymond, 32
Williamson, Judith, 1

"witness wear," 172
Wizard of Oz, 31
Wonder Café of Canada, *94*, 95, *112*, 113
World Health Organization (WHO), 93, *94*
World No Tobacco Day, 93, *94*
World Placeways, *40*
Wright, Derek, 121
Wrigley Field, *117*, 118
Wyclif, John, 53

Xerox "It's a miracle" campaign, 2, 12–14, *13*

Yiddish words, 139
Young & Rubicam agency, 14, *122*, 123, 146–47

Zaltman, G., 206
Zamba, Larry, *119*, 121
Zelinsky, W., 191, 194
Zellman, S., 96

About the Authors

Susan H. Sarapin earned a BS degree in medical illustration from the University of Illinois Medical Center in Chicago, and earned her MA and PhD in media, technology, and society from Purdue University's Brian Lamb School of Communication in West Lafayette, Indiana. Sarapin is an associate professor of journalism and communication at Troy University in Troy, Alabama, and teaches multimedia law, public speaking, intro to mass communication, and holy hype advertising. Her research focuses on the effects of the media, including social media, on the public's perceptions of the law (particularly the First Amendment), the justice system, politics, and advertising.

Pamela L. Morris is an assistant professor in the Department of Communication at Indiana University—Purdue University Columbus. She specializes in media studies and new media. Morris received her PhD in Communication from Purdue University's Brian Lamb School of Communication. Prior to seeking that degree, she studied computer science and worked at IBM as a programmer and project manager. Morris's primary research interests are media law, technology adoption, and uses and effects of technology on communication processes. She particularly enjoys teaching and is passionate about media literacy education and making students good digital citizens.

Milton Keynes UK
Ingram Content Group UK Ltd.
UKHW021331291223
435175UK00010B/112